At the Front Lines of the Welfare System

A Perspective on the Decline in Welfare Caseloads

Irene Lurie

The
Rockefeller
Institute
Press

Cover photo © 2006 by Joanne Hoose.

Rockefeller Institute Press, Albany, New York 12203-1003
© 2006 by the Rockefeller Institute Press
All rights reserved.
Printed in the United States of America

The Rockefeller Institute Press
The Nelson A. Rockefeller Institute of Government
411 State Street
Albany, New York 12203-1003

For Library of Congress Cataloging-in-Publication Data
please contact the publisher

ISBN: 1-930912-17-X (softcover)

To Thad

Contents

List of Tables

Foreword

Richard P. Nathan

Irene Lurie is an economist with a special interest in public finance. She notes in Chapter 1 of this book that it took her years before she pursued her research on welfare by going into the field to dig down and talk with program administrators and observe their offices. She hasn't stopped digging since. This book examines the implementation of the 1996 national welfare reform law at the front lines. It is the product of Professor Lurie's collaborative research, working with local observers (social science graduate students) in four states, supported by the U.S. Department of Health and Human Services and the Rockefeller Foundation. Led by Lurie, the researchers observed the interaction between frontline welfare workers and clients, ultimately yielding a sample of 969 encounters. In this book Lurie describes previous welfare reforms, several of which she studied in the field and found that they fell short in their implementation. But based on her study of the 1996 national welfare reform law, which stresses the "work-first" approach and promotes links to work-facilitation services like child care and transportation, Lurie concludes that to her surprise "it did reach the front lines."

This book carefully describes the process Lurie and her colleagues used to make their observations in local offices and the way work and other requirements of the new law were treated by "street-level bureaucrats" to use a term coined by Michael Lipsky. Lurie's book quotes clients and workers and describes the provision of cash assistance and related benefits and services (Medicaid, food stamps, child care, transportation assistance). Most of all, the book is significant for what it teaches about the real world of social policy. It is also notable methodologically for its patient, persistent effort to get to the bottom line. I have always been impressed and delighted by Irene Lurie's boldness and honest scholarship as an economist who has seen the light. She is a champion social scientist in these terms. We are proud to publish her new book.

Richard P. Nathan is co-director of the Rockefeller Institute of Government, the public policy research arm of the State University of New York. He takes special responsibility for the Rockefeller Institute Press.

Acknowledgments

This study of the front lines of the welfare system is the product of the cooperation, collaborative effort, and support of many individuals and organizations. I thank them all for their contributions during the many stages of this project.

Marcia K. Meyers and Norma M. Riccucci were my collaborators in designing the study, conducting the research at the front lines, and coding the conversations observed. We received generous and timely financial support from the Administration for Children and Families of the U.S. Department of Health and Human Services and the Rockefeller Foundation.

The cooperation of the frontline workers who were willing to be observed as they performed their job in the welfare system was essential to this research. Equally essential was the cooperation of the clients who allowed themselves to be observed during their encounters with workers. The state and local officials who granted us access to their organizations and the administrators, managers, and supervisors who welcomed us into their offices and answered our questions were also vital to this research. Although too numerous to list here, all these individuals deserve my gratitude. In addition, I thank the Schenectady County Department of Social Services for the videos used to train the observers and the Albany County Department of Social Services for facilitating the cover photograph.

Three State Research Coordinators performed the complex tasks of facilitating and scheduling the observations and surveys in the local welfare and workforce offices: Joan Abbey in Michigan, Dan O'Shea in Texas, and Michael Rich in Georgia. The graduate students who observed the frontline workers include Princess Clarke, Sarah Conroy, Renae Cooper, Heather Dash, Stephanie David, Huseyin Gul, Leslie Keyes, Leslie Martin, Zachary Morton, Vanessa Robinson-Dooley, Jessica Runnels, S. Victoria Shire, Sandra Smith-Jackson, Betsy Tessler, and Susan Vorsanger. Our research assistants in Albany, most students at the Rockefeller College of Public Affairs and Policy, include Emmanuel

Barbier, Sooli Choi, Do Han Kim, John Konior, Lepora Flournory Manigault, Ruth McArdle, Charles McCormick, Elizabeth Vogelmann, and Kevin Vogelmann. I hope they value the education they received from their work as much as I value their assistance.

At the Rockefeller Institute of Government, the study relied on the skill, wisdom, and good nature of Thomas Gais, Director of the Federalism Research Group, Project Manager Miriam Trementozzi, Data Manager Jun Seop Han, Project Assistants Maria Augostini and Rebecca Corso, Editor Irene Pavone, and Director of Publications Michael Cooper and his assistant Michele Charbonneau. My colleagues Frank Thompson and Sarah Liebschutz read a draft of this book and offered constructive comments. I also thank three anonymous reviewers, whose comments guided me through a revision.

Most of all, I thank Dick Nathan for getting me into the business of studying implementation, for supporting my research, and for encouraging me to complete this manuscript.

Irene Lurie

1

Why Study Implementation?

On August 22, 1996, in signing legislation to end Aid to Families with Dependent Children (AFDC), President Clinton reminded his audience that the federal law was only the first step to welfare reform. "This is not over," he said, "this is just beginning. The Congress deserves our thanks for creating a new reality, but we have to fill in the blanks. The governors asked for this responsibility, now they've got to live up to it."[1] In other words, the form of the new reality would be created in the states during the process of implementing the law.

The Personal Responsibility and Work Opportunity Reconciliation Act of 1996[2] listed ambitious purposes for the new Temporary Assistance for Needy Families (TANF) block grant. In addition to providing assistance to families with children, state welfare programs were to promote work and marriage, reduce out-of-wedlock pregnancies, and encourage the formation and maintenance of two-parent families. In order for these goals to be realized, many leaders, policymakers, and managers

---

1   Remarks by the President at the signing of the Personal Responsibility and Work Opportunity Reconciliation Act, The White House, August 22, 1996.
2   P.L. 104-193.

needed to act: governors, legislators, welfare administrators, and welfare agency managers and supervisors. They needed to act so that the frontline workers in direct contact with welfare applicants and recipients would deliver a policy consistent with these goals.

The implementation literature examining the process of translating laws into practice amply illustrates the slippage that can occur between a policy goal articulated at the top and its realization at the bottom.[3] This is particularly true in the case of welfare reform. Because welfare policy is complex, controversial, and frequently changed, the risk is high that a reform will fail to become operational at the front lines, where workers have contact with clients. In fact, welfare policy is virtually a case study of factors that contribute to implementation failure: unclear and inconsistent objectives, intractable problems, technical difficulties, inadequate resources, multiple implementing institutions and constituencies, and the short time horizons of responsible officials.[4]

Similarly, the worker in direct contact with welfare clients is the archetype of the street-level bureaucrat who determines the degree and manner of implementing the rules.[5] Empirical research on the implementation of large-scale welfare reforms documents that numerous sources of implementation failure do in fact produce slippage between policy and frontline practice. Formal rules promulgated by legislatures or the upper levels administrative agencies may be misunderstood or ignored by the workers charged with explaining them to clients.[6] Workers may give

3   For a recent summary of the implementation literature, see Thomas Kaplan and Thomas Corbett, "Three Generations of Implementation Research: Looking for the Keys to Implementation 'Success'," in Mary Clare Lennon and Thomas Corbett, eds., *Policy into Action: Implementation Research and Welfare Reform* (Washington, DC: The Urban Institute Press, 2003).

4   Daniel A. Mazmanian and Paul A. Sabatier, *Implementation and Public Policy* (Glenview, IL: Scott, Foresman, 1983); Richard P. Nathan, *Turning Promises into Performance* (New York: Columbia University Press, 1993); Eugene Bardach, "Implementing a Paternalist Welfare-to-Work Program," in Lawrence M. Mead, ed., *The New Paternalism* (Washington, DC: The Brookings Institution, 1997); and Lennon and Corbett, *Policy into Action*.

5   Michael Lipsky, *Street-Level Bureaucracy* (New York: Russell Sage Foundation, 1980); and James Q. Wilson, *Bureaucracy* (New York: Basic Books, 1989).

6   Marcia K. Meyers, Bonnie Glaser, and Karin MacDonald, "On the Front Line of Welfare Delivery: Are Workers Implementing Policy Reforms?" *Journal of Policy Analysis and Management* 17:1 (1998).

more attention to some rules than others or use their discretion to adjust the rules to the circumstances of particular clients.[7] They may not have the resources to deliver the mandated services or monitor clients' behavior.[8] Finally, when legislators cannot resolve their differences in drafting a law, the implementation process itself becomes the context for resolving the resulting conflicts and ambiguities in the law. In this case, instead of policy determining practice, it is practice that creates the de facto policy.[9]

Scholars who have focused on the challenges of implementing welfare programs have all identified the behavior of frontline workers as critical to meeting the program's goals. "The main message of the implementation perspective is that the central focus of policy should be on the point of service delivery," wrote Williams.[10] "When taken together the individual decisions of these [frontline] workers become, or add up to, agency policy," argued Lipsky.[11] The numerous programs designed to promote employment among welfare clients have proved to be particularly challenging to implement. In examining these programs, Behn saw the difficulties facing managers who try to "influence the behavior of those who actually do the agency's work."[12] "Leadership and management are needed to influence the behavior of the bureaucracy," argued Nathan.[13] Bane concluded that altering the behavior of frontline workers to promote employment required a fundamental "culture change" in welfare agencies.[14] When Congress created TANF and devolved responsibility to the states, it intended to change the behavior of welfare agency staff as well as the behavior of welfare recipients.[15]

---

7   Yeheskel Hasenfeld, *Human Service Organizations* (Englewood Cliffs, NJ: Prentice-Hall, 1983).

8   Jan L. Hagen and Irene Lurie, *Implementing JOBS: Progress and Promise* (Albany, NY: Rockefeller Institute of Government, 1994).

9   Evelyn Z. Brodkin, "Policy Politics: If We Can't Govern, Can We Manage?" *Political Science Quarterly* 102:4 (1987-88): 571-87.

10 Walter Williams, *The Implementation Perspective* (Berkeley: University of California Press, 1980), ix.

11 Lipsky, *Street-Level Bureaucracy*, 3.

12 Robert D. Behn, *Leadership Counts* (Cambridge, MA: Harvard University Press, 1991), 67.

13 Nathan, *Turning Promises into Performance*, 6.

14 Mary Jo Bane, "Increasing Self-Sufficiency by Reforming Welfare," in Mary Jo Bane and David T. Ellwood, eds. *Welfare Realities* (Cambridge, MA: Harvard University Press, 1994).

15 Richard P. Nathan and Thomas L. Gais, *Implementing the Personal Responsibility Act of 1996: A First Look* (Albany, NY: Rockefeller Institute of Government, 1999).

To learn whether and how the purposes of the 1996 law were realized, we must examine the practices of the frontline workers at the point of service delivery. This book presents results from a study of TANF implementation designed to answer two broad questions about these practices. First, what were the practices of frontline workers in the welfare system during their face-to-face encounters with clients and to what extent did they conform to the goals for TANF set forth at higher levels? Second, what management factors caused frontline workers to behave as they did? In other words, what was happening at the front lines of the welfare system after TANF and why did it happen this way?

Past Experience Implementing
Work Programs and Requirements

The history of reforming welfare to encourage work among recipients is a history of implementation failure. Like TANF, previous federal welfare reforms sought to transform the welfare system by increasing work effort among welfare recipients. The federal government began supporting work and training programs for welfare recipients in 1962, soon after it gave states the option to extend AFDC to two-parent families headed by an unemployed father. With the expectation that most participants would be unemployed fathers, and that mothers would stay at home with their children, Congress authorized the first welfare employment program, the Community Work and Training Program (CW&T). Like the extension of eligibility to families headed by fathers, the CW&T program was optional for the states. Only 13 states elected to implement the CW&T program and total enrollment was low, peaking at slightly over 27,000 participants.[16]

The idea of encouraging mothers to work, and designing employment and training activities with their needs in mind, gained popularity when AFDC caseloads began to rise rapidly in the mid-1960s (Figure

---

16 Margaret Malone, *Work and Welfare*, 99th Congress, 2nd session (Washington, DC: U.S. Government Printing Office, August 1986). Prepared for the Subcommittee on Employment and Productivity of the Committee on Labor and Human Resources and the Subcommittee on Social Security and Income Maintenance of the Committee on Finance, United States Senate, 29.

Figure 1-1. Families on Welfare

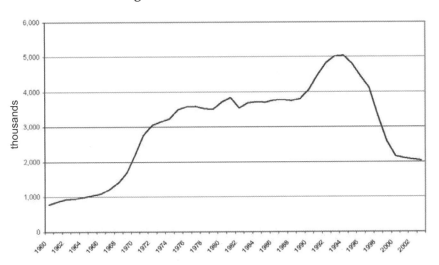

Source: U.S. Department of Health and Human Services

1-1). To curb the expansion of the welfare rolls, the Social Security Amendments of 1967 took several steps to increase the earning capacity and employment of recipients. The law required all states to create a Work Incentive (WIN) program to provide employment and training services to all types of families, including those headed by single mothers. The WIN law also sought to require recipients to work: Welfare agencies were to refer recipients to the WIN program if they did not meet a set of exemption criteria. Individuals who refused without good cause to participate in the program or to accept employment would no longer be counted in determining the amount of the family's welfare benefit. This meant that welfare agencies gained the authority to make participation in the WIN program mandatory, with the threat of a financial sanction, for a large share of the caseload. Finally, the law gave welfare recipients a financial incentive to work by scaling welfare benefits to earnings. Instead of reducing benefits by a dollar for each dollar earned, leaving recipients with the same income regardless of their work effort, states were required to reward work by disregarding a portion of earnings in calculating the amount of the welfare benefit. WIN and the work requirements were altered by laws or regulations in 1971, 1975, 1981, and 1982, each promising to increase the work effort of people on welfare.

WIN ended when the Family Support Act of 1988 created the Job Opportunities and Basic Skills Training Program (JOBS), the final welfare employment program under AFDC. While the Family Support Act was hailed as the most sweeping reform of the welfare system since passage of the Social Security Act of 1935, the JOBS program in fact required only incremental changes in the programs that states operated under WIN. JOBS increased funding for welfare employment services and child care, gave the states clear goals for getting recipients to participate in a work activity, and changed the mix of services to emphasize education. But caseloads rose sharply and state officials, without waiting to learn whether education would pay off in the long run, requested the waivers from federal law that would culminate in the enactment of TANF.

Problems implementing these welfare employment programs and work mandates fall into many of the clusters identified by the implementation literature. Implementation has been hindered by conflicting goals, excessive discretion of workers, inadequate resources, difficulties in coordinating the responsible organizations, unproven service technologies, multiple constituencies, reliance on administrative leadership and motivation, and the impatience of elected officials.

A fundamental conflict in goals is at the heart of the implementation problem. The purpose of welfare is to provide assistance to poor families with children, but providing assistance reduces the incentive for parents to work. Work can be enforced by cutting or eliminating assistance, but these penalties to motivate the parent undermine the goal of helping children. In 1971, soon after WIN was created, the General Accounting Office (GAO) reported, "Local officials have been hesitant to apply the sanctions because such application is administratively time consuming and penalizes the entire family, not just the uncooperative individual.[17]

Impatient with low rates of referral to the WIN program and rising caseloads, Congress enacted amendments in 1971 designed to force welfare agencies to refer people to the WIN program. To reduce their discretion over which individuals were appropriate for referral, the

---

17 U.S. General Accounting Office, *Problems in Accomplishing Objectives of the Work Incentive Program* (WIN), B-164031(3) (Washington, DC, September 24, 1971), 32.

amendments sought to impose a "work test." They sought to make referral to the WIN program mandatory by requiring that everyone, except those specifically exempted by law, register for WIN when they applied for welfare and that registration be completed as a condition of eligibility for AFDC. Parents caring for a child under the age of six were exempt. But despite the mandate to register for WIN, welfare agencies and individual workers continued to exercise considerable discretion in referring recipients to WIN services and in sanctioning those who failed to comply. WIN services, child care, and employment opportunities were in short supply, forcing caseworkers to be selective in their referrals to the WIN program. In addition, when recipients referred to WIN or a job refused to comply, welfare agencies could decide how vigorously to pursue the process leading to financial sanctions. In 1987, 15 years after imposition of the work test, the GAO again noted the high administrative cost of sanctioning, reporting that workers said "they would sanction more frequently if it did not take so much time and energy to document noncompliance."[18]

The JOBS law sought to increase engagement in a work activity by lowering the age-of-child exemption to three years, or one year at state option, and by imposing a mandate on the states that a minimum percent of their nonexempt caseload participate in a work activity. This minimum participation rate rose from 7 percent in 1990 to 20 percent by 1995. By 1995, 43 percent of adult recipients were mandated to work and, of this group, 27 percent were counted as participating. Of all adults, only 14.4 percent were active in a JOBS activity.[19] Sanctioning to enforce compliance was still uneven among the states, welfare offices, and individual workers.[20]

Difficulty enforcing the work requirement was attributed in part to inadequate capacity to deliver employment and training services. Developing the capacity to offer services was perennially hindered by the coordination problems created by the multiplicity of implementing institutions. The CW&T program was administered by the welfare agen-

18 U.S. General Accounting Office, *Work and Welfare: Current AFDC Work Programs and Implications for Federal Policy*, GAO/HRD-87-34 (Washington, DC, January 1987), 62.
19 U.S. House, Committee on Ways and Means, *1998 Green Book*, 484-6.
20 Hagen and Lurie, *Implementing JOBS: Progress and Promise*.

cies, but they lacked experience and staff for operating job training and placement programs.[21] As a result, the 1967 law creating WIN gave responsibility for operating the program to state labor departments. The responsibility of the local welfare agency was to refer AFDC recipients "promptly" to the labor department for enrollment in the WIN program and to provide WIN participants with supportive services such as child care and transportation. The labor department was responsible for delivering all other WIN components.

Difficulties of coordinating the activities of the two organizations soon surfaced. When Congress examined the progress of states in implementing WIN, it found fault with both the welfare and labor agencies for failure to coordinate their activities; some welfare agencies had referred insufficient numbers of recipients to the labor department while others referred too many. In addition, the welfare agencies were not consistently implementing the requirement to refer to the WIN office each person who was "appropriate" for the program. Some agencies defined "appropriate" broadly, others narrowly, so that referrals to WIN varied among the states.[22] According to a nationwide survey of AFDC families in 1971, only 17.6 percent of AFDC families had members referred to the WIN program and only 8.8 percent of families had members currently or formerly enrolled in the program. Southern states lagged noticeably behind others.[23]

With the division of responsibilities between the welfare agency and the labor department identified as a reason for the low rate of referrals to WIN, amendments in 1971 again altered the assignment of tasks. Registration for the WIN program would now take place in the welfare agency, which would make arrangements to provide recipients with child care and other supportive services and "certify" that they were ready to accept WIN services. The labor department would continue to operate the WIN program, providing employment and training services. But it soon became apparent that this arrangement did not ensure that many recipients were, in practice, being exposed to

---

21 Sar Levitan, Martin Rein and David Marwick, *Work and Welfare Go Together* (Baltimore, MD: Johns Hopkins University Press, 1972), 72-4.

22 Malone, *Work and Welfare*, 60-64.

23 U.S. Department of Health, Education, and Welfare, *Findings of the 1971 AFDC Study, Part I. Demographic and Program Characteristics*, DHEW Publication No. (SRS) 72-03756, Tables 38-39.

the employment and training services offered by the WIN program. A nationwide survey of AFDC families in 1973 found that only 16 percent of families living in areas with a WIN program were certified as ready for WIN and that only 5 percent of families were actually engaged in a work or training program; a similar study in 1975 showed virtually no progress.[24]

To further promote exposure to the WIN program, federal regulations issued in 1975 transferred responsibility for WIN registration from the welfare agency to the labor department. Applicants for AFDC applied for assistance at the welfare agency, registered for WIN at the labor department, arranged their child care at the welfare agency, and were assigned to WIN services by the labor department. But critics then argued that this dual administration weakened the program by giving the welfare agency incomplete authority and responsibility for its operation.[25] As a result, amendments in 1981 headed full circle back to the organizational arrangement of the CW&T program by giving state welfare agencies the option to operate a program, called a WIN Demonstration program, on their own independently of the labor department. The Family Support Act of 1988 mandated administration of JOBS by the welfare agency. Still, few welfare agencies had the capacity to offer education, training, and employment services and needed to purchase services from other organizations or bargain to obtain services at no cost.[26]

Federal mandates regarding the mix of education, training, and employment services also ran in cycles, in part due to uncertainty about the effectiveness of these service technologies in increasing employment and earnings. The CW&T program permitted states to offer training and education, but most recipients were simply required to work off their welfare benefit in public or private nonprofit agencies, an arrangement now known as work experience. The WIN program sent the pendulum swing-

24 U.S. Department of Health, Education, and Welfare, *Findings of the 1973 AFDC Study, Part I. Demographic and Program Characteristics*, DHEW Publication No. (SRS) 74-03764, 85 and U.S. Department of Health, Education, and Welfare, *Aid to Families with Dependent Children 1975 Recipient Characteristics Study, Part 4. Social Services*, HEW Pub. No. (SSA) 79-11777, 4.

25 Malone, *Work and Welfare,* 108.

26 Irene Lurie and Jan L. Hagen, *Implementing JOBS: The Initial Design and Structure of Local Programs* (Albany, NY: Rockefeller Institute of Government, 1993).

ing in the other direction, permitting work programs but clearly authorizing education and vocational training. Yet within a few years, members of Congress objected to the emphasis on basic education and classroom training and the lack of job placements, arguing that the main thrust of the WIN program should emphasize immediate work.[27] Amendments in 1971 sent the pendulum in this direction by requiring that states devote at least one-third of their WIN funds to on-the-job training (OJT) and public service employment (PSE). When states responded by enrolling almost half of their WIN clients in these programs,[28] critics argued that WIN was inflexible and that both OJT and PSE, because they entail direct payments to employers, were costly mechanisms for creating work slots.

Legislation in 1981 and 1982 authorized work experience once again and permitted welfare agencies to operate job search programs, an activity previously the exclusive prerogative of the labor department. The 1988 JOBS legislation sent the pendulum back toward education by mandating states to offer recipients basic education, GED (high school equivalency) test preparation, English as a second language instruction, or high school if additional education was appropriate to their employment goal, and states had the option of offering postsecondary education. States could also offer other services, virtually any type of education, job training, or employment activity that could enhance an individual's earning capacity. Many participants were in education, partly because this was a low-cost option to the welfare agency.

During the 1980s and 1990s, however, rigorous evaluations of welfare employment programs decreased the uncertainty about the effectiveness of these service technologies. They found that immediate job search was effective in reducing welfare expenditures. Job search combined with basic education was also effective while work experience, where recipients work in exchange for welfare, was least effective in reducing welfare costs. Riverside, California, operated a particularly effective program that combined "a pervasive emphasis on getting people a job quickly, strong reliance on job clubs but substantial use of basic educa-

---

27 Malone, *Work and Welfare,* 57.
28 U.S. Department of Health, Education, and Welfare and U.S. Department of Labor, *The Work Incentive Program Sixth Annual Report to the Congress* (Washington, DC: U.S. Department of Labor, 1976), 8-9.

tion..., tough enforcement of a participation requirement, close links to the private sector, and a cost-conscious and outcome-based management style."[29] These findings and the model of Riverside would be influential as states designed their programs to implement TANF.

Efforts to create jobs for welfare recipients had been sporadic, hampered by the multiple constituencies of elected officials. One tension was between welfare recipients and other workers. Concern that creating jobs for welfare recipients would reduce jobs for other workers led to language in CW&T, WIN, and JOBS that the programs would not result in "displacement" of regular workers. Legislation, court rulings, and administrative interpretations churned the design details of job creation programs, producing arcane distinctions among "community work programs," "special work projects," "public service employment," "work experience training," a "community work experience program," and an "alternative work experience program." Creating the capacity to educate and train recipients was influenced by other constituencies — the government agencies and nonprofit and for-profit organizations that delivered services and wanted a share of the funds. Their fortunes waxed and waned as the mix of education, training, and employment services cycled over time.

Inadequate resources to serve everyone required to participate in these programs was a chronic problem. Charges that 50 percent federal funding for the CW&T program did not stimulate enough state spending led Congress to provide 80 percent federal funding for the WIN program in 1967, increased to 90 percent in 1971. Yet the total federal allotment for WIN was capped at a level that kept the program strapped for funds. In 1981, when funding for the WIN program peaked, total spending amounted to 3 percent of AFDC payments or only $106 per AFDC family. Many reviews of the WIN program over the years concur that the failure of the program to enable and require large numbers of recipients to participate can be attributed to lack of funds.[30] The federal funding rules

---

29 Judith Gueron, "A Research Context for Welfare Reform," *Journal of Policy Analysis and Management* 15:4 (1996): 552.

30 Mildred Rein, *Work or Welfare?* (New York: Praeger, 1974) 85-86; U.S. General Accounting Office, *An Overview of the WIN Program: Its Objectives, Accomplishments, and Problems*, June 1982 (GAO/HRD-82-55) 12-13; Malone, *Work and*

for JOBS increased the total amount of federal funds available to support the program, but the rules required greater spending by states to claim the additional dollars. States increased their own expenditures too slowly to claim all their federal funds, leaving one-third of them in Washington in 1995.[31] In explaining their decision to limit JOBS expenditures, states cited start-up problems, fiscal problems caused by the 1990-91 recession, and other more pressing budgetary priorities.[32]

A persistent criticism of the WIN program was a lack of funding for child care. Federal legislation earmarked no WIN funds specifically for child care, giving the states a single pool of revenue to divide between child care and other WIN services. A shortage of child care providers was also a problem: good quality care was expensive, spaces in child care centers were scarce, no funds were authorized for the acquisition or construction of child care facilities, and babysitting and other tenuous arrangements broke down.[33] By 1975, the cost of child care and other supportive services absorbed more than one-third of all WIN funds.[34] States soon learned how to shift much of the cost of child care to other funding streams, particularly Title XX of the Social Security Act that funds social services. But when Title XX expenditures mushroomed, amendments in 1981 capped Title XX into a block grant. In the 1980s, program administrators perceived that a lack of child care prevented participation in the program, identifying as problems both lack of providers and shortages of funds to pay them.[35] The 1988 legislation creating JOBS improved access to child care, requiring its availability for all JOBS participants and, on a short-term basis, for recipients who left welfare for employment. Equally important, the federal government began financing child care by the same open-ended matching grant it used to finance cash assistance. Yet shortages in child care funds still limited enrollment in JOBS in some states.[36]

Welfare, 107; U.S. General Accounting Office, *Work and Welfare*, 74; and U.S. Congressional Budget Office, *Work-Related Programs for Welfare Recipients* (April 1987), 62.

31 U.S. House, Committee on Ways and Means, *1996 Green Book*, 413.

32 Hagen and Lurie, *Implementing JOBS: Progress and Promise.*

33 Malone, *Work and Welfare,* 46.

34 *The Work Incentive Program Sixth Annual Report to the Congress*, 21.

35 U.S. General Accounting Office, *Work and Welfare*, 60-1 and 86-7.

36 Hagen and Lurie, *Implementing JOBS: Progress and Promise.*

Inadequate resources to serve everyone required to participate permitted frontline workers to exercise discretion in enforcing the work requirement. Worker discretion in determining eligibility and benefits for cash assistance was reduced when welfare gained the status of an entitlement and a federally mandated Quality Control system encouraged states to routinize the functions entailed in processing cash assistance payments. Many states eliminated "caseworkers" and divided the payment functions among "income maintenance" workers who specialized in a single task such as intake, monthly reporting, redetermination, and food stamps.[37] Yet while workers lost much of their discretion to determine eligibility and benefits for cash assistance, they still retained discretion to determine who was required to work. The ability of workers to exercise this discretion was observed in the early days of WIN and persisted into the JOBS program.[38]

Relying on administrative leadership to overcome these implementation challenges produced uneven results because, inevitably, some leaders had more interest in welfare programs and greater leadership talent than others. Strong administrative leadership in welfare, particularly by the governors, was not the norm in the 1960s and 1970s but it has been a notable feature of the recent history of welfare reform. Beginning with the WIN Demonstration legislation in 1981, which gave the states new options for designing and operating their welfare employment programs, governors took the initiative to craft new programs and present them to the public as innovative and tough-minded solutions to the problem of welfare dependency. Ultimately, with the support of the National Governors Association, their initiatives helped produce the JOBS program. As caseloads continued to rise despite JOBS, their short time horizons made them impatient for results and they requested waivers from federal law to reform their programs further. Similar to the governors' initiatives producing JOBS, gubernatorial leadership in requesting waivers from federal law helped produce TANF. Between 1993 and 1996, 43 states obtained federal approval for waivers, a measure of the governors' activ-

---

37 Thomas J. Kane and Mary Jo Bane, "The Context for Welfare Reform," in Bane and Ellwood, *Welfare Realities*.

38 Rein, *Work or Welfare?*, 89; U.S. General Accounting Office, *An Overview of the WIN Program*, 13-15; U.S. General Accounting Office, *Work and Welfare*, 48-65; Hagen and Lurie, *Implementing JOBS: Progress and Promise*, 165-171.

ism in welfare policy.[39] Governors clearly saw welfare reform as an issue that could generate political capital for them, particularly if they claimed credit for the reforms.

In summary, the history of WIN and JOBS is one of unfulfilled expectations that work programs and requirements would effectively mandate work and reduce welfare caseloads. Implementation problems had created a "WIN funnel" that limited participation in the program to only a trickle of the target population.[40] Few of the large percent of recipients who registered for WIN received an appraisal of their need for services, and even fewer actually engaged in programs, so that many recipients found WIN to be a paper process of registering for services that were not available. JOBS increased funding for services, but it did not impose a widely enforced mandate to prepare for work and find a job. Between the creation of the WIN program in 1967 and the caseload peak in 1994, AFDC caseloads grew from 1.2 to 5.1 million families. Despite repeated tinkering with the programs' designs and increases in federal funding, the states seemed incapable of implementing the program in a way that ensured welfare recipients would prepare for work, accept a suitable job, and leave welfare.

An Overview of TANF

When President Clinton signed the Personal Responsibility Act, liberals felt betrayed. Clinton had followed through on his campaign promise to reform welfare by giving Congress a proposal with a time limit on benefits and other tough provisions to encourage work, but with subsidized jobs for people exhausting their time limited benefits. The Republican Congress, flush with success in the 1994 elections, passed a bill with Clinton's tough provisions but without the safety net of jobs and with an explicit statement that welfare was not an entitlement. The president vetoed the bill twice, but finally played it safe for the 1996 election. When he signed the bill that eliminated AFDC and created TANF, three of his

---

39 U.S. Department of Health and Human Services, Office of the Assistant Secretary for
    Planning and Evaluation, *Setting the Baseline: A Report on State Welfare Waivers*
    (Washington, DC: U.S. Department of Health and Human Services, June 1997).
40 Rein, *Work or Welfare?*, 89.

own welfare administrators resigned in protest. They understood that strong measures were needed to implement work requirements but they objected to the harshest aspects of TANF.

TANF struck a new balance between providing assistance to poor families and maintaining an incentive for parents to work, a fundamental goal conflict in welfare, by limiting assistance. It limited assistance to both states and families. Payments to the states were limited by substituting a block grant, which is a fixed payment to each state, for the AFDC open-ended matching grant, which paid the states a percent of all their expenditures for cash assistance. TANF limited assistance to families by imposing a 60-month lifetime limit on federal financing of payments to individual families. It also explicitly ended the statutory entitlement to welfare that had resulted from decisions of the U.S. Supreme Court. If the block grant became inadequate to finance assistance for all families meeting the eligibility rules, the states could establish waiting lists for assistance.

TANF also strengthened incentives to work by placing greater pressures on both states and families. States were required to engage a higher percent of their caseload in a work activity. It mandated a minimum work participation rate of 25 percent in 1997, rising to 50 percent by 2002. (To avoid forcing states to choose between policies that encouraged work participation and policies that reduced welfare caseloads, states with declining caseloads had to meet lower participation rates.) Recipients were required to work or prepare for work within two years of receiving assistance, or sooner if ready for work. Unlike previous law, TANF listed no mandatory exemptions from the work requirement, although it gave states the option of exempting single parents with a child under age one and reduced the required hours of work for parents with a child under age six. States were required to impose sanctions on people who refused to work without good cause and could even terminate assistance entirely.

To the extent TANF addressed the coordination problems created by the multiplicity of implementing institutions, it did so by giving states more options. The law no longer required that a single state agency have responsibility for welfare. It also gave states new flexibility by allowing them to use charitable, religious, or private organizations to administer and provide services. While one could argue these provisions would in-

crease, not decrease, the number of implementing institutions and coordination problems, the implicit assumption in TANF was that the states
would be better able to manage their programs free of federal control.
TANF also eliminated the Quality Control system designed to reduce errors in determining eligibility and benefits, which had led to the
specialization of welfare workers and the routinization of their tasks.

TANF changed the mix of services again by no longer counting
postsecondary education as a work activity and by limiting participation
in vocational education. The large share of JOBS participants attending
school rather than searching for work had contributed to the sharp increase in caseloads during the late 1980s and early 1990s, and the effectiveness of mandated education was in doubt. Otherwise, the service mix
was similar to JOBS, permitting a wide range of employment and
training activities.

Designing TANF as a block grant was a way of limiting federal
funding but, unexpectedly, the block grant alleviated the chronic lack of
funds for employment and training services that had hindered the implementation of previous work programs. The block grant consolidated federal financing for cash assistance and the JOBS program and gave states
flexibility in deciding how much to spend on cash and work programs.
More importantly, the block grant to each state was based on the amount
of federal funds it received during the years between 1992 and 1995,
when caseloads and hence federal funds were at a historic high. Because
caseloads declined sharply, the block grants were larger than the matching grants states would have received under AFDC, giving states a financial windfall. The windfall was an important source of financing for child
care, transportation, and other assistance to poor families. The Personal
Responsibility Act also increased funding for the Child Care and Development Block Grant, providing an additional source of financing for
child care.

TANF embodied a management philosophy that focused organizations on their mission by rewarding them for performance. Federal legislation and regulations for AFDC contained detailed requirements for the
structure of programs and the processes for operating them. TANF said little about structure and process. Rather, it set a few goals and mandates for
the states and guided their actions with financial penalties and incentives.

The law penalized states that failed to engage a minimum percentage of its caseload in a work-related activity by reducing their block grant. It also set aside funds for bonuses to states that achieved "high performance"[41] and for bonuses to states that reduced out-of-wedlock births while also reducing "the rate of induced pregnancy terminations."[42] As Nathan and Gais argue, TANF sought "to modify two kinds of behavior, the *personal* labor force and sexual behavior of poor family heads and the *bureaucratic* behavior of the agencies that administer welfare and related programs."[43]

Why Study Frontline Workers?

For me, the frequent reforms of the welfare system generated a steady stream of research and an ever-deeper appreciation of the challenges of implementation, but it took years before I went into the field to talk with welfare administrators and observe their offices. In 1972, I used a federal survey of welfare recipients to estimate states' benefit reduction rates and found they did not match the federal rule to disregard $30 of monthly earnings and one-third of the remainder. I explained the deviations from the statutes only by examining published information about state rules, since it never occurred to me to visit a welfare office to see how workers calculate benefits. In 1976, I studied the imposition of federally mandated work requirements, still sitting in my office with published rules, data, and reports. But in 1981, Richard Nathan organized a field network study to examine the states' implementation of Reagan's first budget and sent me out to talk with New York administrators. Seeing federal policies from the state's perspective was an education. New York did not accept federal policies passively but bargained with the federal government and used ingenious strategies to promote or deflect federal goals, enabling it to shape policy to its own ends.[44]

---

41 42 U.S.C. 603(a)(4). The law does not define "high performance."

42 42 U.S.C. 603(a)(2).

43 Nathan and Gais, *Implementing the Personal Responsibility Act of 1996*, 1.

44 Richard P. Nathan, Fred C. Doolittle, and Associates, *Reagan and the States* (Princeton, NJ: Princeton University Press, 1987); Sarah F. Liebschutz, *Bargaining under Federalism* (Albany, NY: State University of New York Press, 1991).

With Jan Hagen, I organized a field network study to examine the implementation of the Family Support Act of 1988 by 10 states and 30 localities.[45] We and our colleagues in the field read laws, regulations, and procedures manuals, interviewed administrators, and collected program data to understand the policy and management choices made to implement the law. The study confirmed the power of politics, resources, and organizational capacity to shape the welfare programs of state and local governments.[46] However, by the final round of the JOBS study in 1992, administrators in many states were trying to transform their welfare agencies by seeking waivers from the federal law and appeared to be taking Behn's advice to change their agencies by articulating new missions and goals. When asked how they were implementing JOBS, I got the sense that some administrators were describing their vision rather than their current program. When the Rockefeller Institute of Government initiated a study of the implementation of TANF by 20 states, I asked Marcia Meyers and Norma Riccucci to join me in a supplemental study of frontline workers. By this time, I was convinced that welfare policy could only be understood fully by looking at the actions of the frontline staff as they work with their clients.

This study examined frontline workers in face-to-face contact with their clients to observe their practices — TANF policy as delivered. In 1998, the study drew a purposive sample of four of the states in the main study, Georgia, Michigan, New York, and Texas, and samples of three local sites in each state. After time spent gaining access to the states and sites (succeeding everywhere but New York City), the study began with interviews of welfare administrators, managers, and staff to learn about goals, policies, resources, organizational relationships, staffing, procedures, and information systems in each site. Trained graduate students then observed approximately 60 hours of face-to-face encounters between workers and clients in each site, yielding a total of 969 encounters. They also administered a survey to all workers in the site who had face-to-face contact with clients. Most of the observations were made

---

45 Jan L. Hagen and Irene Lurie, *Implementing JOBS: Initial State Choices* (Albany, NY: Rockefeller Institute of Government, 1992); Lurie and Hagen, *Implementing JOBS: The Initial Design and Structure of Local Programs*; and Hagen and Lurie, *Implementing JOBS: Progress and Promise.*
46 Behn, *Leadership Counts.*

during the first half of 2000, when welfare caseloads were declining rapidly. A content analysis of the conversation between workers and their clients during these encounters is the primary source of material for this volume. The analysis focuses on the language of the workers and does not systematically examine the client's side of the conversations, such as the problems bringing them to the welfare system and their responses to the workers.

My familiarity with the history of welfare reform implementation made me skeptical about the prospects for TANF. Because no federal welfare reform to encourage work had been fully implemented to meet its goal, my hypothesis about the outcome of the Personal Responsibility Act was that substantive change would be limited. States would implement the law on paper, but achieve less on the ground where policy is delivered. I was wrong.

Policy as Delivered: Summary and Conclusions

To learn whether and how the practices of frontline workers in the welfare system conformed to the goals for TANF set forth at higher levels, the following chapters examine the conversation between workers and clients of greatest relevance to these goals. Chapter 2 describes the samples of local welfare sites and worker-client encounters, the study methods, and the method for analyzing the encounter data. Chapter 3 gives an overview of the conversations between workers and clients, including the topics mentioned in the conversations and the activities of workers regarding these topics. Chapters 4 through 8 focus more narrowly on selected topics of conversation to see how the welfare system implemented policies designed to reduce reliance on welfare and encourage work, such as the time limits, the mandates on clients' behavior, and, in particular, the work-related mandates imposed on TANF applicants and recipients. The observations revealed that, in addition to implementing the policies in TANF, welfare offices were using increasingly sophisticated information systems to reduce reliance on welfare, as described in Chapter 9. Chapter 10 examines the management strategies employed by the states and local welfare offices to influence the practices of frontline workers so they conformed to the goals of TANF. Chapter 11 concludes by summarizing how TANF policy as delivered at the frontlines pushed families away from the welfare system.

At the front lines, the welfare systems in the four states differed in numerous respects. Yet in all four states, the policy as delivered by frontline workers — the policy that can change clients' personal behavior — discouraged families from long-term reliance on TANF as a source of income. They discouraged families from relying on TANF not by explicitly denying them entry to the welfare system but by imposing behavioral mandates as a condition of entry. A work-related mandate on applicants, imposed with few exceptions, became an embodiment of TANF's provision that welfare is no longer an entitlement. Work-related mandates on recipients were also imposed, although with more exceptions, and were supported by financial assistance for child care and transportation. After decades of reform of the welfare system that sought to reduce reliance on welfare, the wide imposition of mandates to attend a work-related activity represents a major accomplishment of the 1996 legislation.

Imposing work-related mandates on applicants and recipients was accomplished by bureaucratic procedures, or processes, within the welfare system. These processes structured the behavior of staff to ensure they implemented policies to mandate work. Workers were able to follow these procedures because the welfare systems, aided by the financial windfall from the block grant, created the capacity to provide the work-related activities, child care, and other services families need to conform to the work mandates. TANF modified the personal behavior of poor families by permitting and encouraging the agencies to modify their bureaucratic behavior, achieving the two kinds of behavioral change identified by Nathan and Gais.

While the states used the work mandate to encourage employment and discourage reliance on welfare, they made less effort to achieve other stated purposes of the TANF legislation. States were cautious in promoting marriage, reducing the incidence of out-of-wedlock pregnancies, and encouraging the formation and maintenance of two-parent families. Common barriers to implementation were still standing in the way of meeting these goals. Public support for using the welfare system to intervene in decisions about marriage and childbearing was not solid, nor had proven service technologies been developed for intervening in these decisions. Workers in Georgia referred clients to information about family planning, but this was the only initiative taken to pursue these goals in the four states.

The sharp decline in welfare caseloads from a high of 5.1 million families in 1994 to a low of 2.0 million families in 2003 is also evidence that TANF was, in fact, implemented (Figure 1-1). The decline was unprecedented, resulting from the fortuitous combination of welfare reform and a strong economy. From 1991 to 2001, the nation's economy experienced sustained growth, generating jobs for families affected by the welfare policy changes. The confluence of the booming economy, the waivers from federal welfare law, and the 1996 law was powerful. In proposing legislation to reauthorize the 1996 law, the Bush Administration wrote, "The results of these reforms, which were implemented during one of the hottest economies of recent decades, are nothing short of spectacular."[47] Never before have the results of welfare reform been hailed as "spectacular."

How much of the decline in caseloads was due to TANF and how much to the economy is not well understood. The long economic expansion of the 1990s generated jobs for both welfare recipients and people at risk of becoming recipients and raised labor force participation among single women with children. At the same time, expansions of the Earned Income Tax Credit made low-wage jobs more attractive to workers, as did expansions in Medicaid and federal assistance for child care. While it is likely that all these factors contributed to the drop in caseloads, the relative importance of each of them is far less certain. Moreover, TANF is not a single policy but a set of policies implemented together, greatly complicating efforts to identify the relative importance of each. With numerous factors operating simultaneously to decrease caseloads, Blank conceded, "There remains debate as to how much of these results were due to a strong economy, to program reform, or to their interactive effects."[48]

---

47 "Working Toward Independence," February 26, 2002, press release, http://www.whitehouse.gov/news/releases/2002/02/welfare-reform-announcement-book.html.
48 Rebecca M. Blank, "Evaluating Welfare Reform in the United States," *Journal of Economic Literature* XL (December 2002): 1159. See Blank for a comprehensive re-

Looking at welfare caseloads over the past 40 years, a longer period than the time frame of recent studies on the determinants of the drop in caseloads, the trends suggest the strength of noneconomic factors (Figure 1-1). Between 1966 and 1972, the number of families receiving AFDC increased from 1 million to 3 million families. Caseloads increased by 12 percent in 1967, 16 percent in 1968, 20 percent in 1969, 30 percent in 1970, 25 percent in 1971, and 10 percent in 1972. Economic conditions were strong as caseloads began to rise, not weakening until the recession of 1970-71. Caseloads settled down after 1972 as states allowed the value of benefits to be eroded by inflation, with modest recession-induced changes until a spike beginning in 1990. Then beginning in 1994, coinciding with a surge of state waivers from federal law, and continuing after the 1996 TANF legislation, caseloads plummeted at the suddenness with which they rose in 1966-1972.

Research on the 1967-1972 caseload explosion debated its underlying and more proximate causes, but most observers agreed it resulted primarily from legal and regulatory actions and the response of families to them. Many states increased benefits during this period, raising income eligibility levels and making more families eligible for assistance. Decisions by the U.S. Supreme Court established guarantees of equal protection and due process in welfare administration, thereby establishing the principal that individuals who met the eligibility criteria for welfare were entitled to benefits. This made access to welfare easier for poor families and encouraged more potentially eligible poor families to apply for assistance.[49] Among eligible families headed by women, the proportion that actually received assistance increased from around 60 percent in

---

view of factors explaining the decline in caseloads and the increase in labor force participation among single mothers.

49 Frances Fox Piven and Richard A. Cloward, *Regulating the Poor* (New York: Vintage, 1971); Irene Lurie, "Legislative, Administrative and Judicial Changes in the AFDC Program, 1967-1971," in *Studies in Public Welfare*, U.S. Congress, Joint Economic Committee (U.S. Government Printing Office, 1973); Daniel P. Moynihan, *The Politics of a Guaranteed Income* (New York: Vintage, 1973); Michael R. Sosin, "Legal Rights and Welfare Change, 1960-1980," in Sheldon H. Danziger and Daniel H. Weinberg, eds. *Fighting Poverty, What Works and What Doesn't* (Cambridge, MA: Harvard University Press, 1986); and R. Shep Melnick, *Between the Lines: Interpreting Welfare Rights* (Washington, DC: Brookings Institution, 1994).

1967 to nearly 90 percent in 1971.[50] In other words, the "take-up" rate for welfare increased. A structural shift caused by these legal and regulatory reforms and the response of poor families to them appears to be the major explanation for the caseload increase during this period, not overall economic conditions.[51]

The 1996 legislation was another structural shift, one that permitted states to reverse the legal liberalizations made three decades earlier. By changing federal financing from a matching grant to a block grant and devolving authority to the states, TANF gave states new financial incentives and the ability to make new institutional arrangements to deliver services. By saying that welfare is not an entitlement and imposing a time limit on benefits, TANF permitted states to design policies and procedures that made welfare more difficult to receive. As the take-up rate increased after welfare became an entitlement, the take-up rate decreased after TANF ended the entitlement. Among eligible single-parent households, the proportion that actually received assistance decreased from an estimated 81 percent in 1996 to an estimated 57 percent in 2000.[52] Certainly economic conditions and tax policies contributed to the decline in caseloads since 1994, but they did so during a fundamental overhaul of the welfare system.

---

50 Irwin Garfinkel and Sara S. McLanahan, *Single Mothers and Their Children* (Washington, DC: The Urban Institute Press, 1986), 111.

51 Robert Moffitt, "Historical Growth in Participation in Aid to Families with Dependent Children: Was There a Structural Shift?" *Journal of Post-Keynesian Economics* 9:3 (1987).

52 Anu Rangarajan, Laura Castner and Melissa A. Clark, *Public Assistance Use Among Two-Parent Families: An Analysis of TANF and Food Stamp Program Eligibility and Participation*, Final Report (Princeton, NJ: Mathematica Policy Research, Inc., January 2005), 23.

2

Samples, Methods, and Data Analysis

Selecting the 969 encounters to be observed required drilling down from large to small entities, drawing samples of ever smaller units of analysis. A sample of four states was selected first, followed by samples of geographic areas within the states, offices within the geographic areas, workers within the offices, and, finally, encounters between these workers and their clients. This chapter describes the approaches to drawing these samples. It also summarizes the methods used to collect information about management and practices within the welfare system. In the process, it describes characteristics of the states, offices, and workers that may help to understand why frontline workers behaved as they did.

After observing the encounters and creating a written record of the conversation, the content of the conversation was analyzed with three sets of codes. Codes were developed for 1) the primary purposes of the encounters, 2) the topics of conversation during the encounters, and 3) the worker's activities regarding the topics. The coding process and subsequent method of data analysis are described here. The frequency of the codes will be discussed in later chapters.

States and Sites

State welfare programs have always had very different policies about who is eligible for assistance, what rules people must follow to receive assistance, and the amount of assistance they receive. In selecting the sample of states for the study, one objective was to choose states that would be likely to illustrate the diversity of responses to the TANF legislation. The four states in the sample — Georgia, Michigan, New York, and Texas — provide variation in several characteristics expected to influence the state's response: the generosity of welfare benefits, state political culture, and geographic region (Table 2-1). Georgia and Texas provided low TANF benefits by national standards, while Michigan and New York provided relatively high TANF benefits. Similarly, on a scale of political culture measuring states' policy liberalism, Georgia and Texas were relatively conservative while Michigan and New York were relatively liberal. Geographic regions included the northeast, midwest, south, and southwest.

The states also varied considerably in the amount of TANF funds available to serve their poor residents. The basic TANF block grant, which was based on the previous level of federal funding for AFDC, was $331 million annually in Georgia, $775 million in Michigan, $2,443 million in New York, and $486 million in Texas. Basing the block grants on historical funding levels meant that no state suffered a decrease in federal funding, but it perpetuated the wide differences in federal funding per poor resident that existed under AFDC. In 1994, annual federal AFDC funds per poor resident were $1,020 in New York, $663 in Michigan, $389 in Georgia, and $169 in Texas. The Personal Responsibility Act gave supplemental grants to states with low expenditures per poor resident or high rates of population growth and both Georgia and Texas qualified for these grants, but the grants were small, supplementing the basic block grant by less than 10 percent.[1]

A second objective was to select states using new organizational arrangements for delivering welfare services. TANF no longer required states to give overall responsibility for welfare programs to a single gov-

---

1   U.S. Congress, Committee on Ways and Means, *2004 Green Book*, 7-15 to 7-20.

Table 2-1. Criteria for Selecting States

Benefit for 3-Person Family, 1997[1]	Political Culture[2]	Welfare Agency Structure	Workforce Agency Structure
		GEORGIA	
$280	-1.04	State administration/some county role	State-level contract with state labor department for applicant job search
		MICHIGAN	
$459-$489	1.18	State administration/county divisions	State workforce commission/local workforce boards contract with public or non-profit service providers
		NEW YORK	
$577-$703	2.12	County administration	County option
		TEXAS	
$188	-0.65	State administration/regional divisions	State workforce commission/local workforce boards contract with public, non-profit or for-profit service providers

1   U.S. Congress, Committee on Ways and Means, *1998 Green Book*, 416-17.
2   Robert S. Erikson, Gerald C. Wright, and John P. McIver, *Statehouse Democracy: Public Opinion and Policy in the American States* (Cambridge University Press, 1993). Political culture is a measure of states' policy liberalism. Policy liberalism is a composite of state policies on the following eight issues: education, Medicaid, AFDC, consumer protection, criminal justice, legalized gambling, equal rights amendment, and tax progressivity. Over 167,000 responses from national public opinion surveys conducted between 1976 and 1988 are aggregated to arrive at this measure. The scale runs from most conservative (Arkansas at -1.54) to most liberal (New York at 2.12).

ernment agency, reflecting perceptions that the organizations in the welfare system were themselves impediments to meaningful welfare reform. States could administer welfare through several government agencies or through contracts with charitable, religious, or private organizations. Diversity in the organizational arrangements for delivering services, particularly employment services, influenced the selection of the states and, in some cases, the local sites.

The sample included two states with centralized welfare administration (Michigan and Texas), one that combined state-centered administration with some county-level control (Georgia), and one where welfare was administered by counties under state supervision (New York). The organizational arrangements for delivering employment services were more diverse. In Georgia, local offices of the state Department of Labor provided job search and job placement services for TANF applicants. In Michigan, employment services were overseen at the state level by the public Michigan Jobs Commission, which decentralized responsibility to local Michigan Works! agencies operating under the direction of local workforce development boards. The Michigan Works! agencies, in turn, contracted with nonprofit or school-affiliated agencies to provide "Work First" services to TANF clients. Texas created a similarly decentralized system. State oversight was the responsibility of the public Texas Workforce Commission, which decentralized responsibility through grants to local workforce development boards. The local workforce development boards, in turn, contracted with nonprofit or for-profit agencies to operate Texas Workforce Centers. Texas was included in the sample because several counties, including Dallas, contracted with a large for-profit corporation, Lockheed Martin, to operate its workforce centers. In New York, where welfare is administered by counties, arrangements for employment services varied by county.

Within each of the states, the sample included two or three local sites, listed in Table 2-2, where a site was defined to include one welfare office and the employment and child care agencies serving the clients of this office. Because major metropolitan areas contain a large share of the nation's welfare population and many bureaucracies to provide services, these areas faced more complex management challenges in coordinating services for their caseloads than did smaller areas. In drawing the sample, the goal was to include two local sites within a major metropolitan area of each state and a third site in a smaller metropolitan or suburban area of the state.

This goal was met in Georgia, with participation by two welfare offices in Fulton County (Atlanta) and the single welfare office in Bibb County (Macon). The willingness of office directors to participate in the study determined the selection of the two Fulton offices. This goal was also met in Texas, with two offices in Dallas County and the single wel-

Table 2-2. Functions of Organizations in the Local Sites

Determine Eligibility for Welfare	Arrange Child Care Financing	Provide Employment-Related Services
GEORGIA		
Fulton County: Northwest Area Office, Fulton County Department of Family and Children Services	Welfare office	Georgia Department of Labor: job search for applicants Welfare offices contract for other employment services
Fulton County: Southwest Area Office, Fulton County Department of Family and Children Services	Welfare office	Georgia Department of Labor: job search for applicants Welfare offices contract for other employment services
Bibb County Department of Family and Children Services	Welfare office	Georgia Department of Labor: job search for applicants Welfare offices contract for other employment services
MICHIGAN		
Wayne County: Glendale/Trumbull Office, Michigan Family Independence Agency	Welfare office	St. Clair Shores/Born Center (nonprofit)
Macomb County: Sterling Heights Office, Michigan Family Independence Agency	Welfare office	Jewish Vocational Services (nonprofit); Operation HELP (nonprofit)
Hillsdale County: Hillsdale Office, Michigan Family Independence Agency	Welfare office	Community Action Agency (nonprofit)
NEW YORK		
Albany County Department of Social Services	Welfare office	Albany County Department of Social Services contracts for all employment services
Suffolk County: Smithtown Office, Suffolk County Department of Social Services	Welfare office via telephone	Suffolk County Department of Labor
TEXAS		
Dallas: Masters Office, Texas Department of Human Services	Texas Child Care Management System	Texas Workforce Center operated by Lockheed Martin Corporation (for-profit)
Dallas: Grand Prairie Office, Texas Department of Human Services	Texas Child Care Management System	Texas Workforce Center operated by Lockheed Martin Corporation (for-profit)
Denton: Denton Office, Texas Department of Human Services	Texas Child Care Management System	Texas Workforce Center operated by North Texas Human Resources Group, Denton Center (nonprofit)

fare office in Denton County, north of Dallas. The regional welfare administrator selected the offices in Dallas. In New York, however, the state's largest city was not included because New York City administrators refused to grant access; instead, the sites included the welfare office in a moderate size city, Albany, and a welfare office in Suffolk County on Long Island. A county welfare administrator selected the welfare office in Suffolk. In Michigan, state officials selected the sites: only one welfare office in Wayne County (Detroit); one office in Macomb County, a Detroit suburb; and the third in rural Hillsdale County, which was an early participant in the state's Project Zero initiative that sought to employ all adults on welfare. If the involvement of administrators in selecting sites created a bias, the bias is presumably toward sites they thought were well-managed.

By design, the workforce offices in the sample took a variety of organizational forms. In Michigan, the Glendale/Trumbull welfare office in Wayne County referred clients to two nonprofit agencies, a community-based organization (Operation Help) and a social service agency (Jewish Vocational Services); the Sterling Heights welfare office in Macomb County sent clients to a school-affiliated center housing the area's alternative middle and high schools and adult education programs (St. Clair Shores/Born Center); and the Hillsdale County welfare office sent clients to the local Community Action Agency. In Texas, the welfare offices in Dallas referred their clients to workforce centers operated by Lockheed Martin, a for-profit firm, while the welfare office in Denton sent clients to a workforce center operated by a nonprofit corporation (North Texas Human Resources Group). All welfare offices in Georgia sent TANF applicants to the state Department of Labor and, to obtain services for recipients, contracted with other specialized service providers. In New York, the Suffolk County welfare agency contracted with the county Department of Labor to serve as the lead agency for employment services for all offices, including Smithtown. The Albany County welfare agency retained lead responsibility for employment services and contracted itself for specific services with individual nonprofit and for-profit agencies. Arranging child care financing for clients was the responsibility of the welfare agency in all states except Texas, which operated a Child Care Management System independent of the welfare agency. As a result, as shown in Table 2-2, the number of organizations constituting a site ranged from one to three, and varied from purely public to a combination of public and nonprofit or public and for-profit organizations.

One purpose for selecting states with different organizational arrangements for delivering employment services was to examine whether performance based systems influenced the behavior of frontline workers. States varied in their use of performance mechanisms (Table 2-3). In Georgia, the state Department of Labor subjected its local offices to goals for job placements. In Michigan and Texas, local contracts included performance goals such as the percent entering employment, the percent entering employment whose hourly wage rate is at least a specified amount, the percent employed at follow-up of 30, 60, or 90 days, and the average wage at follow-up. Project Zero in Michigan, a special initiative to promote employment, granted additional funds to sites for the purpose of employing the entire caseload. The New York Department of Labor allocated some funds on a performance basis, but most funds were allocated by the state welfare agency to county welfare agencies and did not contain performance goals. Similarly, the state welfare agency in Georgia did not impose performance goals on the funds allocated to county welfare agencies.

In summary, the states can be characterized along three dimensions: 1) the degree of centralization, 2) the level of TANF resources, and 3) the use of performance incentives. Michigan was most centralized and made greatest use of performance incentives. The state welfare agency operated the local welfare offices and, while overall responsibility for workforce activities was lodged in another state agency that decentralized operations to the local level, the local workforce agencies operated under performance goals set by the state. TANF funds were relatively generous and the state welfare agency allocated a portion for Project Zero, which had the single performance goal of employing the entire caseload. Texas used similar organizational arrangements, with state operation of local welfare offices and decentralized workforce agencies operating under state performance goals, but TANF funds to serve the state's poor population were most limited. Georgia was in the middle along all dimensions. The state Department of Labor served TANF applicants under performance goals, but county welfare agencies had some authority to design their operations and the work activities of TANF recipients. Georgia received more TANF funds per poor resident than Texas but less than the

Table 2-3. Accountability Mechanisms for Employment Services

Agency Responsible for Meeting the Federal Participation Rate	Lead State Agency for Employment Services	Lead Local Agency for Employment Services	Accountability Mechanisms for Employment Service Providers
GEORGIA			
County welfare agency	Applicant job search: Georgia Department of Labor (DOL)	County welfare agencies and DOL form a local partnership for applicant job search County welfare agencies contract for other education and training services	DOL: job placement goal Local contracts: some have performance goals*
MICHIGAN			
State welfare agency	Michigan Jobs Commission	Local workforce development boards contract for all services with public or nonprofit organizations	Performance goals* Project Zero: zero unemployment
NEW YORK			
County welfare agency	New York Department of Labor (NYDOL)	Albany: welfare agency contracts with public, nonprofit and for-profit services providers Suffolk: welfare agency contracts with Suffolk County Department of Labor (SDOL)	Albany: local contracts, some with performance goals* Suffolk: contract with SDOL is not performance based; some funds from NYDOL have performance goals*
TEXAS			
Local workforce agency	Texas Workforce Commission	Local workforce development boards contract for all services with public, nonprofit or for-profit workforce agencies	Participation rate and performance goals*

* Performance goals vary by site and may include the percent entering employment, the percent entering employment whose hourly wage rate is at least a specified amount, the percent employed at follow-up of 30, 60, or 90 days, and the average wage at follow-up.

other two states. New York was the only state with full decentralization of welfare administration to the local level. The state received the most TANF funds and made the least use of performance incentives.

Management Interviews

Visits to each of the sites were made between August 1998 and August 1999 to learn more about the agencies and to lay the groundwork for observing the frontline workers. Interviews were conducted with the senior administrators of the welfare and employment agencies and with purposive samples of midlevel and program managers, one or more direct supervisors of frontline workers, and between two and ten frontline workers. During these three to four day site visits, an interview protocol guided the collection of information about the local understanding of goals; local policy and program characteristics; the relationships among the organizations providing assistance and work activities; the specialization of job roles; the training, monitoring, and evaluation of frontline workers; the discretion given to workers; the use of management information systems for program operations and client tracking; and mechanisms to ensure that clients receive fair and equitable treatment. Management documents such as policy transmittal letters, interagency contracts, personnel policies, management information systems documentation, policy manuals, training manuals, standardized documents, and forms used to track and monitor clients were also collected. To prepare for the systematic observations of frontline workers, the rosters of staff in each office were collected along with notes about which staff had direct contact with clients. Also to prepare for the next phase of the study, observations were made of a small number of frontline workers meeting with clients.

Survey of Workers

When the observations were conducted, the observers administered a pencil and paper survey to all frontline staff who had direct, face-to-face contact with TANF applicants or recipients in the welfare, employment, and child care agencies. The survey elicited staff responses to questions about their understanding of the primary program goals for their office, their receipt of training in the prior three years, the extent of supervision and performance rewards, the extent of professional judgment they were expected to exercise in their work with clients, their assessment of the agency's management and leadership practices, their personal opinions about welfare and about clients, and their demographic and professional characteristics. A total of 354 surveys were distributed and 256 were returned, for a 72 percent response rate.

Frontline Workers and Encounters

To see a complete picture of frontline practices, it was necessary to observe all types of workers with face-to-face contact with clients. Every worker who had direct contact with TANF applicants and recipients potentially had the power to influence their experience with the welfare system. The most highly skilled staff such as case managers, eligibility workers, and job counselors were clearly influential, but less skilled staff such as receptionists and clerks who had the initial contact with clients could also be influential by providing information that steered people toward or away from the welfare system. For this reason, the sample included encounters between clients and frontline workers in all job positions where workers had face-to-face contact with TANF applicants and recipients.

An encounter was defined as any type of face-to-face contact between a worker and a TANF applicant or recipient. Encounters were of three types: 1) a one-on-one meeting, 2) a group meeting like an orientation or a training session in job search, and 3) a stream of clients coming to a reception desk or checkpoint. The encounter could be for any purpose, such as eligibility determination, recertification of eligibility, orientation to work activities, job search and placement, monitoring of work activity, conciliation and sanctioning, and arranging child care financing. Workers in any job position entailing face-to-face contact with TANF applicants and recipients were included. Interactions over the telephone were not included because only the worker's half of the conversation could be observed.

The first step in sampling the frontline workers and their encounters with clients was to identify job positions entailing face-to-face contact with TANF clients. Table 2-4 lists these job positions and the number of staff in each position in each site. In the welfare agencies in Michigan and Texas, a single position performed all the agency's functions for TANF clients, so applicants and recipients met only with office receptionists and these workers. In Georgia and New York, where local welfare offices had more discretion over job design, the offices divided staff into more specialized positions. With the exception of Georgia, the local workforce offices had discretion over job design and organized their staff in a variety of configurations. The Albany County welfare agency contracted with several public and private organizations for specialized employment services but because these organizations did not have overall responsibility for the employment function, their workers were not observed in the study.

When the observers arrived at a site, they conducted a brief survey of a sample of workers in each position in the site that asked how many hours they spent in face-to-face contact with TANF applicants or recipients each week. Multiplying the number of staff by the number of hours gave an estimate of the total number of weekly hours of client contact by workers in each job position. Table 2-4 shows the number of weekly hours of client contact in each job position in each site.

In every site, the majority of the staff who dealt directly with TANF clients were employed by the welfare agencies (Table 2-4). Except for New York, the percent employed by the welfare agencies were similar within each state: 92 percent of staff in Georgia, 75 to 81 percent in Michigan, and 70 to 81 percent in Texas. The two New York sites varied more substantially, with 100 percent of staff working in the welfare office in Albany County, where the welfare agency retained responsibility for arranging the client's employment activity, and 71 percent of staff working in the welfare office in Suffolk County. The distribution of staff contact time was generally similar to the distribution of staff. In Georgia, welfare staff accounted for 88 to 92 percent of total direct contact time with TANF clients at the site level; in Michigan, 70 to 79 percent; in Texas, 81 and 88 percent in two sites and 63 percent in Masters; and in New York, 53 percent in Suffolk County and 100 percent in Albany County.

**Table 2-4. Distribution of Staff and Staff Time with
TANF Clients by Agency and Job Position**

GEORGIA

	Number of Staff	Percent of Site Total	Staff Time With TANF Clients (Total Hours Per Week)	Percent of Site Total
		BIBB	*	
Welfare (DFACS)				
Screener	5	10	121	10
Intake (Eligibility)	11	22	278	23
"Challenger" Case Manager	4	8	103	9
Ongoing Case Manager	12	24	286	24
Employability	6	12	152	13
Work Experience Program	4	8	100	8
Child Care	4	8	71	6
Subtotal	*46*	*92*	*1,111*	*92*
Employment (DOL)				
Service Specialist	4	8	94	8
Subtotal	*4*	*8*	*94*	*8*
TOTAL	*50*	*100*	*1,205*	*100*
	FULTON Northwest			
Welfare (DFACS)				
Ongoing	17	44	192	46
Intake	5	13	37	9
Child Care	6	15	67	16
Reception	8	21	83	20
Subtotal	*36*	*92*	*378*	*92*
Employment (DOL)				
Service Specialist	2	5	31	8
Employment (DRS)*				
Workshop Leader	1	3	4	1
Subtotal	*3*	*8*	*35*	*8*
TOTAL	*39*	*100*	*413*	*100*
* Department of Rehabilitative Services				
	FULTON Southwest			
Welfare (DFACS)				
Eligibility	18	47	187	32
Employment	4	11	88	15
Receptionist	7	18	99	17
Child Care	6	16	138	24
Subtotal	*35*	*92*	*512*	*88*
Employment (DOL)				
Service Specialist	3	8	71	12
Subtotal	*3*	*8*	*71*	*12*
TOTAL	*38*	*100*	*583*	*100*

Table 2-4. Distribution of Staff and Staff Time with
TANF Clients by Agency and Job Position (Continued)

MICHIGAN

	Number of Staff	Percent of Site Total	Staff Time With TANF Clients (Total Hours Per Week)	Percent of Site Total
HILLSDALE				
Welfare (FIA)				
Family Independence Specialist	7	58	70	68
Reception	2	17	3	2
Subtotal	*9*	*75*	*73*	*70*
Employment (Community Action Agency)				
Case Manager	1	8	17	17
Job Developer	1	8	8	7
Support Services	1	8	6	6
Subtotal	*3*	*25*	*31*	*30*
TOTAL	*12*	*100*	*103*	*100*
MACOMB				
Welfare (FIA)				
Family Independence Specialist	24	75	353	63
Reception	2	6	52	9
Subtotal	*26*	*81*	*404*	*72*
Employment (St. Clair Shores/Born Center)				
Community Resource Specialist	1	3	28	5
Job Club & Retention	2	6	55	10
Job Readiness	1	3	26	5
Job Search	1	3	29	5
Assessment	1	3	22	4
Subtotal	*6*	*19*	*160*	*28*
TOTAL	*32*	*100*	*564*	*100*
WAYNE				
Welfare (FIA)				
Family Independence Specialist	49	78	964	76
Reception	2	3	39	3
Subtotal	*51*	*81*	*1,003*	*79*
Employment (Jewish Vocational Services)				
Retention Specialist	4	6	101	8
Case Coordinator	3	5	72	6
Employment (Operation Help)				
Orientation	1	2	20	2
Job Developer	4	6	80	6
Subtotal	*12*	*19*	*273*	*21*
TOTAL	*63*	*100*	*1,276*	*100*

**Table 2-4. Distribution of Staff and Staff Time with
TANF Clients by Agency and Job Position (Continued)**

NEW YORK

	Number of Staff	Percent of Site Total	Staff Time With TANF Clients (Total Hours Per Week)	Percent of Site Total
ALBANY				
Welfare (DSS)				
Eligibility	15	43	45	38
Intake	8	23	42	35
Reception Clerk	9	26	29	24
Child Support Investigation	1	3	1	1
Mental Health Barriers	2	6	3	2
TOTAL	*35*	*100*	*119*	*100*
SUFFOLK				
Welfare (DSS)				
Eligibility	7	37	53	31
Reception Clerk	3	16	24	14
Employment	1	7	1	1
Fraud Control	2	11	12	7
Subtotal	*13*	*71*	*90*	*53*
Employment (DOL)*				
Assessment	3	14	51	30
Registration	1	4	9	5
Job Readiness Training	1	4	4	2
Job Development/OJT	1	3	5	3
Job Placement	1	3	11	6
Subtotal	*5*	*29*	*79*	*47*
TOTAL	*19*	*100*	*169*	*100*

* *Proportional share for Smithtown office*

A quota of 60 hours of observations was assigned to each site to be
allocated across the job positions according to contact time. Because a
few job positions accounted for large shares of the total contact time, allocating the quota of 60 hours across positions in proportion to the distribution of time would yield many hours of observation of some positions
but few hours, or even just minutes, of others. To reduce variation in
hours of observation, the square root of the weekly hours of contact time
by workers in each position was calculated and the quota of 60 hours was
distributed among the job positions in proportion to the percent distribution of the square root of hours. Later, when analyzing the encounters,
each one was weighted to reflect the distribution of time of workers in
that position. Encounters with workers in positions that had been un-

**Table 2-4. Distribution of Staff and Staff Time with
TANF Clients by Agency and Job Position (Continued)**

	Number of Staff	Percent of Site Total	Staff Time With TANF Clients (Total Hours Per Week)	Percent of Site Total
TEXAS				
DENTON				
Welfare (DHS)				
Texas Works Advisor	12	60	150	77
Reception	2	10	7	4
Subtotal	*14*	*70*	*157*	*81*
Employment (TWC)				
Career Development	2	10	29	15
Workshop Facilitator	1	5	6	3
Resource Coordinator	1	5	2	1
Customer Service Rep	2	10	0	0
Subtotal	*6*	*30*	*37*	*19*
TOTAL	*20*	*100*	*194*	*100*
GRAND PRAIRIE				
Welfare (DHS)				
Texas Works Advisor	11	69	141	82
Reception	2	13	10	6
Subtotal	*13*	*81*	*151*	*88*
Employment (TWC)				
Career Counselor	1	6	8	5
Seminar Leader	1	6	12	7
Child Care	1	6	2	1
Subtotal	*3*	*19*	*21*	*12*
TOTAL	*16*	*100*	*172*	*100*
MASTERS				
Welfare (DHS)				
Texas Works Advisor	17	74	102	57
Reception	1	4	10	6
Subtotal	*18*	*78*	*112*	*63*
Employment (TWC)*				
Career Counselor	3	13	45	25
Seminar Leader	1	2	6	3
Resource Room Monitor	1	2	8	4
Child Care	1	3	8	4
Subtotal	*5*	*21*	*67*	*37*
TOTAL	*23*	*100*	*179*	*100*

* Proportional share for Masters office

der-observed were given a higher weight, while encounters with workers who were over-observed were given a lower weight.

The observers were given the quota of hours for each job position and instructed to randomly select workers within each position for observation. To do this, a list of all workers within each position was constructed from the agency rosters, and each worker was assigned a random number. Observers were instructed to select workers for observation beginning with the lowest number. Observers then explained the study to the selected workers, asked them to participate and, if they agreed, asked them to sign a form giving informed consent. Observers then waited until workers met with clients. Each worker was observed with clients for a minimum of three hours and a maximum of six hours, which were not always on the same day. The encounters observed during these hours constituted the sample. Many encounters were brief, so that 60 hours of observation time in each of the 11 sites produced a usable sample of 969 encounters.

The observers were graduate students from local universities who were trained to conduct the research. Officials in Michigan and Texas granted permission for them to use tape recorders during the observations, as did the Departments of Labor in Georgia and Suffolk County. In the other sites, the observers took handwritten notes, producing detailed records of the conversation between workers and clients. Observers asked the workers to introduce the client to them and to give the client an informed consent form, written in both English and Spanish, to be signed. Observers sat close enough to the worker and client to operate the tape recorder or hear the conversation, but they were instructed not to say anything during the encounter. If the worker left the client and observer alone, the observer was free to converse with the client but not to engage in any substantive conversation.

During the encounter, the observer began to complete the Encounter Worksheet (see Appendix), noting the client's race, gender, and spoken language. After the encounter, the observer conducted a debrief of the worker to learn the primary purpose for the client's visit to the office, what actions occurred as a result of the encounter, what factors explained the disposition of the case, and whether the worker believed the disposition entailed any professional judgment. The observer also gathered information about the gender, ethnic background, and educational background of the worker. Most observations were made between January and June 2000.

Analyzing the Content of the Conversation

With 969 encounters in the sample, it was necessary to develop a systematic method for analyzing the content of the conversation between the workers and clients. The method consisted of coding the conversation with two sets of codes: one set for the topic being discussed and the other set for the activity of the worker or client regarding the topic. The codes were developed by reading a sample of the encounters and identifying topics and activities of greatest relevance to the implementation of the TANF legislation. Coders were instructed to give a segment of conversation first a topic code and then an activity code, making it possible to identify what the workers were doing when they discussed each topic. The frequencies of these codes indicate the degree of attention workers gave to the topics.

In addition to coding these two dimensions of the conversation, codes were applied to indicate the primary purpose of the encounter, such as applying for assistance or attending job readiness training. A fourth set of codes was applied to indicate the actions taken by the worker as a result of the encounter, but these codes proved to be incomplete because the resulting actions were frequently not apparent from the conversation. Often, workers were unable to inform the client of the action to be taken because more information was needed to reach a definitive decision about the case.

Five trained graduate students applied the codes to the encounters using Atlas.ti, a software package designed to analyze qualitative data. A former welfare caseworker then checked the topic codes, applying and removing codes to improve accuracy. After the coding was completed, an analysis of the inter-rater reliability of the activity codes applied by the five coders showed which of the 34 worker activity codes were reliable. Unreliable activity codes were grouped together to achieve sufficient reliability or, in the case of codes that did not fit into any reliable group, dropped from the analysis. Grouping yielded 9 reliable worker activity codes; 13 codes were dropped from the analysis. The topic codes for education and training were combined, yielding a total of 42 topic codes. Appendix Tables 1 and 2 list and define all the codes.[2]

Topic and activity codes were then combined to answer the question: What was the worker doing regarding the topic? For example, if a worker and client were discussing the TANF time limit, was the worker explaining the rule or exempting the client from the rule? Atlas.ti has the capacity to identify segments of text marked with two codes and mark it with a third code, a "supercode." Supercodes combining a topic code and an activity code were defined and then applied automatically by Atlas.ti to segments of text.

The next step was transforming the topic codes and supercodes into variables. The choice here was between defining a variable to be the *number* of segments of text in an encounter marked with a particular code or supercode or creating a dummy variable indicating whether or not *any* text in the encounter was marked with a particular code or supercode. For example, a variable could be the number of segments of conversations in which the worker explained the time limit rule during the encounter or a dummy variable indicating whether or not the worker explained the rule at all during the encounter. A reading of a sample of encounters indicated that the number of times the worker explained the rule depended more on the organization of the conversation than on the emphasis given to the rule, since workers could express the rule forcefully even if they mentioned it only once. For this reason, the variables analyzed here are dummy variables indicating whether or not the entire encounter included any segment of text marked with particular topic codes or supercodes. The codes and supercodes from 969 encounters were imported from At-

---

2 The intraclass correlations among the activity codes were calculated using a method described in Patrick Shrout and Joseph Fleiss, "Intraclass Correlations: Uses in Assessing Rater Reliability," *Psychological Bulletin* 86:2 (1979): 420-428. This exercise revealed that all but 5 of the 34 worker activity codes were unreliable, where reliability was defined as an intraclass correlation (ICC) score of .6 or higher. An exercise in combining the other 29 codes to form broader codes found that 15 of the activity codes with a score below .6 could be grouped together into 4 broader codes with acceptable reliability, producing a total of 9 reliable activity codes. Due to its importance, the code "MIS verification" was analyzed even though its ICC score was below the .6 cutoff. To narrow the scope of this volume, the only reliable client activity code, inquiring about rules or benefits, was not analyzed. See Appendix Table 2 for the original and combined codes used here.

las.ti into an SPSS database, where they were transformed into dummy variables and their frequencies were tabulated.

Limitations of the Encounter Data

The encounter data suffer from several limitations in describing the practices of frontline workers.

First, the decision to exclude telephone conversations from the sample means that some interactions between workers and clients were not observed. Also unobserved were indirect contacts between workers and clients, such as letters and notices sent by the agency and office visits clients made to drop off paperwork without seeing a worker. These unobserved interactions were part of the treatment of clients by the welfare system and, to the extent they were significant, the encounter data fail to describe the treatment completely.

Second, the study did not track individual clients over multiple encounters with the welfare system, another reason why the encounter data are not a complete record of the treatment of the client by the welfare system. Workers often met with clients several times and had some flexibility in timing their discussion of particular topics. The absence of discussion of a particular topic in one encounter does not imply the topic was never discussed with the client. More generally, the data tell us what happened during the encounters but not what should have happened and did not.

Third, the tape recorders used in Michigan and Texas produced a more complete record of the conversation than the handwritten notes taken in Georgia and New York. The amount of text per minute of encounter was greater in Michigan and Texas than in Georgia and New York, suggesting that the observers taking handwritten notes missed some of the conversation. In addition, the use of multiple observers within Georgia and New York is a potential source of bias in the data. With no information about the nature of this potential bias, however, the analysis makes no adjustments for it.

Fourth, because the workers knew they were being observed, they might have altered their behavior toward their clients. One client made this argument to the observer when the worker left the office for a few minutes:

> *Client:* Now you know a lot of these workers are only being nice because you're here. A lot of them treat you like you're dirt because you come here.

> *Observer:* Mm-hmm.

> *Client:* A lot of them make you feel like you're bothersome to them. But she's the first polite one I've met, the first one. But a lot of them makes you feel like horrible. I have seen some of them make you cry.

This suggests that, to the extent the workers altered their behavior when the observers were present, they became more humane and generous in the treatment of their client.

Finally, the observations of frontline workers during their face-to-face encounters with clients do not give a complete view of the treatment of clients by the entire welfare system. The observations show the conversations of the workers and the responses of the client while they were together, including whatever decisions were mentioned at that time. A great deal of activity occurred during these encounters, as documented below. But the observations showed that certain final decisions, particularly those about eligibility, benefit amounts, and the imposition of sanctions, were often made when the client was not present with the worker. Frontline staff needed to gather additional information about the client and confer with supervisors before making a final decision to grant or withhold services. Supervisors and other back office staff reviewed decisions for accuracy before the decision became final. Computer systems generated decisions based on the information entered by staff and sent letters to recipients about benefits and about behavioral requirements, such as appearing at the welfare office for an assessment or recertification, that could affect their welfare eligibility. For these reasons, even the extensive observations of the encounters cannot paint a complete picture of the actions taken by the entire welfare system.

3

An Overview of Practices and Conversations at the Front Lines

A s in the nation as a whole, welfare caseloads declined sharply in Georgia, Michigan, New York, and Texas after the passage of TANF. Between 1995 and the first half of 2000, when the sites were observed, caseloads fell in the four states and all 11 sites in the sample (Table 3-1). Unemployment rates also declined in every state and site over this period, quite substantially in most places. Compared with the nation as a whole, the caseload declines in the sites were generally greater than the national decline of 53 over this period. Their unemployment rates generally declined more and were lower than the national rate of 4.0 percent in the first half of 2000. Yet the sites were not at the extremes and are broadly representative of the nation's experience, making them a relevant sample for examining the caseload decline from the perspective of the front lines of the welfare system.

This chapter gives an overview of practices and conversations in the welfare and workforce offices in the 11 sites. The overview begins to answer one of the questions posed earlier: To what extent did the practices

Table 3-1. Unemployment Rates and Caseloads

State and Locality	Unemployment Rate 1995 Percent	Unemployment Rate 2000 Percent	AFDC Cases 1995	TANF Cases Jan-June 2000	Percent Change in Caseloads 1995-2000
GEORGIA	4.9	3.7	137,314	52,015	-62.1
Bibb County	5.4	4.8	5,150	1,787	-65.3
Fulton County	5.4	3.7	21,984	8,259	-62.4
MICHIGAN	5.3	3.6	201,336	72,714	-63.9
Hillsdale County	4.8	3.8	480	138	-71.2
Macomb County	4.7	3.1	5,863	1,972	-66.4
Wayne County	6.0	3.9	88,618	31,840	-64.1
NEW YORK	6.3	4.6	451,633	258,181	-42.8
Albany County	4.2	2.8	4,362	2,498	-42.7
Suffolk County	5.4	3.2	12,339	5,016	-59.3
TEXAS	6.0	4.2	270,125	123,483	-54.3
Dallas	5.1	3.5	28,703	10,766	-62.5
Denton	3.4	2.0	1,218	319	-73.8
U.S. Total	5.6	4.0	4,798,309	2,259,608	-52.9

Sources: U.S. Department of Labor, Bureau of Labor Statistics. Local Area Unemployment Statistics. http://www.bls.gov/data/home.htm. State caseload data provided by the states. Federal caseload data: http://www.acf.dhhs.gov/programs/ofa/caseload/2000/family00tan.htm.

of frontline workers in the welfare system conform to the goals for TANF set forth at higher levels? Specifically, did workers give equal attention to all the goals of TANF in the federal law — to provide assistance to families with children; end dependence on government assistance by promoting job preparation, work, and marriage; reduce out-of-wedlock pregnancies; and encourage the formation and maintenance of two-parent families — or did they give selective attention to the provisions of the law?

This chapter first uses the encounter data to examine why people came to the welfare and workforce offices. Because the most common reason was to apply for assistance, it draws on the management interviews to describe the application process designed by the states or sites. It then uses the frequencies of the topic codes to summarize the attention workers gave to various policies, services, and family problems during their conversations with clients. The frequencies of the activity codes summarize the nature of the workers' activities during these conversations. These summaries permit some broad conclusions about the sites' responses to the goals of TANF stated in the federal law.

Primary Purpose of the Encounter

Arriving at a welfare office in 2000, clients might have picked up signals about the new goals of the welfare system. A big banner in the lobby of one office in Georgia proclaimed "Welcome Job Seekers!" Framed posters in the waiting room said "You Have A Choice, Choose A Job — Work First"; "Work First so that your child is not the next generation on welfare"; "Life works if you Work First"; and "There is a better alternative: Work First." The message was the same in the waiting room of a Texas welfare office: "Job Seekers Welcome!" and, in English and Spanish, "Time is Running Out/Welcome Job Seekers, Your independence is our success." The Suffolk County, New York, welfare agency covered the walls of its waiting room with Department of Labor job postings. Both clients and staff could not help but see these physical statements of the agency's goals. Only in Michigan were the waiting rooms of the welfare agencies bare of exhortations to work.

In Georgia, the welfare offices in Fulton County were modern multi-story buildings, easily accessible by Atlanta's rapid transit system. In Bibb County, the welfare office was surrounded by the office's own child care center, its teen center, its center for remedial education, and a satellite office of the Department of Labor. In Texas, welfare offices in Dallas were small and located in rented space, one in a spacious carpeted office on an upper floor of a bank building not served by public transportation, the other in a slightly dilapidated one-story building shared with a bingo parlor until the workforce office rented the space to serve TANF clients. The Texas welfare agency invested modestly in its offices, but the workforce offices serving the general population in Texas occupied large and modern buildings. Welfare offices in Michigan were in nondescript office buildings, while the workforce agencies were located in community agencies — a school, a crowded urban storefront, a social services agency, and a community action agency. As in Texas, the welfare office in Suffolk County was located in a less imposing building than the workforce office. The newly renovated welfare office in Albany County gave clients a number to form an orderly queue, a priority of the county executive whose name was written on the door in gold letters. Guards and metal detectors were common at the entrances to the welfare offices but not the workforce offices.

Because the purpose for a client's visit to the welfare system structures the conversation between the worker and the client, it is useful to begin by asking why people came to meet with a worker. The primary purposes for visits to the welfare and workforce offices in the states are shown in Table 3-2. Between 36 and 50 percent of the encounters took place in the welfare offices for the purpose of applying for TANF, food stamps, or Medicaid, making these the most common reasons for coming to the welfare office. Applications for TANF, food stamps, and Medicaid are grouped together because workers often determined a family's eligibility for the three programs simultaneously. Smaller numbers of encounters were for the purpose of applying for other types of assistance, such as transportation assistance and, in Michigan and New York, emergency housing assistance. In addition, families already receiving assistance came to the welfare office periodically to recertify their eligibility. Families leaving welfare did not need to come to the welfare office for an exit interview and the encounters captured few encounters for this pur-

Table 3-2. Distribution of Encounters in Welfare and Workforce Offices by Their Primary Purpose

	GEORGIA		MICHIGAN		NEW YORK		TEXAS	
	welfare	workforce	welfare	workforce	welfare	workforce	welfare	workforce
	percent		percent		percent		percent	
Eligibility Determination								
Application for TANF, Medicaid, or Food Stamps	36	0	40	0	41	0	50	1
Application for Other Assistance	0	0	5	1	7	1	0	2
Recertification/Exit Interview	13	0	9	0	18	1	15	1
Oversight								
Monitoring Compliance With Mandates	1	0	4	1	0	1	0	3
Attendance Problems/Conciliation or Sanctioning	6	0	3	0	2	0	0	1
Suspected Fraud	0	0	1	0	1	0	0	0
Employment-Related Meeting								
Group Orientation	2	0	1	0	0	1	0	3
Assessment	12	3	7	3	1	4	0	1
Application for Child Care Assistance*	18	0	3	0	1	1	0	10
Attending Job Readiness/Job Search Activity	3	5	1	10	1	5	0	7
Other								
Other Client-Initiated Visit	0	0	3	0	7	1	0	2
Other	1	1	6	1	3	2	0	4
Purpose Unclear	0	0	0	0	0	0	0	0
Total	91	9	82	18	82	18	65	35

* In Texas, Child Care Management System workers were stationed in workforce offices.

pose. Altogether, between 49 and 69 percent of all encounters took place in order to determine eligibility for some form of assistance.

People also came to the welfare or workforce office, frequently in response to a letter, for purposes of oversight by workers. Workers monitored their compliance with rules, discussed penalties for noncompliance, and investigated fraud. Encounters for oversight purposes were between 4 and 9 percent of the total.

Another group of encounters were directly related to the client's potential employment and took place in either welfare or workforce offices. Most workforce offices held group orientations to explain work requirements, the availability of services to support work, and other topics related to work. Welfare and workforce offices called in clients for assessments related to their potential employment, education, or training. People came in to apply for child care assistance in order to work or attend another work-related activity. In addition, workforce offices and a few welfare offices held various types of individual and group meetings to prepare clients to search for work and help them find jobs. The percent of encounters for these employment-related purposes ranged from 14 percent of all encounters in New York to 43 percent in Georgia.

Encounters in the "other" category were related to eligibility (such as reporting missing checks or incorrect benefits, delivering or picking up documents, and adding children to the case), employment (such as picking up a bus pass or a job referral, reporting a new job or a job loss, or changing child care provider), housing assistance (resulting from an eviction, utility shut-off, or moving) and so forth. Finally, some encounters served multiple purposes; for example, a person who came to the welfare office for the primary purpose of applying for TANF might also apply for child care assistance or a client who came to the workforce office to attend an orientation might also be offered child care assistance so she could begin job search.

Of all the encounters in the welfare system, the majority occurred in welfare offices, ranging from 65 percent in Texas to 91 percent in Georgia (Table 3-2). The variation among the states in the percent of encounters occurring in welfare offices reflects the division of responsibilities between the welfare and workforce agencies and, not surprisingly, mirrors the distribution of staff between the welfare and workforce offices (Table 2-4). For example, the main responsibility of the welfare agencies in Texas was to determine eligibility for assistance, while the welfare agencies in Georgia also had responsibility for authorizing child care assistance and referring recipients to employment and training activities. With this division of responsibilities, the primary purpose of all the encounters in the Texas welfare agencies was application or recertification for assistance, while little more than half the encounters in the Georgia welfare agencies were for these purposes. In Georgia, almost a third of the encounters in the welfare agencies were for the primary purpose of authorizing child care assistance or assessing recipients in order to determine their employability and refer them to an employment activity.

By the same token, the workforce agencies had greater responsibilities in some states than others. The Texas workforce agencies handled all tasks related to employment, including monitoring compliance with work mandates. Stationed in these agencies were also the workers responsible for authorizing child care assistance. The Georgia workforce agencies had the narrowest set of responsibilities, only job readiness and job search assistance for TANF applicants. In Michigan and New York, their primary tasks were assessing clients and providing employment and training services.

The distribution of encounters by their primary purpose shows that determining applicants' eligibility for assistance was the context for a large share of the encounters in welfare offices. Although TANF caseloads declined sharply, applications for assistance declined much less rapidly. The slower decline in applications meant that determining eligibility continued to impose a heavy demand on the time of frontline staff in the welfare agency. Furthermore, many staff reported that the time required to process an application for assistance had increased with the mandates in TANF.

The Application Process

In responding to TANF, state and local officials realized that the procedures for determining eligibility were potential levers for reducing reliance on the welfare system. Restrictive rules for receiving assistance have always caused welfare agencies to design complex application procedures to screen out people who are not eligible. "Demeaning qualification tests and tedious administrative procedures" have created "ordeals" for applicants to target assistance on families with the least ability to earn income and to deter more able families.[1] In the years leading up to TANF, some states had added to the process by requiring welfare applicants to search for work or had experimented with diverting applicants from assistance by offering them a lump sum payment in lieu of welfare. With welfare no longer an entitlement, welfare agencies were free to design an application process that made access to welfare more demanding or that offered alternatives to welfare.

Determining Eligibility

Although specific procedures varied across the 11 sites, the basic elements of the welfare application process were similar. Welfare applicants began the process by visiting a local welfare office, in person, to obtain an application for TANF. Reception staff provided a multipage application form — typically a combined application for TANF, food stamps, and Medicaid — that required applicants to report extensive information about their financial circumstances, recent work history, living arrangements, and family composition. Computers were replacing paper forms in Georgia and Texas, reflecting the increased use of computers in welfare administration generally.

The second step in the intake process involved an in-person meeting at the welfare office, often on another day, to verify the application information, collect additional information, and explain the rules and requirements of the welfare system. One or more eligibility staff met with each applicant to review the completed application and collect documentation verifying income, family, housing, and other information. TANF applicants were required to provide extensive personal and financial information at this stage; eligibility workers used written or computerized application forms to collect information about the family's composition

---

1   Albert L. Nichols and Richard J. Zeckhauser, "Targeting Transfers through Restrictions on Recipients," *American Economic Review* 72:2 (May 1982): 376.

and its members' place of birth, citizenship status, address, current and recent income, current and recent employment, living expenses, and so on. Much of this information had to be documented, and the eligibility worker collected, reviewed, and often copied identification and citizenship cards, drivers' licenses, birth, marriage and divorce certificates; current and recent pay stubs, bank statements, tax records, proof of income from self-employment, family members or other sources; proof of address, rent, utility bills, and other expenses; documentation of assets such as car registrations and bank records; and any other documents bearing on their eligibility for assistance.

Applicants typically arrived with standard types of required documentation — such as social security cards or birth certificates. Other forms of verification were unique to the welfare application process and often required the applicant to make personal contact with a variety of other individuals and/or agencies and bring documents to the welfare office. Those with recent employment, for example, had to visit past employers to obtain statements verifying both their employment and the reason for their termination. Those who received financial assistance from ex-partners or from family members had to obtain signed statements documenting this support. In some sites, those with young children had to obtain medical records from their doctors and those with school-aged children had to obtain attendance records from their children's schools. Because the housing arrangements of very poor individuals are often complicated, verifying address and living arrangement was often time-consuming, requiring letters or signed statements from landlords, neighbors, and relatives. Special circumstances often required particular documentation — probation records, death certificates, eviction notices, medical proof of pregnancy, proof of their own or their children's disability, and so forth. Because applicants typically arrived at their intake appointments without one or more pieces of required documentation, the eligibility worker made a list of required documents for the applicant to bring to her next review. Applications were "pended" until the welfare worker received all required verification and were closed without a determination of eligibility if the documentation was not provided.

The rigorous verification of information was motivated in part by the Quality Control system in the food stamp program. Prior to TANF, the federal government's Quality Control system imposed financial penalties on states with excessive rates of error in determining AFDC eligibility and benefits. Quality Control in cash assistance ended with TANF, but the Department of Agriculture continued to penalize states with high rates of error in administering food stamps.[2] Because eligibility for food stamps and cash assistance were determined jointly, gathering accurate information from TANF applicants continued to be a priority of state and local welfare offices.

All welfare offices were also alert to the possibility of fraud by people applying for assistance. Measures to detect and deter fraud were particularly evident in New York and Texas, where welfare staff electronically fingerprinted all applicants. The welfare offices in New York required workers to refer cases with suspicious information to a Front End Detection System (FEDS) fraud investigator. Most new applicants in Suffolk County were referred to FEDS and required to have an in-office interview and sometimes a home visit by a FEDS worker. In Texas, the welfare information system was integrated with other state data systems and with a database of financial information collected by a private company (described by staff as a "data broker"), all accessible through the computer on the worker's desk. Eligibility workers were responsible for cross checking a number of client claims — including recent earnings, child support, car ownership, and citizenship — against automated employment tax records, records from the Attorney General's Office and the Department of Motor Vehicles, and state birth records. Using the private database, the workers could find the client's credit information, criminal history, neighbors' addresses and phone numbers, and other private information. In both states, evidence of misrepresentation by the applicant was grounds for closing the application and could lead to a more extensive investigation and prosecution for fraud.

If the applicant was a single parent, the eligibility worker reviewed her compliance with relevant child support enforcement requirements. Additional procedures varied with the type of case and by site. If the applicant was a single parent with a child support order in place, the eligibility worker typically verified the order and all income received from

---

2   Federal legislation in 2002 revised the Quality Control system and gave states options for simplifying the Food Stamp program.

the absent parent. If an order was not in place or if payments had not been made, the applicant was required to cooperate with finding the absent parent and assigning an order. Another set of workers or another agency generally had responsibility for child support enforcement, but the eligibility worker had authority to refer the applicant to the child support office and deny TANF benefits for failure to appear at the office.

Work First

In Georgia, Michigan, and Texas, the eligibility determination process included an explicit employment component called Work First. The introduction of a work component into the eligibility process was a major reform resulting from TANF, one that signaled applicants that welfare clients were expected to work. While the specific form of these employment activities varied across and sometimes within the states, they all put the applicant in contact with the workforce agency staff prior to receiving assistance.

✦ In Georgia, applicants for welfare were required to participate in a Work First program before welfare could be authorized. Unless applicants were already working or going to school, they had to search for a job before they could be certified eligible to receive TANF. Fulton County put the application "on hold" for three weeks while the applicant searched for work, while Bibb County held the application for 45 days. During this time, staff from the Department of Labor gave applicants training in job search and information about available jobs, while the welfare agency provided funds for child care and transportation to help them search for work. If the applicant complied with job searching during this period, the eligibility worker processed her application.

Administrators in all sites said the goal of job search for applicants was to divert them from assistance. One administrator said, "We take a TANF application and set it aside. We try to get them to work right away. If they don't get a job, then we do the application."

✦ In Michigan, the welfare agencies referred all applicants to a group orientation conducted jointly by the welfare agency and the local workforce agency. The orientation explained the welfare rules and the services available to support employment. Applicants then met individually with a worker who assigned them to an initial Work First activity, generally job search, and arranged assistance for child care. When the applicant attended the first day of the work activity, the workforce agency notified the welfare agency and the welfare agency authorized TANF.

In the view of administrators, diversion was not the goal of Work First. The goal was to give applicants the message they would be required to work and that barriers to work would be removed. "Our goal is to get customers to self-sufficiency, but they can't be thinking about getting a job if they are hungry, so we open a case as soon as possible."

◆ In Texas, as in Michigan, all applicants for welfare were required to attend a group orientation at the local workforce agency. The orientation described the workforce agency's program for TANF recipients (named Choices) and the supportive services available at the agency. Workforce staff stamped a form to document their attendance and scheduled a return meeting on a future date after assistance would be authorized. In some sites, the workforce staff followed the orientation with a brief individualized employment assessment and referral on the spot. The welfare eligibility worker "pended" the application until the applicant returned with signed proof of attendance at the orientation. If the applicant failed to provide proof, the application for welfare was closed.

In the initial phase of TANF implementation, the welfare agency designed a process to "redirect" applicants from welfare to employment before they met with an eligibility worker — to divert applicants even before referring them to Work First. When applicants registered with the receptionist, the receptionist was to refer them immediately to a resource room or a computer with job listings. Some welfare offices also invited employers into their lobby to recruit potential applicants. By the time of the observations, however, the welfare offices had abandoned this initiative to "redirect" applicants before they met with an eligibility worker to complete their application for assistance.

When asked whether the goal of Work First was more about getting people off welfare or getting them into jobs, one supervisor said, "It's more about getting people off welfare. It's no secret; it's in the newspapers. But that is politically incorrect, so they say it is about getting people jobs." An administrator said, "Getting to work and getting off welfare mean the same thing in Texas because grants are so low."

✦ In New York, the state did not mandate a Work First approach and each county designed its own application process. In Suffolk County, frontline welfare workers decided which of several mandatory referrals the applicant would receive at the point of application. In most cases, the worker sent the applicant to an orientation meeting at the Department of Labor. If the applicant claimed to have a disability (and was not already receiving Social Security or Supplemental Security Income), the worker referred her to the Department of Health for an assessment. If the eligibility worker suspected a drug or alcohol problem, she referred the applicant to the Department of Alcohol and Substance Abuse for a mandatory assessment. Failure to cooperate at this point was grounds for benefit denial. Each of these referrals could result in a plan for ongoing, mandatory activities. Labor Department staff, for example, developed and monitored an employment plan specifying activities such as job search or work experience. Likewise, staff at the Departments of Health or Alcohol and Substance Abuse devised treatment plans for clients determined to have health or substance abuse problems.

In Albany County, welfare intake workers met with applicants to collect information about their situation and screen them for substance abuse and domestic violence. If a screening was positive, the applicant was referred for an assessment at the Department of Mental Health or to the liaison for domestic violence. Other applicants received a job search booklet with directions for a self-directed job search. The intake worker then scheduled an appointment for a full eligibility interview in five to seven days. The welfare agency retained lead responsibility for employment activities, contracting with several agencies for specific education, training, and employment services.

Albany County gave workers the discretion to offer applicants cash diversion payments as an alternative to ongoing assistance. With this exception, the goal was to require and support work but not to divert applicants from assistance.

In addition to enforcing employment-related eligibility requirements and linking applicants to employment services, welfare eligibility workers in many sites were responsible for discussing a "personal responsibility agreement" (PRA) with new applicants. A PRA was typically reviewed and signed during one of the face-to-face meetings. Its provisions often required the applicant to work, comply with child support enforcement, and obtain and return verification of additional activities, e.g., attendance at parenting classes, immunization, and well-child exams. Once a client signed the agreement, the welfare agency could sanction someone who failed to comply with it.

Definition of "Applicant"

To examine encounters with TANF applicants, it was necessary to define an "applicant" broadly to include anyone with children who came to the welfare office to apply for TANF, food stamps, or Medicaid. Grouping applicants for TANF, food stamps, or Medicaid together was necessary because workers determined eligibility for these programs in a single process. Families came to apply for food stamps or Medicaid and learned they might also be eligible for cash assistance, or they came for welfare but learned they were eligible only for food stamps or Medicaid. Part of the worker's task was collecting information from the potential applicant in order to identify the program or programs the family might qualify for.

Importantly, in some of the encounters with applicants for TANF, food stamps, or Medicaid, people did not complete a formal application for TANF. This happened for a number of reasons. In some cases, with only a few questions, the worker could determine the client was ineligible because her income was too high, because she was too young to apply on her own and had to apply as a member of her parent's family, or because she failed to meet some other eligible rule. In a few cases, families learned about the program's requirements and decided not to apply for assistance. In others, families left the office without deciding whether they would apply for assistance. These conversations were all part of the TANF application process and worth examining regardless of whether or not the individual ultimately completed a formal TANF application.

Defining applicants broadly complicates the interpretation of the quantitative data on encounters, particularly those on the frequency of discussion of topics of conversation with applicants. These frequencies are surprisingly low if one expects topics of importance to TANF to be discussed in all encounters with applicants, with frequencies of 100 percent. But a prior presumption that workers would discuss a topic with everyone applying for some sort of assistance is unwarranted. When workers determined that a family was ineligible for TANF, they generally stopped treating the family as a TANF applicant. To some unknown extent, workers did not implement the provisions of TANF because the people in front of them did not qualify for TANF. This occurred more frequently in Michigan and New York than in Georgia and Texas. Michigan and New York provided emergency housing assistance to people threatened with an eviction, a shut-off of their utilities, or another housing problem. In these states, particularly in New York, the availability of housing assistance drew to the welfare office families whose incomes exceeded the limits for TANF. When workers learned that the family's income disqualified them from TANF, they no longer focused on the TANF rules and mandates.

Even in encounters with applicants who were likely to be eligible for TANF, workers did not discuss the TANF rules and mandates in every encounter. When a client appeared to satisfy the eligibility conditions, workers often asked the applicant to bring in a document verifying the information she provided, such as a pay stub, job termination letter, or eviction notice. When the applicant returned to the welfare office with the document, the worker did not explain all the mandates again. Because multiple visits gave workers multiple opportunities to discuss rules and mandates, workers did not discuss them in every encounter.

In addition, the encounters captured people reapplying for TANF, food stamps, or Medicaid in cases when they lost their electronic benefit or Medicaid card and mistakenly concluded they were no longer eligible, or when assistance was interrupted for other reasons. Although they were coded as applicants, they were in fact already recipients. Unless the worker was recertifying their eligibility at that time, an explanation of the rules and mandates might not have been necessary or appropriate.

With certain families, discussion of several of the TANF rules and mandates was not appropriate. Workers did not discuss all the mandates when the adults in the household were receiving payments only for the children. The adults in these "payee only" cases were parents receiving Supplemental Security Income (SSI), grandparents, and other relatives or caretakers. Because they were not receiving assistance to meet their own needs, several mandates, particularly the ones regarding work and child support enforcement, did not apply to them. About 4 percent of the encounters were coded as payee-only cases, one-quarter of which were applicants.

Finally, none of the encounters in the workforce agencies for orientations and job search activities were coded as encounters with applicants. Because these were group encounters, not individual encounters, a decision was made not to code these as encounters with applicants. As a result, the instances where rules and mandates were discussed during the application process are undercounted, since staff at the workforce agencies explained and emphasized many of the rules and mandates during these encounters.

In interpreting all the encounter data, including encounters with both applicants and recipients, it is important to distinguish between encounters and clients. The data were drawn from a sample of encounters, not a sample of clients. The frequencies presented below indicate the likelihood a topic was discussed in an encounter, not the likelihood that a client would experience a discussion of the topic. Because clients may have had more than one encounter with workers over the course of their contact with the welfare system, they may have had multiple opportunities to experience a discussion of the topic. The absence of a topic from a particular encounter does not imply the client never heard about the topic, so the frequencies understate the discussion of the topic with a client over the course of the client's experience with the welfare system.

Topics Discussed

How much attention did workers give to the goals of TANF in their conversation with clients? As described in the previous chapter, the conversation was coded with two sets of codes: one for the topic being discussed and the other for the activity of the worker or client regarding the topic. The frequencies of the topic codes, which are presented here, are a measure of the attention workers gave to each of the TANF goals. Later chapters on the individual policies include quotations from the conversation that show the content of the discussion in more detail.

The 42 topic codes are listed in Table 3-3, where they are clustered into five groups. (See Appendix Table 1 for the full definitions of the topic codes). "Welfare rules" includes eligibility rules like time limits, sanctions, entitlement and fraud, and behavioral rules like participating in mandated activities, cooperating with child support enforcement, signing a Personal Responsibility Agreement, and immunizing children. "Work-related" topics include employment and training activities, supportive services like child care and transportation, and the financial incentives to work provided by the earned income tax credit and earnings disregards. "Other assistance and services" includes a variety of government services other than TANF, like SSI and unemployment insurance, as well as food stamps, Medicaid, health insurance, services in the community, and the availability of cash, Medicaid, food stamps, and child care for people who do not receive TANF. "Family-related topics" include absent parents, family problems such as domestic violence, pregnancy-related topics, and marriage. "Client problems" include health problems, problems with housing and utilities, crime, and substance abuse.

Table 3-3a shows the percent of all encounters in which each of the selected topics was discussed at least once during the encounter. Similar percentages for the encounters with applicants for TANF, food stamps, or Medicaid are shown in Table 3-3b. As stated above, the use of tape recorders in Michigan and Texas produced a more detailed record of the conversation, and hence more coding, than the handwritten notes in Georgia and New York. The average number of topic codes per encounter is 9.8 in Michigan and 11.3 in Texas, compared to 8.0 in Georgia and

Table 3-3a. Frequency of Discussion of Topics
All Encounters

(Number of Encounters)	MICHIGAN (269)		TEXAS (229)		GEORGIA (202)		NEW YORK (264)	
	Percent	Rank	Percent	Rank	Percent	Rank	Percent	Rank
Welfare Rules								
Participation	66	3	56	6	54	3	32	6
Child Support Enforcement	35	13	55	7	44	5	25	11
Personal Responsibility Agreement	14	24	39	13	22	16	0	39
Immunization of Children	9	29	33	16	26	13	0	40
School Attendance of Children	8	32	29	17	12	23	10	22
Sanctions	14	25	15	25	11	24	14	18
Time Limits	7	33	28	18	15	19	3	32
Entitlement or Self-Sufficiency	18	20	16	24	6	29	4	30
Family Cap	0	42	0	40	15	18	0	42
Earnings Disregards	4	35	0	40	0	40	1	36
One-Time Diversion Assistance	6	34	0	39	0	41	2	33
Fraud	3	36	6	33	3	35	7	26
Work-Related Topics								
Employment — Current and Future	72	1	66	3	58	2	52	1
Child Care	54	5	52	10	67	1	33	5
Transportation	56	4	69	1	50	4	25	10
Employment — Past	51	7	68	2	39	7	39	3
Job Readiness/Job Search — Current or Future	67	2	55	8	35	8	27	8
Education or Training — Current or Future	36	12	44	12	43	6	22	13
Education or Training — Past	22	17	25	20	32	10	15	16
Education/Employment Unclear — Current or Future	11	27	10	30	6	28	7	27
Job Readiness/Job Search — Past	10	28	8	32	5	32	3	31
Work Experience — Current or Future	2	37	1	38	4	34	9	23
Education/Employment Unclear — Past	2	38	4	34	0	39	0	41
Earned Income Credit	1	40	2	36	1	37	1	34

Table 3-3a. Frequency of Discussion of Topics
All Encounters (Continued)

(Number of Encounters)	MICHIGAN (269)		TEXAS (229)		GEORGIA (202)		NEW YORK (264)	
	Percent	Rank	Percent	Rank	Percent	Rank	Percent	Rank
Other Assistance and Services								
Other Government Services	52	6	52	9	28	12	41	2
Food Stamps	50	8	61	5	31	11	29	7
Medicaid	2	9	63	4	21	17	26	9
Community Services	20	18	11	29	6	30	10	21
Benefits Without TANF	16	21	19	23	5	33	5	28
Emergency Assistance	11	26	2	37	0	41	5	29
Health Insurance	18	19	34	14	10	26	8	24
Family-Related Topics								
Absent Parent	27	15	51	11	35	9	17	14
Family Problems	23	16	23	21	24	14	16	15
Pregnancy	15	22	15	26	13	20	12	19
Parenting	8	31	13	28	3	36	1	35
Family Planning	1	39	3	35	13	22	1	37
Marriage	1	41	0	40	1	38	1	37
Client Problems								
Health, Disability, and Mental Health — Client	40	11	19	22	23	15	23	12
Housing and Utilities	40	10	14	27	9	27	36	4
Health, Disability, and Mental Health — Others	28	14	34	15	13	21	14	17
Crime	15	23	27	19	10	25	12	20
Substance Abuse	9	30	9	31	6	31	8	25

Table 3-3b. Frequency of Discussion of Topics
Encounters with Applicants for TANF, Food Stamps, or Medicaid

(Number of Encounters)	MICHIGAN (111)		TEXAS (115)		GEORGIA (72)		NEW YORK (110)	
	Percent	Rank	Percent	Rank	Percent	Rank	Percent	Rank
Welfare Rules								
Participation	79	2	57	10	65	3	22	12
Child Support Enforcement	50	11	85	4	76	1	36	6
Personal Responsibility Agreement	21	21	56	11	39	15	0	38
Immunization of Children	17	24	49	13	39	14	0	38
School Attendance of Children	4	34	39	16	19	22	9	23
Sanctions	12	26	12	30	11	26	12	20
Time Limits	7	30	28	21	19	23	2	29
Entitlement or Self-Sufficiency	19	22	22	24	10	27	1	34
Family Cap	0	41	0	39	35	17	0	38
Earnings Disregards	4	35	0	39	1	39	1	35
One-Time Diversion Assistance	4	33	0	39	0	40	2	30
Fraud	4	32	10	31	1	38	12	21
Work-Related Topics								
Employment — Current and Future	79	4	76	5	63	4	47	3
Child Care	56	8	46	14	71	2	22	11
Transportation	52	10	73	7	55	7	16	15
Employment — Past	72	6	92	1	61	6	55	1
Job Readiness/Job Search — Current or Future	79	3	60	9	51	10	25	9
Education or Training — Current or Future	32	16	37	17	37	16	13	18
Education or Training — Past	19	23	34	18	51	9	7	25
Education/Employment Unclear — Current or Future	10	29	7	33	7	32	4	28
Job Readiness/Job Search — Past	6	31	8	32	2	37	2	31
Work Experience — Current or Future	2	37	1	38	3	34	1	35
Education/Employment Unclear — Past	1	38	2	35	0	40	1	35
Earned Income Credit	0	41	2	37	3	35	0	38

Table 3-3b. Frequency of Discussion of Topics
Encounters with Applicants for TANF, Food Stamps, or Medicaid (Continued)

(Number of Encounters)	MICHIGAN (111)		TEXAS (115)		GEORGIA (72)		NEW YORK (110)	
	Percent	Rank	Percent	Rank	Percent	Rank	Percent	Rank
Other Assistance and Services								
Other Government Services	72	5	69	8	44	12	41	5
Food Stamps	84	1	90	3	54	8	49	2
Medicaid	70	7	91	2	44	13	45	4
Community Services	25	18	14	29	9	28	7	24
Benefits Without TANF	21	20	18	26	8	31	5	26
Emergency Assistance	12	27	2	35	0	40	4	27
Health Insurance	36	15	55	12	24	21	13	17
Family-Related Topics								
Absent Parent	43	13	74	6	63	5	26	8
Family Problems	32	17	33	19	44	11	23	10
Pregnancy	23	19	22	22	25	20	18	14
Parenting	3	36	17	27	6	33	0	38
Family Planning	1	39	6	34	29	19	1	32
Marriage	1	39	0	39	2	36	1	32
Client Problems								
Health, Disability, and Mental Health — Client	46	12	22	23	31	18	18	13
Housing and Utilities	55	9	18	25	15	25	34	7
Health, Disability, and Mental Health — Others	38	14	44	15	9	29	12	19
Crime	17	25	32	20	15	24	14	16
Substance Abuse	10	28	16	28	8	30	11	22

6.0 in New York. While differences in the actual conversations may explain a portion of these differences in the number of codes, the amount of detail in the record strongly suggests that a portion is due to the method of recording the conversation. To permit comparisons between the states where tape recorders were used and those where they were not used, the tables also include the rank of the topics by their frequency within each state.

Looking at the rank of the topics by their frequencies, it is clear that workers gave more attention to the employment goals of TANF than to its goals to promote marriage and two-parent families and to reduce out-of-wedlock pregnancies. Work-related topics include the most frequently discussed topic in every state: child care in Georgia, transportation in Texas, and current and future employment in Michigan and New York. Among the welfare rules, the rule discussed most frequently in every state was the requirement to participate in a mandated activity. These mandated activities, as discussed in Chapter 4, were most commonly employment or a work activity arranged by the welfare system.

Marriage and family planning, in contrast, were discussed infrequently. Workers discussed family planning in 13 percent of the encounters in Georgia, but workers in the other states gave this topic almost no attention. Discussion or activity that appeared to promote marriage and the formation of two-parent families occurred in one percent or less of the encounters in all the states.

Importantly, many topics of conversation were not coded: identifying information like names, addresses, and social security numbers; demographic information such as the number and ages of children in the family; and financial information about amounts of income, assets, and expenditures on specific items. Conversation about these topics consumed a large portion of the time of many encounters, particularly those for the purpose of applying for assistance. When a client was applying for assistance, the worker asked a series of questions to learn whether the client met the eligibility rules for TANF, Medicaid, and food stamps. Workers asked for the names, ages, addresses, and telephone number of all family members and absent parents. They collected numerous documents: birth certificates, immigration papers, drivers' licenses, rent receipts, utility receipts, eviction notices, bank statements, and paychecks. They inquired about sources of income: earnings, Social Security, unemployment insurance, contributions from household members, child support, contributions from relatives and friends, and so forth. They asked about expenditures: rent, mortgage payments, utility bills, payments for cable TV, car payments, loan payments, credit card payments, unpaid medical bills, insurance payments, expenditures on gasoline and public transportation, arrangements for sharing food expenditures, and so forth.

The decision not to code identifying, demographic, and financial information means that counts in Tables 3-3 and elsewhere understate the amount of attention welfare agencies devoted to determining eligibility for assistance. Although not indicated by the code counts, the task of determining eligibility continued to absorb much of the time of the frontline workers in the welfare agencies.

Workers' Activities

To learn what workers were doing when they covered a particular topic, coders assigned an activity code to every segment of conversation that had been assigned a topic code. Descriptions of the coded activities are contained in Appendix Table 2, and Chapter 2 describes how they were combined into broader activities to achieve sufficient interrater reliability among the coders. Table 3-4 shows the percent of encounters in which each of the ten activities was coded at least once. To permit comparisons between the states where tape recorders were used and those where they were not used, the table also includes the rank of the activities by their frequency within each state.

Chapters 4-8 on TANF rules and work-related topics cover the activities of workers regarding specific topics. For the purpose of that discussion, the activity codes were grouped into the seven broader categories listed in Table 3-4. Several objectives motivated the grouping of the activity codes. One objective was to differentiate among welfare offices according to their "culture" as defined by Bane and Kane, who distinguished between "an organizational culture in which the dominant ethos is centered around eligibility and compliance" and a culture en-

Table 3-4. Frequency of Worker Activities — All Encounters

(Number of Encounters) Worker Activities	Type of Attention	MICHIGAN (269) Percent	Rank	TEXAS (229) Percent	Rank	GEORGIA (202) Percent	Rank	NEW YORK (264) Percent	Rank
Collecting Information or Documents									
Collecting Information About Circumstances	R	92	1	91	1	80	1	81	1
Collecting Documents	R	21	7	25	7	19	8	11	6
Explaining Rules	R	84	2	85	2	68	2	54	2
Asking Clients to Complete or Sign Forms	R	65	5	74	3	60	3	34	5
Verifying or Monitoring									
Verifying	R	65	4	69	4	50	5	45	4
MIS Verification	R	14	9	40	6	22	6	11	7
Excepting or Exempting	I	9	10	14	8	8	9	5	10
Advising or Assessing									
Advising	I	78	3	69	5	54	4	48	3
Assessing	I	24	6	8	10	19	7	10	8
Providing Employment Services	I	16	8	11	9	6	10	8	9

R: Routinized activity
I: Individualized activity

couraging and supporting work.[3] They argued that the focus of the welfare agency on accurate eligibility determination and compliance with rules diverted its attention from serious efforts to prepare welfare clients for employment. The groupings of activities also drew on previous research by Hasenfeld and Weaver and by Mead seeking to identify factors increasing the likelihood of client compliance with program requirements.[4] Mead, in particular, argued that close monitoring of clients increases program effectiveness.

Determining eligibility and enforcing compliance involve the first five activities in the table — "collecting information or documents," "explaining rules," "asking clients to complete or sign forms," "verifying or monitoring," and "excepting or exempting." The activity code "collecting information or documents" means the worker was asking for information about the client's circumstances, needs, and intentions or the worker was collecting documents from the client to verify this information. "Explaining rules" means the worker was explaining rules, requirements, benefits, services, or procedures. When the worker asked the client to fill in or sign a form, the code "asking clients to complete or sign forms" was applied. "Verifying or monitoring" included several mechanisms for verifying the information provided by the client and for monitoring the client's activities. These included sending the client to someone or somewhere to obtain a document or signature; contacting an employer, service provider, or landlord to verify information or monitor the client's activity; or using computer systems containing information about the client. "Excepting or exempting" means the worker was telling the client an exception or exemption was being made or was postponing enforcement of a rule.

Encouraging and supporting work involve these activities as well, but also entail "advising or assessing" and "providing employment services." "Advising or assessing" is a combination of advising clients by collecting information about the client's intentions, plans, and needs

---

3   Kane and Bane, "The Context for Welfare Reform."

4   Yeheskel Hasenfeld and Dale Weaver, "Enforcement, Compliance, and Disputes in Welfare-to-Work Programs," *Social Service Review* 70:2 (1996); Lawrence M. Mead, "Welfare Employment," in Lawrence M. Mead, ed., *The New Paternalism* (Washington, DC: The Brookings Institution, 1997).

other than cash assistance; explaining options among the activities, programs, or providers available to the client; invoking the worker's personal beliefs; advising the client based on an interpretation of the rules or how the rule applies in the client's particular circumstances; and using professional expertise to advise and counsel the client. Assessing is a combination of evaluating the need for education, training, and employment services and for other types of services like child care, transportation, substance abuse programs, and so forth. "Providing employment services" is a combination of two codes, providing job placement and providing job readiness and job search services.

Another conceptual framework reflected in Table 3-4 is the distinction made in the literature on effective management practices between routinized and individualized attention by frontline workers. Bloom, Hill, and Riccio hypothesize that giving clients routinized attention that "focuses on collecting and processing information about clients and using that information in accordance with prescribed rules" may be less effective than giving them personalized attention that "emphasizes attitudinal and behavioral changes."[5] They find that the degree of personalized attention workers give to clients significantly increases the impacts of welfare-to-work programs, suggesting that the distinction between routinized and personalized activities is meaningful for program effectiveness.[6] The first four activities in the table are often routinized. The other three activities — excepting or exempting, advising or assessing, and providing employment services — are more likely to be individualized.

The most routinized activities — collecting information or documents, asking clients to complete or sign forms, and verifying information — are discussed here. Another routinized activity — explaining rules — has more policy content and is discussed in the context of various topics. Individualized activities are also discussed in the context of particular topics.

---

5   Howard S. Bloom, Carolyn J. Hill, and James Riccio, "Modeling the Performance of Welfare-to-Work Programs: The Effects of Program Management and Services, Economic Environment, and Client Characteristics," MDRC Working Papers on Research Methodology (New York: Manpower Demonstration Research Corporation, May 2001), 10.
6   Bloom, Hill, and Riccio, 40.

Routinized Activities

In the conversations between workers and clients, collecting information about the circumstances of the client was the most common activity in all the states. Collecting information was most common even though information about the identity of family members and other demographic and financial information was ignored in the coding and hence not included in the count of topic or activities codes. Workers collected information from clients in 92 percent of the encounters in Michigan, 91 percent in Texas, 80 percent in Georgia, and 81 percent in New York (Table 3-4). This activity was central to the process of determining the eligibility of applicants, redetermining the eligibility of recipients, enforcing behavioral requirements, providing supportive services, providing employment and training services, and virtually every other task of workers in the welfare system.

Collecting documents from the client to verify information was less common, occurring in 21 percent of encounters in Michigan, 25 percent in Texas, 19 percent in Georgia, and 11 percent in New York. Workers collected documents about current employment (employment verification letters and pay stubs); past employment (separation notices from employers and pay stubs); current education and training (school attendance forms, report cards, and verification of enrollment in training classes); forms verifying attendance at workforce orientations; documentation of job search; letters explaining lack of attendance at school or training; letters from physicians about the client's health, ability to work, or pregnancy; immunization records; bills from child care providers; sanction letters; work plans; death notices; divorce decrees; and so forth. Again, workers requested additional documents to identify the clients and to obtain demographic and financial information for purposes of determining eligibility and benefits.

The majority of encounters in every state but New York entailed at least one form to be completed or signed by the client. Many of these forms were used to determine eligibility and benefits but some of them served other functions as well. In Texas, for example, the welfare agencies routinely asked applicants to complete the following: (1) Application for Assistance (Form 1010); (2) Parent Profile Questionnaire (Form

50) for each absent parent; (3) Household Financial Statement — Monthly Expenditures and Income (Form CSS-05-088-4/012-6); (4) Assignment of Child/Medical Support Rights and Authorization for Child/Medical Support Services (Form 1712); (5) Landlord Verification (Form 1857); (6) Job History Information (Form 1108); (7) Texas Works! Identification Sheet and Employment Profile (Form 1181); (8) School Attendance Verification (Form 1155); (9) Personal Responsibility Agreement (Form 1073); and (10) Head of Household Verification (Form 03-1450) if the applicant was not the head of household. In addition, applicants were required to ask someone familiar with the family to complete (11) Request for Domicile Verification (Form 1155) and applicants could register to vote using (12) Opportunity to Register to Vote (Form 1350). The other states used a similar set of forms. Unlike the others, New York did not use a Personal Responsibility Agreement, although it did ask clients to sign forms designed to screen them for substance abuse and domestic violence. In Georgia, the only state with a family cap policy denying an increase in benefits for a child conceived while the mother is receiving welfare, the welfare agency asked clients to sign a Notice of the Family Cap Rule (Form 786).

These forms served several functions: to collect information needed to determine eligibility and benefit amounts, verify information provided by the client, enforce child support obligations of absent parents, obtain legal authority to transfer child support payments to the state, obtain the client's written agreement to engage in required behaviors so she could later be sanctioned if she failed to comply, monitor the client's behavior, learn whether the client had a problem that would interfere with work activity, and inform the client about features of the program. The multiplicity of forms, however, limited the amount of time workers could devote to each. The Personal Responsibility Agreement, the forms designed to learn whether the client had a problem that would interfere with work activity, and the forms used to inform the client about features of the program often became pro forma. Rather than discussing the issue, the worker often simply asked the client to sign the form.

Workers verified the information provided by the client or monitored the client's behavior using several methods. Collecting documents from the client, as discussed above, was one method. Another common method was sending the client to someone or somewhere to obtain a document or signature verifying the information provided, like a letter from a previous employer or a signature from a landlord. The client had to leave the welfare office to obtain the document or signature, imposing a cost on the client in terms of time and potentially delaying the determination of eligibility. Because the worker's activity in sending the client away could affect the receipt of welfare, it was important to count the frequency of this practice. To do so, this type of activity was coded "sending for verification" even when the topic was a type of identifying, demographic, or financial information that was not coded. The activity "verifying" in Table 3-4 consists primarily of "sending for verification." Other methods to verify information and monitor the behavior of clients, including the use of computers and finger-imaging systems (electronic fingerprinting), are discussed in Chapter 9.

Summary and Conclusion

The sites implemented TANF by giving selective attention to the stated purposes of the federal law. Providing assistance to families with children, the first purpose listed in the TANF legislation, had always been a purpose of the AFDC program and required little change in welfare agencies. Providing assistance continued to focus the attention of workers in the welfare agencies on the complex and time-consuming process of determining eligibility.[7] Eligibility determination and redetermination dominated the work of the welfare offices, accounting for half or more of all the encounters observed in the sites. Ending welfare dependence by promoting job preparation and work, another purpose of TANF, was a focus of attention in both welfare and workforce offices. Building Work First into the process of determining eligibility ensured that staff would discuss job preparation and work with TANF applicants.

The other purposes of TANF — promoting marriage, reducing out-of-wedlock pregnancies, and encouraging the formation and mainte-

---

7   The same conclusion is reached by Janet Quint et al., *Big Cities and Welfare Reform, Early Implementation and Ethnographic Findings from the Project on Devolution and Urban Change* (New York: Manpower Demonstration Research Corporation, April 1999), 189-91.

nance of two-parent families — received little or no attention. The lack of attention to these purposes of TANF was not surprising. With the majority of middle-income mothers participating in the labor force, the public supported work by low-income mothers applying for welfare or already receiving welfare. Increasing their work effort had been an objective of welfare reform for decades, and high-quality research had identified programs that were effective in moving them into the labor force. Not only was public support for using the welfare system to intervene in decisions about marriage and out-of-wedlock childbearing weaker, but research had not identified interventions with proven effectiveness in changing the behavior of people facing these decisions.

Without firm public support and knowledge of proven interventions, administrators in the four states had not set policies to respond to TANF's goals for marriage and out-of-wedlock childbearing. The only state to get near this issue was Georgia, which imposed a "family cap" on TANF benefits that denied families an increase in benefits after the birth of an additional child. Consistent with the family cap, the welfare offices instructed workers to refer clients to information about family planning and, as a result, family planning was discussed more often in Georgia than the other states (Tables 3-3).

Much of the activity of workers was highly routinized, in part because so much of the activity of workers in the welfare offices revolved around the routinized process of determining eligibility. Collecting information or documents, explaining rules, signing forms, and sending clients to obtain verification of information was central to the task of eligibility determination. The sheer volume of information, rules, and forms forced workers to devote much of their time to these routinized tasks and generated a vast amount of paperwork, which has long been a source of complaint by both workers and clients. Even delicate questions that might justify an individualized conversation, like inquiring whether the client faced a substance abuse problem that interfered with employment, frequently became a routinized task of asking the client to sign a piece of paper.

Yet, while routinization undermined the effectiveness of some procedures, the routinization of other procedures had the salutary effect of ensuring they were implemented. In particular, by making compliance with Work First a routine and a verified component of the process of applying for welfare, responsibility for informing applicants of the work mandates was no longer at the discretion of individual workers. Equally important, Work First conveyed the mandate by requiring an activity by the client, not just by words and a piece of paper that could be signed and then forgotten.

4

Limiting Welfare Use Directly and Indirectly

The TANF legislation permitted states to limit the use of welfare both directly and indirectly. By stating that welfare is not an entitlement and by imposing a 60-month time limit on assistance funded by the block grant, TANF permitted states to limit welfare directly by restricting access or terminating benefits. The end of the entitlement, in turn, gave states new authority to restrict the use of welfare indirectly by imposing mandates and rules designed to influence the behavior of applicants and recipients. Without an entitlement, a client's compliance with mandates designed to influence her behavior, like mandates to search for work or attend school, could be a condition of receiving assistance. If the mandate succeeded in changing her behavior, like increasing her work effort or earning capacity, it limited the use of welfare by reducing the family's need for assistance. If the mandate did not change her behavior, workers could reduce assistance by imposing a sanction that cut benefits.

Viewed in a historical context, these limitations raised the prospect that states might return to the kind of practices that the U.S. Supreme Court ended when it decided that welfare was a statutory entitlement. In order to restrict access to welfare, states had denied welfare to unwed mothers by declaring their homes to be "unsuitable" and by denying assistance to families with a "man in the house" regardless of his responsibility for the children.[1] Denying assistance to recent migrants into the state was another approach to restricting access. Even in states without these restrictions, the discretion of workers in determining eligibility and benefits had been wide and often arbitrary.[2] Although it was unlikely that states would adopt the same practices they had used earlier, TANF gave them vastly more authority to limit access to welfare.

This chapter first examines the responses of states and workers to two provisions of TANF that could limit the receipt of welfare directly: the lack of an entitlement to TANF and the time limit on assistance. It also examines a state-initiated policy permitting workers to limit the receipt of welfare directly by offering applicants a one-time cash payment to divert them from ongoing assistance. Did frontline workers use these rules to limit assistance directly by restricting access or terminating benefits? Did they use these rules for other purposes? The chapter then examines the workers' discussions of the mandates imposed on the behavior of applicants and recipients as a condition of receiving assistance. Did some mandates receive more attention than others? How did these mandates support the goal of TANF to end welfare dependence by promoting job preparation and work? How might these mandates have contributed to the decline in welfare caseloads?

Limiting Welfare Use Directly

The Personal Responsibility Act was emphatic that TANF was not an entitlement for individuals or families, stating this at the beginning and the end of the title creating the block grant.[3] Terminating the entitlement was such a major reform that it was difficult to predict how states would use this provision in formulating policy and how workers would interpret it in treating their clients. Would workers deny assistance to ap-

1   Winifred Bell, *Aid to Dependent Children* (New York: Columbia University Press, 1965).
2   Joel F. Handler and Ellen Jane Hollingsworth, *The "Deserving Poor": A Study of Welfare Administration* (Chicago: Markham Publishing Company, 1971).
3   Personal Responsibility and Work Opportunity Reconciliation Act of 1996, Title I, Sections 103(a)(1) and 116©).

plicants or cut recipients off assistance by telling them it was not an entitlement, or would the end of the entitlement play out in less direct ways? Two other mechanisms — time limits and one-time diversion assistance — were also ways to limit welfare use directly. The frequency of discussion of these three topics and the frequencies of the activities of workers regarding these topics show whether and how workers used these mechanisms. Quotes from the conversations show in detail what the workers were saying when they discussed these topics. To provide a context for understanding and interpreting the behavior of workers, the states' formal rules are summarized in the tables presenting the frequencies of the topic and activity codes.

No Entitlement to Welfare

The states' formal rules about the entitlement to welfare were more ambiguous than the federal law (Table 4-1). Federal law stated "This part shall not be interpreted to entitle any individual or family to assistance under any State program funded under this part."[4] Statutes in Michigan and Georgia explicitly stated that welfare was not an entitlement. The entitlement to welfare remained in force in New York, where the state's constitution guarantees assistance to the poor. Statutes were silent regarding an entitlement in Texas. However, the states' operating policies contained language about the authorization of benefits that did not always conform to the statutory language. Explicit language in state policy continued to authorize benefits to all eligible families in Georgia and Texas. In Michigan, state policy language authorized benefits subject to funding. In New York, language in state policy authorized benefits to all eligible families while other language authorized benefits subject to funding.

Text was coded "entitlement" when the worker said that 1) welfare is no longer an entitlement or 2) the client is expected to become self-sufficient, i.e., get off welfare. In the 969 encounters, only once did a worker explicitly tell someone that welfare is not an entitlement. This occurred in Bibb County, Georgia.

---

4   42 U.S.C. 601(b).

Table 4-1. Discussion of Entitlement or Self-Sufficiency
All Encounters and Encounters with Applicants for TANF, Food Stamps, or Medicaid

	MICHIGAN		TEXAS		GEORGIA		NEW YORK	
Explicit entitlement provision[1]	No entitlement — explicit in statute		Statutes silent		No entitlement — explicit in statute		State constitution guarantees assistance to the poor	
Explicit language in state policy[1]	Benefits subject to funding		Benefits for all eligible families		Benefits for all eligible families		Benefits for all eligible families/ benefits subject to funding	
	Percent of encounters discussing entitlement or self-sufficiency							
(Number of Encounters)	*All (269)*	*Applicants (111)*	*All (229)*	*Applicants (115)*	*All (202)*	*Applicants (72)*	*All (264)*	*Applicants (110)*
Any worker activity	17.5	18.9	16.2	21.7	6.6	10.1	3.4	0.9
Explaining rules	13.4	14.7	8.3	10.7	4.0	5.0	2.7	1.1

Source: [1]Center for Law and Social Policy/Center on Budget and Policy Priorities, State Policy Documentation Project, Cash Assistance Entitlement Policies, State Summaries as of October 1999, www.spdp.org/tanf/entitlement.htm. The source explains it is unclear how the two provisions in the New York statute are intended to be read together.

> **Georgia** *(Bibb) welfare worker:* When you apply for TANF, TANF is no
> longer an entitlement even if you have children under 19.... They
> have a 4-year limit. You could only receive it for 4 years, no more.

Workers did use the word "entitlement," but only in discussing other
programs, such as child care, transportation assistance, transitional child
care, transitional Medicaid, Social Security, SSI, Unemployment Insurance, Home Energy Assistance Program (HEAP), and veterans' benefits.
Clearly, the federal law ending the welfare entitlement did not play out
through explicit statements to clients about their eligibility for assistance.

Apart from this one instance in Georgia, all the conversations given
the code "entitlement" were expressions of an expectation that clients
would become self-sufficient and independent of welfare. Most frequently, the workers defined self-sufficiency in terms of immediate employment. Less frequently, workers discussed self-sufficiency while
giving clients the option of GED preparation, training, or other preparation for employment. While the relative emphasis on immediate employment versus education and training varied among the sites, expressions of
the importance of self-sufficiency were widespread.

> **Michigan** *(Hillsdale) welfare worker:* Michigan's welfare laws have
> changed and if you're capable of assignments you're expected to
> work so that you're self-sufficient.

> **Texas** *(Denton) workforce worker:* We are here to hopefully give you the
> connections to get back into the work force, to make informed deci-
> sions, and to become self-sufficient again. OK?

> **New York** *(Suffolk) workforce worker:* So the goal is to find a job, now. Be
> self-sufficient.

In summary, workers did not invoke the federal law stating that
TANF is not an entitlement. The end to the entitlement permitted states to
change their eligibility rules and impose additional behavioral mandates
on applicants, which are discussed below, but state policy continued to
authorize benefits to all families conforming to the rules and mandates.
The possibility that inadequate funding would lead states to establish
waiting lists for assistance did not materialize. As caseloads fell, funding
from the block grant was adequate to provide assistance to everyone conforming to the rules and mandates. The end of the entitlement did not
become a direct tool for limiting the receipt of welfare.

Table 4-2. Discussion of Time Limits
All Encounters and Encounters with Applicants for TANF, Food Stamps, or Medicaid

	MICHIGAN		TEXAS		GEORGIA		NEW YORK	
	All	Applicants	All	Applicants	All	Applicants	All	Applicants
State policy regarding time limits[1]	No time limit		For adults:12, 24, or 36 months depending on education and work experience For children: 60 months		48 months		60 months of TANF followed by Safety Net Assistance with no time limit	
State policy regarding exemptions from time limits[2]	NA		Federal limit: no exemptions State limit: elderly, disabled, caring for disabled family member or young child, victim of domestic violence		No exemptions		Federal limit: no exemptions	
(Number of Encounters)	*(269)*	*(111)*	*(229)*	*(115)*	*(202)*	*(72)*	*(264)*	*(110)*
					Percent of encounters discussing time limits			
Any worker activity	6.7	7.2	27.6	27.8	14.6	18.8	2.7	2.7
Collecting information or documents	1.4	3.1	7.6	10.1	5.2	8.2	1.7	2.4
Explaining rules	4.6	4.2	17.3	17.1	8.4	9.8	1.4	0
Completing or signing forms	1.2	0	3.9	7.2	3.3	6.8	0	0
Verifying or monitoring	0	0	5.1	7.8	2.7	4.4	0	0
Advising or assessing	1.8	0	5.2	1.4	3.1	3.9	1.0	0
Excepting or exempting	0	0	0	0	0	0	0	0

Sources: [1]Management interviews.
[2]U.S. Department of Health and Human Services, Administration for Children and Families, *TANF Program Third Annual Report to Congress* (August 2000).

Time Limits

The observations of the encounters did not capture any discussions in which workers informed recipients that their assistance was being terminated due to a time limit. In Georgia, Michigan, and New York, this is explained by state policy. Georgia's four-year time limit did not trigger terminations until 2001, so families had not yet reached the termination date. Michigan had not imposed any time limit on assistance and New York operated a Safety Net Assistance program financed by state and local funds to aid families after 60 months of TANF. Texas had introduced time limits for adults that were as short as 12 months (Table 4-2). Workers in Texas were observed telling recipients the number of months of assistance remaining, but no one was observed informing clients they had reached their limit. Similarly, none of the observations captured a worker discussing an exemption from a time limit.

While no workers were observed triggering a time limit, workers in all states discussed it, even in the states that had not imposed one. Workers discussed the time limit more often in Georgia and Texas, which had a clear time limit policy, than in Michigan and New York, but some workers in all four states mentioned it regardless of state policy.

When discussing the time limit, workers were most often explaining its rules. Workers explained rules about time limits in 17.3 percent of all encounters in Texas, and 8.4 percent of all encounters in Georgia (Table 4-2).

> **Texas** *(Denton) workforce worker:* They changed AFDC to TANF because they wanted to emphasize the "T"; it's temporary, OK? And I'm gonna discuss that further with you because the state put time limit restrictions as to how long a person could receive TANF. And, uh, I'll give you a little handout in a minute that's gonna tell you which category you may fall into.

> **Georgia** *(SW Fulton) welfare worker:* We're at a critical point — everyone here's been on TANF for 30 months. Under welfare reform, there's a lifetime cap of 48 months of welfare benefits. So we're collaborating with DRS [Department of Rehabilitative Services] to help us determine how we can best serve you.

Workers in Georgia generally explained the 48-month time limit accurately. The rules were more complex in Texas: the federal 60-month limit applied to children while the limit for adults was 12, 24, or 36 months depending on their level of education and work experience. A few workers were observed making mistakes in explaining the time limit, overstating the number of years. The workforce office in Denton prepared a handout that explained the time limits. In a workforce office in Dallas, the worker drew a clock for a client who had exhausted 4 of her 12 months and used the picture to show how she had 8 months left.

Not surprisingly, this topic received less attention in Michigan and New York. Workers in Michigan explained rules about time limits in 4.6 of the encounters, usually suggesting the state might introduce one.

> **Michigan** *(Macomb) welfare worker:* Federal funding is now limited to five years in your lifetime. In Michigan you may be eligible for cash assistance beyond the five-year limit … but this could change.

In New York, workers explained time limit rules in only 1.4 percent of all encounters, a low frequency consistent with continued aid under the state's Safety Net Assistance program. In the few instances when they mentioned a time limit, they did not give a full and accurate explanation of the state's time limit policies. A few workers invoked the federal time limit without mentioning that state Safety Net Assistance would be available after 5 years.

> **New York** *(Suffolk) workforce worker:* Our goal here is to get you off public assistance because now there is a 5-year limit on it.

No workers explained that Safety Net Assistance would be available after 60 months of TANF. In two encounters, workers mentioned Safety Net Assistance in passing, but without any discussion of what it was.

The immediate use of the time limit rules was to convince clients to change their behavior, in particular to search or prepare for employment. In explaining these rules, workers used them as a rationale for work or work-related activity, invoking the time limit as a reason why clients should focus their attention on finding employment or preparing for it.

> **Michigan** *(Wayne) welfare worker:* Work is mandatory for all cash assistance recipients. They're trying to phase out FIP [Family Independence Program], so they will be seeking a job for you at the Work First program.

> **Texas** *(Grand Prairie) workforce worker:* Once your benefits are gone, that's it — no transportation, child care, or financial assistance. So you need to think about what is important: "Do I want to go to work?"

> **Georgia** *(NW Fulton) welfare worker:* You'll be allowed to be on assistance for four years for your whole life. Now we want you to be self-sufficient, because four years isn't long, especially in the life of a child and what they need. It's easy to be lackadaisical, but that four years can fly by. We're requiring you to do GED — you're under 21, so it's mandatory. Now, try to get this in your head — it's not punishment, but we want you to get an education, so you can get a better job and be self-sufficient.

Workers urged clients to seek work immediately, sometimes telling them they could bank their months of assistance for later use.

> **Michigan** *(Hillsdale) workforce worker:* Work First is a program that is designed to help those people who are applying for assistance to go to work. You need to be working now because we don't know what will happen later on. If you've already used up your five year limit, who knows what will happen down the road.

> **Texas** *(Denton) workforce worker:* The quicker you can get a job, the quicker you can get off of the TANF benefits and save yourself some time limits.

> **Georgia** *(SW Fulton) welfare worker:* The 48 months is why I am so adamant about you getting a job. You don't want to exhaust your 48 months of cash benefits. If something happens, you may want to come back and get TANF for a few months.

Advising and assessing individuals in connection with time limits occurred in 5.2 percent of encounters in Texas and 3.1 percent in Georgia, the states with time limits, and less often in Michigan and New York (Table 4-2). In advising and assessing individuals in this context, work and preparation for a job were again the primary topics of conversation.

> **Michigan** *(Hillsdale) welfare worker:* I'm going to push when there's no reason for you not to be working.

> *Client:* Right.

> *Worker:* I will push because I don't know what Michigan is going to do in another four years as far as your eligibility.

> **Texas** *(Masters) workforce worker:* You got eighteen months, and the reason that's good to know is that you, you can kind of pace yourself as

to what you want to do with those eighteen months. Like get your GED.

Georgia (SW Fulton) welfare worker: You know when your checks will end?

Client: Oh yes, I know.

Worker: You know it's coming up. We need to be working with you to get you ready to put you on work plan, get your assessment to see where you need to be working.

In Texas and Georgia, workers generally had computers on their desk, which provided information about the months on assistance. They were observed referring to these data and informing clients about the number of months remaining. Verifying or monitoring in the context of time limits occurred in 5.1 percent of encounters in Texas and 2.7 percent in Georgia, but never in Michigan and New York. The observations provide no evidence that workers in Michigan or New York had access to information about the number of months that clients had been on assistance. Administrators in New York reported the state had not yet come up with a plan to track the time on assistance. Workers in New York who were collecting information about clients in the context of time limits were often simply inquiring about whether the individual had received assistance before.

In summary, while language about entitlement to welfare did not enter the workers' lexicon, the less ambiguous concept of a time limit to welfare was a policy that workers did incorporate into their conversations with clients. The time limit in TANF gave workers a concrete tool for changing the behavior of welfare applicants and recipients. They used it not to cut recipients off welfare but to motivate people to work or prepare for work, to emphasize that Work First was not just a requirement but was an activity in their long-term interest.

This absence of observations of families reaching a time limit and the absence of discussions about exemptions from a time limit are consistent with reports that time limits were infrequently triggered during the initial years of TANF implementation.[5] The welfare agencies in Georgia

---

5   By mid-2000, an estimated 60,000 families had lost benefits due to time limits. Liz Schott, "Ways that States Can Serve Families that Reach Welfare Time Limits" (Washington, DC: Center on Budget and Policy Priorities, June 21, 2000).

apparently did not count the months on assistance prior to TANF implementation toward the limit. The absence of observations of triggers in
Texas is more perplexing since the state had obtained permission to impose time limits under a waiver from the pre-TANF federal law. Perhaps
Dallas and Denton were late in implementing it. Perhaps the welfare
agency terminated clients by a letter, not by calling the client in to a meeting at the welfare office. In any case, the workers in Texas were observed
discussing the time limit but not actually imposing it.

Cash Diversion Payments

Because welfare was no longer an entitlement, federal law implicitly
permitted states to operate a cash diversion program, where applicants
were offered a one-time cash payment on the condition they withdrew
their application for ongoing assistance. Georgia and Michigan chose not
to offer cash diversion assistance while Texas and New York, like the
majority of states, chose to permit this option (Table 4-3). Workers could
offer diversion assistance to applicants who in their judgment could
avoid ongoing assistance if they had cash to meet a short-term crisis, af-
fording workers a powerful vehicle for exercising discretion in
distributing cash.

**Table 4-3. Discussion of Applicant Cash Diversion Programs
Encounters with Applicants for TANF, Food Stamps, or Medicaid**

	MICHIGAN	*TEXAS*	*GEORGIA*	*NEW YORK*
State policy regarding cash payment[1]	No cash pay-ment	Up to $1,000	No cash pay-ment	Cash payment at county op-tion Albany: yes Suffolk: no
(Number of Encounters)	*(111)*	*(115)*	*(72)*	*(110)*
Any worker activity	3 encounters	0	0	2 encounters

Sources: [1]Michigan, Texas, and Georgia: Gretchen Rowe, *Welfare Rules Databook:
State TANF Policies as of July 1999* (Washington, DC: The Urban Institute, 2000);
New York: management interviews.

Administrators in Texas mentioned the cash diversion policy but no observations captured workers discussing it with applicants. In New York, where cash diversion was a county option, Albany County but not Suffolk County permitted workers to issue cash diversion payments. Permitting diversion assistance was one of the major changes Albany made in response to TANF. According to an Albany administrator, the welfare office replaced the clerks who had done the initial eligibility screening — called "pre-screening" — with more skilled eligibility workers who could decide whether cash diversion was appropriate. Cash diversion assistance was clearly at the discretion of the worker. As one of the workers doing pre-screening noted, "Some workers do diversion, some don't."

The observations captured two instances of workers issuing a one-time cash payment that they termed grant diversion.

> *New York (Albany) welfare worker [to a woman who was laid off for the summer from her job in a high school and wants help paying her rent]:* I talked with your Family Assistance Worker. If you can prove you are going back to work, we'll pay your rent for two months. Get a letter verifying that you are going back to work. Come back in a week. Bring in the employer's form, an eviction request, and a copy of your health insurance.

The worker explained she was using "TANF grant diversion" to keep the client from being evicted and needing more assistance from the welfare agency. In assessing the magnitude of this policy change, it is worth noting that the state's longstanding policy of providing emergency housing assistance could also have justified this payment. Although the worker called it diversion, it could also have been called an emergency housing payment.

The second example of grant diversion illustrates a misuse of the policy — a worker issued a diversion payment to someone who was already receiving TANF. The worker explained that the client had been receptive to the worker's help and was now employed. Because the client had made an effort, the worker made an extra effort to assist her with car repairs to make transportation to the job easier.

> *New York (Albany) welfare worker:* If your car is worth more than $500 it's worth fixing it up. If not you should try to find something else, because the $500 is a one shot deal.

Michigan did not have a policy of diverting applicants with cash payments, but the observations captured several workers discussing "employment support services" and "post-employment services" available to people who were not receiving assistance but were working. Provided applicants were employed, these served the purpose of diverting them from ongoing assistance.

> **Michigan** *(Wayne) welfare worker:* OK. You're applying for everything.
>
> *Client:* You know, I don't want to apply for everything.... She said, when I come here, apply for everything because that's the only way they could help me in getting my car fixed.
>
> *Worker:* Ah, that's not true.
>
> *Client:* Oh. So I can erase all of that then. 'Cause I don't want the money....
>
> *Worker:* If you want to repair the car ... I need you to bring the title, showing that the car is in your possession, car insurance ... and recent paycheck stubs....This is employment support services, so you need to show that you're working.
>
> **Michigan** *(Hillsdale) welfare worker:* If you get any kind of a full-time job at minimum wage, you're not going to be eligible for cash assistance, but you will be eligible for food stamps and those post-employment services that I just talked about [child care, work clothes, a ride to work and home, car purchase, car repairs, insurance].

In summary, Albany County appeared to be the only site with a formal policy permitting cash diversion payments. An administrator explained that diversion payments were still in an early stage, with no tracking of the number of diversions and considerable variation in practice among the workers. The workers' mixed interest in cash diversion added another source of variation in the treatment of clients by a policy that, in its nature, requires workers to exercise discretion. State policy in Texas permitted diversion payments but no workers were observed discussing them. Their use in Albany County but not in Texas is consistent with the location of these sites at polar extremes in the degree of formal discretion allotted to workers. The Albany County welfare office, which had responsibility for all components of TANF including cash, employment and training activities, and child care, required workers to select the client's package of services, giving them more formal discretion than any other welfare office. Welfare workers in Texas operated within a process structured by a computer system (see Chapter 9) that limited their authority to make any decisions. Introducing diversion payments into this process would have required a new set of skills among workers whose tasks were more clerical than those of workers in the other states.

Michigan's offer of services to TANF applicants who found employment instead of coming onto welfare, a policy akin to diversion payments, is consistent with a state initiative called Project Zero. Under Project Zero, the state gave additional funds to welfare districts to pursue the goal of zero unemployment among their caseload. Hillsdale County was an early Project Zero site, while Wayne County became a Project Zero site just before the period of the observations. As reflected in the workers' discussion of numerous topics below, Project Zero put the sites under pressure to move all employable clients, both applicants and recipients, into a work activity.

TANF does not mention cash diversion payments, a silence that permitted states to create this mechanism. This was one way the lack of an entitlement was operationalized. It was also operationalized by rules and mandates imposed on applicants and recipients as a condition of receiving assistance. To clients, these rules and mandates increased the cost of receiving assistance in terms of their time, the behavioral change required, and the stigma imposed by the eligibility process and the mandated services. They worked indirectly to make welfare less attractive.

Limiting Welfare Use Indirectly

States used their broad authority under TANF to impose a variety of mandates on the behavior of applicants and recipients. For instance, states designed mandates to require applicants for TANF to search for work and to require recipients of TANF to immunize their children, keep their children in school, and attend money management, parenting, and family planning classes. Without an entitlement, states had the authority to deny assistance to applicants who failed to participate in the mandated activity and to sanction recipients who failed to comply with these mandates, even by withdrawing assistance completely.

The Personal Responsibility Act creating TANF encouraged states to impose obligations on recipients by giving states the option of requiring them to sign an "individual responsibility plan"[6] as a condition of receiving assistance and sanctioning those who failed to comply with the plan without good cause. Georgia, Michigan, and Texas opted to use this tool, which they called a Personal Responsibility Agreement (PRA), and designed a formal document listing the client's responsibilities and requiring her signature. Workers in Georgia and Texas asked applicants to sign the PRA when they applied for assistance, while workers in Michigan usually discussed the PRA at their first visit to the client's home after assistance began. The PRA was mentioned in 56 percent of the encounters with applicants for TANF, food stamps, or Medicaid in Texas and 39 percent of applicants in Georgia (Table 3-3b). Only 21 percent of the encounters with applicants in Michigan captured discussion of the PRA, perhaps because home visits might have been under-observed during the study. New York did not adopt this administrative tool for inserting a discussion of mandates into the process of determining eligibility for assistance.

Presenting mandates in the context of the PRA encouraged workers to discuss the mandate but it also routinized the discussion. Workers in Georgia and Michigan had discretion to tailor the responsibilities to the client's circumstances by checking selected items off a list and, in Michigan, by adding items to the list. Workers had no discretion in Texas, where the list of responsibilities was printed on a PRA form. This meant that the list was identical for everyone and could include responsibilities of no relevance to the client, for example making sure her children attended school even if she had no school-age children. This made the presentation of the PRA particularly routinized in Texas, with workers generally reading the list of responsibilities at the end of the eligibility interview with little explanation.

To analyze the content and frequency of conversation about mandates, this section uses the topic code "participation." The code "participation" was defined as "client's participation in mandatory education/employment activity, substance abuse program, or other mandated activity. Failure to participate without good cause results in a sanction." Text marked with "participation" and a topic code for a potentially mandated

---

6   42 U.S.C. 608(b).

Table 4-4. Discussion of Participation Mandates
All Encounters and Encounters with Applicants for TANF, Food Stamps, or Medicaid

(Number of Encounters)	MICHIGAN		TEXAS		GEORGIA		NEW YORK	
	All (269)	Applicants (111)	All (229)	Applicants (115)	All (202)	Applicants (72)	All (264)	Applicants (110)
	Percent of encounters discussing participation mandates							
Any discussion of participation mandates	66.2	79.6	55.8	56.7	53.7	65.1	32.0	22.0
Job readiness/job search; workforce orientation	54.4	74.9	43.3	49.6	23.4	44.8	17.3	14.1
Employment	30.6	31.9	18.5	15.1	13.5	11.2	14.0	5.0
Education or training	12.7	11.4	14.1	7.2	13.8	14.8	8.4	1.2
Work activity, unclear	5.4	5.7	6.1	2.9	4.3	5.9	4.2	0.0
Other government services	9.9	10.7	6.9	9.2	3.4	6.3	1.2	0.6
Family problems	4.6	2.9	0.2	0.0	3.1	4.6	1.4	0.0
Parenting	2.7	1.6	4.8	5.0	0.0	0.0	0.3	0.0
Family planning	0.0	0.0	0.0	0.0	3.8	8.8	0.0	0.0
Immunization of children	0.5	1.3	7.2	11.3	1.4	3.8	0.3	0.0
School attendance of children	0.8	1.3	4.5	5.0	4.0	7.4	2.0	1.2
Health, disability, and mental health — client	9.5	8.6	4.7	5.8	5.0	14.0	3.1	0.6

activity was automatically given a third code, or "supercode," by the At-las.ti software. For example, text marked with the codes "participation" and "job search" was given a supercode indicating the worker was discussing a mandate to search for a job. The purpose here is to identify the mandates that were most commonly imposed on clients. Enforcing mandates requires another set of tasks: monitoring the compliance of clients and imposing sanctions. The methods for monitoring compliance with mandates and the use of sanctions are discussed in Chapters 6 and 9.

The observations show that workers frequently discussed participation in a mandated activity during their encounters with recipients and applicants (Table 4-4). Participation in a mandated activity was a topic of conversation in more than half the encounters in all states except New York. Workers discussed one or more mandates in 66.2 percent of all encounters in Michigan, 55.8 percent in Texas, 53.7 percent in Georgia, and 32.0 percent in New York. The discussion of mandates with applicants was higher in every state but New York: 79.6 percent of applicants in Michigan, 56.7 percent in Texas, 65.1 percent in Georgia, and 22.0 percent in New York. Due to the definition of an "applicant" for welfare, which also includes applicants for food stamps and Medicaid, these percentages understate the discussion of mandates with actual welfare applicants.

Mandates to Participate in a Work-Related Activity

Of all the mandates on clients, the activities mandated most frequently at the front lines involved work and preparation for work. These mandated work activities included orientation at a workforce agency, job readiness training, job search, employment, and education or training, either immediately or at some time in the future (Table 4-4). Of these, workers most frequently discussed the mandate to attend an orientation at a workforce agency or engage in job readiness and job search activities. Workers in Michigan discussed this requirement in 54.4 percent of all encounters and in 74.9 percent of encounters with applicants. Workers in Texas mentioned this requirement in 43.3 percent of all encounters and in 49.6 percent of encounters with applicants. Workers in Georgia and New York were observed discussing this requirement less frequently, in 23.4 percent of all encounters and 44.8 percent of encounters with applicants in Georgia, and in 17.3 percent of all encounters and 14.1 percent of encounters with applicants in New York, but job readiness/job search activities were still the most common mandated activity in these states.

The requirement to engage in regular paid employment ranked next in frequency. Workers mentioned a work requirement in 30.6 percent of all encounters in Michigan, 18.5 percent in Texas, 13.5 in Georgia, and 14.0 percent in New York. Less frequently, workers told people they must engage in education and training in 12.7 percent of all encounters in Michigan, 14.1 percent in Texas, 13.8 percent in Georgia, and 8.4 percent in New York. The mandate to participate in a work activity, where the worker did not mention a specific work activity, was mentioned in 4 to 6 percent of all encounters.

Because mandates related to a work activity were a major tool for reducing reliance on welfare and promoting employment, they are examined in detail in the next chapter. Compared to these mandates, the other mandates in TANF were discussed less frequently by workers and resulted in fewer immediate referrals to services and less monitoring of compliance. Moreover, some of these were discussed in a routinized manner, mentioned only briefly when the worker drilled down the list of responsibilities in the PRA.

Mandates Regarding Other Government Services

Workers rarely required clients to apply for, or participate in, government services other than those provided by the welfare office or the workforce office. Other government services for low-income families included cash programs like unemployment insurance, Supplemental Security Income (SSI), and Social Security, and in-kind programs like the Home Energy Assistance Program (HEAP) and housing subsidies. This code was also applied to government services such as foster care and child protective services. Mandates regarding these services occurred in 9.9 percent of encounters in Michigan, 6.9 percent in Texas, 3.4 percent in Georgia, and 1.2 percent in New York. Furthermore, a reading of the encounters shows that over half the encounters with this code were not true instances of a mandate to participate in a government service.

When workers mandated clients to apply for another government service, they were most frequently discussing unemployment insurance or SSI. Workers explained that an applicant who is covered by unemployment insurance must file a claim for benefits before applying for TANF. Discussions of SSI or Social Security Disability Insurance in this context were with clients who wanted an exemption from the work requirement due to a disability, prompting workers to explain they must apply for disability benefits. In several cases where clients had already applied for disability benefits but had been denied, workers urged them to appeal their denial. Mandating participation in government services for other reasons was uncommon. One worker told a mother who had recently been released from prison that her children should be referred to Protective Services. In no instance did workers mandate an application for housing subsidies or for HEAP. Because the conversations often revealed waiting lists for housing subsidies, it is not surprising that workers did not mandate applications for housing programs.

Mandates in the Context of Family Problems, Family Planning, and Parental Responsibilities

Workers discussed mandates in the context of several of the family-related topics listed in Table 3-3, including family problems, problems in parenting, and family planning. Workers also discussed welfare mandates on clients in their role as parents, particularly the rules regarding children's immunization and school attendance.

Family problems included client's problems with a spouse or partner, relationship problems with other family members, and domestic violence. Discussion about mandates in this context occurred in 4.6 percent of encounters in Michigan, 3.1 percent in Georgia, 1.4 percent in New York, and in only one encounter in Texas. Some of these family problems created difficulty in meeting mandates while others served as valid excuses for not meeting mandates. Relationship problems within the family created difficulties in meeting the work mandate and mandates for attendance at substance abuse programs and children's attendance in school. Disabled children and deaths of relatives interfered with attendance at work or training.

Victims of domestic violence could be exempted from work participation according to the formal policies of all four states. Workers in Texas, however, did not screen for domestic violence and were not observed making exemptions. Observations in Georgia, Michigan, and New York captured workers considering the domestic violence exemptions for their clients, granting an exemption in some cases and denying it in others. In the one observation in Georgia, the worker learned a father was in jail for child molestation and ascertained from the mother that this would not interfere with her employment. Workers in Michigan informed women they would waive the requirement to participate in a work activity. For evidence of violence, workers used a mother's residence in a domestic violence shelter, a mother's status as a client in the child protective system, and a police report of a father's attack. Workers in Albany did not have authority to waive the participation requirement but instead referred women to an assessment by a specialized domestic violence worker. They also referred to this specialized worker the women who wanted a domestic violence exception from the mandate to cooperate in child support enforcement. In the one observation in Suffolk, the welfare agency referred the client to the workforce agency for an assessment for a possible exemption from the work requirement. The assessment took place over the phone. The specialist at the other end concluded the father's behavior did not interfere with the mother's employment and did not grant a waiver.

Mandates regarding family planning were discussed only in Georgia. Elsewhere, state administrators and legislators sidestepped this policy area, and several local welfare administrators expressed reluctance to take any initiative. In Georgia, where the state required workers to discuss family planning with TANF clients, mandates were discussed in 8.8 percent of encounters with applicants. Georgia was also the only state opting to impose a "family cap" on welfare benefits, which caps a family's benefit so it is not increased with the birth of an additional child. Workers in Georgia mentioned the family cap in 15 percent of the encounters (Table 3-3). Consistent with the family cap policy, workers in Georgia were far more likely than workers in other states to mention family planning in any context, with discussion in 13 percent of all encounters in Georgia compared to 3 percent in Texas and 1 percent in Michigan and New York (Table 3-3). The link between the family cap and family planning was explicit. When workers in Georgia informed clients about the family cap rule, they asked them to sign a Notice of the Family Cap Rule. At the bottom of the form in block letters was the question, "What services are available to help my family with family planning?" and the answer, "If you want family planning services, the Department of Family and Children Services can tell you where you can receive free or reduced rate services in your area."

Most discussion of family planning in Georgia was in the context of the PRA. Workers told applicants they must see their own physician for family planning counseling or attend family planning classes at the Health Department. In one encounter, a mother was told her teenage daughters must attend a class at the Health Department. Of the 19 encounters in Georgia where family planning was discussed, four women reported having had their tubes tied. Of the four encounters in Texas where family planning was discussed, two women said their tubes were already tied and the other two women said they were considering it.

Mandates on clients in their role as parents also varied considerably among the states. Workers in Georgia and Texas devoted considerable attention to requiring parents to immunize their children. Texas routinely included this requirement in the Personal Responsibility Agreement signed by all applicants, which accounts for the 11.3 percent of encounters with applicants where this mandate is mentioned, higher than the other states. In addition to these encounters, workers in Georgia and Texas monitored compliance with this mandate by asking to see the children's immunization records. Because requests for these records were not coded as mandates for immunization, Table 4-4 understates the attention given to this mandate. Workers in Georgia routinely asked to see current immunization records, while workers in Texas were sometimes satisfied with school attendance records since immunizations were needed for school attendance. Workers in these states mentioned that immunizations were needed both for the children's health and for their attendance at child care, suggesting the goal of employment helped drive the emphasis on this mandate. In Michigan, workers discussed immunizations but this did not appear to be a universal mandate and workers did not ask for documentation. Because New York did not require immunizations, they received no attention.

The parents' responsibility for their children's school attendance, or "learnfare," was also routinely included in the Personal Responsibility Agreement in Texas and was a mandate that could be included at the worker's discretion in the PRAs in Georgia and Michigan. The observations captured workers in Georgia and Texas including this mandate in their PRA, but they captured workers asking for a form verifying school attendance only in Texas. Workers in Michigan and New York discussed this mandate infrequently.

Mandates regarding parenting classes and other parenting services were at the discretion of the worker in all the states. As part of the PRA, workers in Texas routinely told applicants they must attend parenting skill classes "if requested to do so" and workers in Georgia explained this mandate selectively. The observations captured workers in all the states referring clients to parenting classes or referring the family to Child Protective Services, but these referrals were uncommon.

Mandates in the Context of Client Problems

Discussion about mandates in the context of the health, disability, or mental health of a client occurred in 9.5 percent of encounters in Michigan, 4.7 percent in Texas, 5.0 percent in Georgia, and 3.1 percent in New York. In almost all cases, the client was describing medical problems that prevented or restricted work participation. In the few cases where a worker imposed a mandate on clients in this context, it was to document their disability status so they would be exempt from work. Because Georgia mandated immediate job search for applicants, the highest frequency of discussion of medical problems in the context of mandates, 14.0 percent, was with applicants in Georgia.

Participation in substance abuse treatment programs was mentioned in 2.3 percent of encounters in Michigan, 1.9 percent in both Georgia and New York, and in no encounters in Texas. The content of these encounters indicate that workers in Georgia and New York were more aggressive in responding to drug and alcohol abuse than workers in the other states. Observations in Georgia and New York captured workers making referrals to screening for substance abuse and to substance abuse treatment programs. Workers also discussed participation in a substance abuse program as a condition of eligibility or lifting a sanction. In New York, state law required welfare agencies to screen all applicants for substance abuse, refer suspected abusers to a formal assessment, and if they were unable to work due to their problem refer them to treatment. Georgia did not require substance abuse screening for all applicants, but the welfare agencies viewed substance abuse as a serious problem and engaged facilities to provide assessment and treatment.

State law in Michigan required a urine screening for applicants and mandated treatment for substance abusers, making it the first state in the nation to attempt large-scale drug testing of applicants, but a lawsuit and injunction halted the testing during the period of the observations.[7] Workers were circumspect in discussing drug treatment, saying drug treatment was available but they could not force anyone to attend.

In Texas, as seen in Table 4-4, no encounters discussed mandates regarding substance abuse. The only mention of substance abuse was in the Personal Responsibility Agreement signed by all applicants in which they agreed "not to use, sell, or possess controlled substance or abuse alcohol." Workers generally reviewed the agreement quickly without asking the client whether they would be able to conform to each of its numerous provisions. Unlike the other states, where several clients admitted to having a substance abuse problem, none of the observations in Texas show a client mentioning a current substance abuse problem. Although administrators said that drug abuse was common, they explained that the Dallas/Denton region had taken no action regarding this issue and that the state has the capacity to treat only a small number of people. They said each welfare office had information on the services available in the area and could make a "cautious" referral, without making assumptions about abuse. A workforce administrator said her office referred clients to a program "gingerly." None of the observations in Texas captured a referral.

Summary and Conclusion

Invoking the lack of an entitlement to welfare and imposing time limits did not directly prevent families from receiving TANF in the encounters observed in this study. Rather, these laws permitted and sup-

---

7   Kristin S. Seefeldt et al., *Recent Changes in Michigan Welfare and Work, Child Care, and Child Welfare Systems*, State Update No. 4, (Washington, DC: The Urban Institute, July 2001).

ported other policies, processes, programs and tools that had the power to discourage entries to welfare and encourage exits. Together with the greater flexibility given to the states by the TANF block grant, the lack of an entitlement to TANF benefits gave welfare agencies greater authority to mandate behavior that would reduce reliance on welfare. Simultaneously, the time limit impressed upon the welfare agencies the need to change their own behavior with welfare recipients, to make greater efforts to prepare them for a life without welfare.

In discussing behavioral mandates, workers gave the most attention to topics regarding job preparation and work. Several other topics were addressed in the context of mandates because they interfered with the ability to work. Health, disability, and mental health problems of clients were addressed in the context of mandates primarily because health problems interfered with the mandate to work, not because workers were mandating clients to address these problems. The highest frequency of discussion of these problems among applicants was in Georgia, where a requirement that applicants search for work immediately raised discussion about them. To a lesser extent, substance abuse was discussed because it interfered with employment. Similarly, family problems received some attention in the context of mandates because they interfered with participation in a work activity. The mandate to immunize children was driven in part by the prospect that children would need immunizations in order to be placed in child care while their parents worked.

This means that of all the mandates discussed by workers, participation in a work-related activity was most likely to have contributed to the decline in caseloads. This mandate could have deterred applicants from applying for welfare or encouraged recipients to work, hastening their exit from welfare. Because the activities of workers to implement the mandates regarding job preparation and work were so common, they are examined in greater detail in the following chapters.

5

Mandating
Work-Related Activities

Despite repeated federal reforms in work programs and requirements for welfare recipients, the work requirement had been implemented unevenly around the country. States had the authority to require work, but a work mandate had not been consistently imposed at the front lines. Participation in work activities increased when the JOBS program replaced WIN in 1988, driven by a federal mandate that a minimum percent of each state's nonexempt caseload participate in the JOBS program.[1] Yet in the year before TANF was enacted, only 14.4 percent of adults were active in a JOBS activity.[2]

TANF tightened the work requirement by changing the rules for both people and states. It specified that parents receiving assistance engage in work activity as soon as they were determined to be ready for work. Welfare agencies could also impose a work-related mandate on applicants for assistance and, with welfare no longer an entitlement, could deny eligibility to people who failed to comply. A work-related mandate

1   Irene Lurie, "A Lesson from the JOBS Program: Reforming Welfare Must be Both Dazzling and Dull," *Journal of Policy Analysis and Management* 15:4 (Fall 1996).
2   U.S. Congress, Committee on Ways and Means, *1998 Green Book*, 484-6.

on applicants could also deter them from following through on their welfare application, thereby diverting them from assistance. The age of the child in the family was no longer grounds for an exemption from the work requirement, although states had the option of exempting parents with a child under the age of one year.

To encourage the states to mandate work, TANF increased the minimum percent of the state's nonexempt caseload required to participate in a work activity from 20 percent in the final years of the JOBS program to 25 percent in 1997, rising to 50 percent in 2002 and beyond. Participation in a work activity, which had been defined as 20 hours of work per week under JOBS, increased to 30 hours per week in 2000. Single parents with a child under age 6 were required to work for only 20 hours per week.

Although TANF subjected states to much higher participation rates, another TANF provision gave them an escape hatch. The law lowered the participation rate that each state must meet by a percentage point for each percentage point decline in the caseload since 1995, provided the decline was not due to changes in the state's eligibility criteria. Congress gave states credit for declines in their caseloads to lessen the conflict a state might face in choosing between policies that encouraged work participation and policies that reduced caseloads. (People in work programs must be on welfare in order to be counted as participants.) Because caseloads declined sharply in the four states examined here, as they did around the country, the percentage of the caseload actually participating in a work activity did not need to reach the minimum rate set in federal law.

Imposing a work requirement takes more than simply invoking a rule — it takes a capacity to serve the client. In order to mandate work, frontline staff must be able to place clients in a job search program to help them find immediate employment, in an education or training program to increase their earning capacity, or in a regular or subsidized job. Staff must have some assurance that the client's young children will have child care while the parent is participating in a work activity. Transportation is necessary if the work activity is not within walking distance of home. A lack of capacity to offer these programs and services to clients can undermine a work requirement by driving frontline staff to be lenient in granting exemptions or to ignore the requirement altogether.

This chapter and Chapters 6 and 7 examine the conversations of frontline workers to learn the extent to which they had this capacity and how stringently they imposed the TANF work requirement on applicants and recipients. This chapter analyzes the workers' activities regarding two of the topics of conversations listed in Table 3-3: 1) job readiness/job search — current or future and 2) education or training — current or future. The workers' conversations in discussing these topics reveal the mechanics of imposing the work requirement on applicants and recipients, the range of choice workers gave recipients when placing them in a work activity, the opportunities they offered for education or training to increase clients' earning capacity, and the treatment of long-term recipients who were not participating in a work activity. Chapter 6 examines the financial inducements for clients to work or participate in a work activity, including the positive inducements of wages and the negative inducements of sanctions. Chapter 7 examines the workers' discussions regarding the availability and financing of child care and transportation to support work.

Work Mandates for Applicants

Applicants for TANF often came to the welfare office with an imperfect understanding of the rules for receiving assistance, not always certain about their decision to apply. How did frontline workers present the connection between work and welfare to applicants? How vigorously did they implement work mandates at this point and in what time frame? Did they in practice find reasons for exempting applicants from the work mandate for reasons other than those specified in state policy, in particular a shortage of Work First activities or child care? What evidence do the observations offer that work mandates on applicants diverted them from welfare?

Each state designed its own process for imposing a work mandate on applicants, devolving the design to the local level to a greater or lesser degree. The designs of these processes, generally called Work First, were described in Chapter 3 and are summarized in Table 5-1. Although the designs of Work First varied, all the welfare agencies in Georgia, Michigan, and Texas were similar in expecting their workers to send applicants to a workforce agency. In Michigan, the process called for the welfare agencies to refer all applicants to a group orientation conducted jointly by the welfare and workforce agencies followed by an individual orientation where the applicant was assigned to an initial work activity. Only after the applicant attended the first day of the work activity, and the workforce agency notified the welfare agency of the applicant's attendance, did the welfare agency authorize assistance. Texas designed a similar process, although the orientation was conducted by the workforce agency alone. When the applicant attended the orientation, the workforce agency worker stamped a form that the applicant brought back to the welfare agency. At that point, the welfare agency could authorize assistance. During the orientation, the workforce agency also set up an appointment for the client to return after benefits were authorized.

Georgia was the only state to require a job search by all adult applicants before the welfare agency could authorize assistance. Exemptions from job search were limited to teen parents, parents with a medical problem, and parents with a young child who chose to take a once-in-a-lifetime exemption from work until their child was 12 months of age. (Of the four states, only Georgia took advantage of the option in TANF to exempt parents with a young child from work and disregard these individuals in calculating the state's work participation rate.) The workforce agency provided job search assistance, while the welfare agency monitored the applicant's compliance. County welfare agencies had some authority to set the period of job search and design other features of Work First.

New York State, at the other extreme, permitted Work First activities but did not mandate them on its county welfare agencies. The Suffolk County welfare agency routinely referred applicants to the workforce agency unless they explained they could not work. The Albany County welfare agency gave its staff the discretion to mandate a period of unassisted, unsupervised job search. In both counties, applicants saying they were unable to work due to health, mental health or substance abuse problems were immediately referred to health and mental health agencies for an assessment by specialized staff. With assessments of employability done by other agencies, the staff of the welfare agencies no longer had the discretion to exempt clients from work.

**Table 5-1. Discussion of Workforce Orientation and
Job Readiness/Job Search
Encounters with Applicants for TANF, Food Stamps, or Medicaid***

	MICHIGAN	TEXAS	GEORGIA	NEW YORK
State policy regarding an orientation at a workforce agency or job search by applicants	Orientation required for all applicants First day of attendance at a Work First activity required for nonexempt applicants	Orientation required for all applicants	Job search required for non-exempt applicants	Neither required
Local policy regarding an orientation at a workforce agency or job search by applicants	Same as state policy	Same as state policy	Bibb: 30-40 days of job search Fulton: 14-21 days of job search	Albany: no orientation; unsupervised job search at worker's discretion Suffolk: orientation at workforce agency required for nonexempt applicants
State policy regarding age of child exemptions from work	Child under 3 months	Child under 3 years (permitted by a waiver from federal AFDC law)	Child under 12 months, one time exemption only	Child 3 to 12 months at county option
State policy regarding education and training by teen parents	Mandated under age 18	Mandated under age 19	Mandated under age 20	Mandated under age 18
	Percent of encounters discussing orientation and job readiness/job search — current or future			
(Number of encounters)	*(111)*	*(115)*	*(72)*	*(110)*
Any worker activity	79.3	60.0	50.9	25.4
Explaining rules	64.2	44.5	42.7	14.1
Advising or assessing	36.5	23.0	15.0	5.1
Excepting or exempting	7.6	16.3	5.4	1.2

* All encounters with these applicants occurred in welfare offices.
Source of policy information: management interviews.

Georgia

Workers in the welfare offices discussed job search in 50.9 percent of their encounters with applicants for TANF, food stamps, or Medicaid (Table 3-3b and Table 5-1). In 42.7 percent of encounters with these applicants, they explained the rules about job search.

> **Georgia** *(NW Fulton) welfare worker:* You have to do job search first, because you're over 20. If you were under 20, your primary activity would be school.
>
> *Client:* How'm I gonna get a job without a GED? I tried that job search before, it didn't work out. You see what I'm saying?
>
> *Worker:* I hear you, but we can't get around the rule. You've got to do the job search.
>
> **Georgia** *(Bibb) welfare worker:* When you apply for TANF you have to do a job search. You have to put in four applications a day.
>
> *Client:* So you'll help me find a job?
>
> *Worker:* Well, you're really finding a job on your own, we just make sure that you are looking. You'll have to come in every day between 8 and 10 A.M. Sign in and bring in your job contacts.
>
> **Georgia** *(Bibb) welfare worker:* I'll be your employment services case manager. My goal is to help you get employed before you get benefits. It's a 30-45 day process before you start getting benefits. You'll have to participate in full time job search. Four jobs a day — checking in every day.

Workers in the welfare offices advised or assessed clients about job search in 15.0 percent of encounters with applicants. The advice in this conversation was generally a reinforcement of the job search mandate; there was no assessment of the appropriateness of job search as an initial work activity.

> **Georgia** *(NW Fulton) client:* I just want to go to school.
>
> *Welfare worker:* Under the new rules, the situation is, you have to do three weeks of job search first. Under the worst case, if you don't find a job, we could enroll you in something like Atlanta Tech for GED and skills training…. I think your GED is the most important. I'm a real believer in education. I wish I could just send you over there now. But we have to put you on job search first.

> ***Georgia** (Bibb) welfare worker [to an applicant currently engaged in a job search]:* You got your GED?
>
> *Client:* No.
>
> *Worker:* How close are you to completion, are you close?
>
> *Client:* I had 9 quarters left.
>
> *Worker:* Do you think you possess the skills to pass the test or you need some brushing up?
>
> *Client:* I need some brushing up.
>
> *Worker:* You may want to do your job search in the morning and do your GED in the afternoon so check into that.

Workers from the employment services unit in the Bibb County welfare office met with new applicants to ask them briefly about their employment history and goals, but their primary task at this point was to refer them to the Department of Labor for job search. DOL workers were stationed in the Bibb welfare agency to register applicants immediately in the DOL computer system, which entailed questions about their education, previous employment, and interests. Apart from the exemptions in state policy, the job search was imposed on all applicants.

Workers discussed exemptions from applicant job search in 5.4 percent of encounters with applicants. Applicants were exempt from job search if they were teenagers, if they or their children had physical or mental health problems, or if they were in late pregnancy. Parents with a child under 12 months of age could take a one-time exemption from the work requirement, an option frequently offered by workers.

> ***Georgia** (SW Fulton) welfare worker:* Since you are in Project Connect [a substance abuse center], you don't have to see DOL or do job search.
>
> ***Georgia** (Bibb) welfare worker:* I'm not gonna put you in any activity because you're due next month, but when your baby turns 6 weeks old, we have to put you in an activity.
>
> ***Georgia** (SW Fulton) welfare worker:* You don't have a work requirement because you have a child under 12 months. You can take a one-time exemption to not have to participate.... If you take the exemption, you don't have to do work requirement until your baby turns 12 months. If you don't take it, you're mandatory for work.

Workers at the Department of Labor did an assessment of clients when they met with them individually, but the assessment was geared to immediate job placement rather than the client's need for education or training. The assessment included questions about previous jobs, interests, and work goals, but did not include a reading or math test. In Bibb County, workers from the Department of Labor were located in the welfare office to assess all applicants at the beginning of the application process.

Job search could divert applicants from assistance in several ways: they could find a job raising their income above the eligibility level, they could be deterred from welfare by the prospect of working, they could be working off the books and risk losing that job if they spent time searching for another one, or they could encounter difficulty getting to the job search program. Because the study did not track the experience of individual clients, it could not measure the effect of job search in diverting applicants from TANF. But it did observe encounters in the welfare offices where job search kept people off assistance.

> **Georgia** *(SW Fulton) welfare worker [to a woman cut off assistance]:* Were you under the impression you couldn't reapply?
>
> *Client:* I came to reapply, then I had to go to Work First, but you're not supposed to bring children, and I've got two small children....
>
> *Worker:* Did you let them know?
>
> *Client:* I called, but there was no answer.

Michigan

Workers in the Michigan welfare offices discussed Work First in 79.3 percent of their encounters with applicants for TANF, food stamps, or Medicaid. In 64.2 percent of the encounters with applicants, they explained the rule that attendance at the orientation conducted jointly by the welfare and workforce offices was mandatory before cash assistance could be authorized. Workers generally explained that applicants also had to attend the first day of the Work First program before assistance could be authorized. Although the program frequently entailed job readiness and job search, the Work First agencies could provide other work activities and, perhaps for this reason, workers did not always tell people what would happen at Work First.

Michigan *(Macomb) welfare worker:* Before I can give you any money, you're going to have to go to our Work First program. You have to go to an orientation, uh, where they'll explain all the work programs to you. What the requirements are. The following Monday, you will be assigned to attend the Work First class. The way the policy is set up right now, I cannot give you any money until after you have gone to the Work First class.

Michigan *(Wayne) welfare worker:* You know you need to go Work First, but they're not going to take you with this baby coming any second.... You're going to be exempt from working until the baby gets three months. And then you have to go to Work First or have you a job.... Due to your pregnancy, I'll just send you to the orientation part.

Michigan *(Hillsdale) welfare worker [to a pregnant woman saying she has complications from pregnancy]:* I can't open your case until you attend Work First now. All cash assistance cases, no matter if they're gonna be exempt from work or not, must go to the orientation for Work First. If you're exempt, all you'll have to go to is the orientation until the exemption is lifted.

Workers in the welfare offices advised or assessed clients about Work First in 36.5 percent of encounters with applicants, more than any other state. This conversation consisted of various types of advice that reinforced the mandate to participate in Work First and to work. Workers urged applicants to attend the Work First orientation so their case could open, to go there soon, and to get there early. To varying degrees, they encouraged applicants to participate in Work First by describing the supportive services and the education and training options available through the program and by warning them about tougher sanctions if they failed to cooperate. They advised applicants about working more hours, not quitting a job, and about the availability of transitional benefits when they left welfare. They advised two-parent families how they could achieve 35 hours of work and, in one case, how a two-parent family could cope with a disabled child.

Michigan *(Hillsdale) welfare worker:* You can always look for another job, but you can't quit a job. Especially within the first two months. If a person quits a job within the first two months while they're on cash assistance, then they are no longer eligible. So, it benefits you to stay employed until you find, you know, something that you like and then, and then, you know make a change.

> ***Michigan** (Macomb) welfare worker [to an unemployed husband]:* The
> Work First program is designed to help you find employment — put
> you in touch with employers, help you with your resume. You either
> have to work 35 hours per week or be at the Work First office 35
> hours per week. You have to attend one orientation session — you
> have a choice between these four offices. They'll explain the Work
> First program.

> ***Michigan** (Wayne) welfare worker:* Here's that form that will get you into
> Work First. It's only on Wednesdays. They have a morning session
> and an afternoon session. And you will go this next Wednesday. The
> sooner you go, the sooner we'll be able to get your case open.

Workers exempted few applicants from the Work First orientation
and, on the instructions of administrators, they used the word "deferred"
not "exempt." Observations captured workers granting exemptions to
pregnant applicants close to their due date, a mother with a newborn, and
to a recovering drug abuser who had been court-ordered to go to
parenting classes, drug treatment, and GED classes. They also exempted
applicants who were threatened by domestic violence, consistent with
Michigan's decision to elect this option in TANF.

> ***Michigan** (Wayne) welfare worker:* Once upon a time we didn't request or
> require people to work, but being that things have changed, society
> has changed, they're requiring that now. We don't require you to go
> to Work First because you probably will have this baby within the
> next two weeks. It is mandatory, normally, for people to go to Work
> First orientation and to the Work First program.

> ***Michigan** (Wayne) welfare worker [to a client who fled a domestic vio-*
> *lence situation and is afraid to leave the house]:* You got police pa-
> pers with you? You got it with you? 'Cause that way I can defer
> you.... Right now you will be deferred from Work First because of
> the situation you're in ... I'll call you, see how things are coming and
> then, if things seem to be doing better, no incidents or anything, you
> know, nothing happens, then I'll send you to Work First, OK? If you
> feel it is safe.

The observations did not capture applicants who were diverted from
welfare by Work First, but they did capture an applicant being denied assistance because she had quit her job.

> ***Michigan** (Hillsdale) welfare worker:* There is nothing I can do to help you
> since you are a voluntary job quit. Because of the law I have to turn
> you down.

> *Client:* Why are you treating me like dirt?

> *Worker:* What do you want me to do different? How differently can I tell you that the law won't let me help you?

New York

Workers in the New York welfare offices discussed an immediate work-related activity with 25.4 percent of applicants for TANF, food stamps, or Medicaid, considerably less than the other states. Without a formal Work First process, workers explained that applicants must go to the workforce office or search for work in only 14.1 percent of the encounters. Applicants saying they were unable to work due to a health problem, a disability, a substance abuse problem, or domestic violence were referred to an assessment by the health department or the domestic violence liaison. Employable applicants in Suffolk were routinely referred to the Department of Labor. In Albany County, where the welfare agency contracted with several agencies for specific services, the workers used their discretion in referring applicants to a work activity.

> **New York** *(Suffolk) welfare worker:* You're gonna have to go to DOL, you understand that, right?
>
> *Client:* Yes.
>
> *Worker:* Do you have a problem with that?
>
> *Client:* (hesitates)
>
> *Worker:* Well, let's put it this way, you don't have much choice.
>
> **New York** *(Albany) welfare worker:* Do you realize you have to job search?
>
> *Client:* Yes.
>
> *Worker:* This is the Job Search book. Fill in six jobs weekly and come back in two weeks.
>
> **New York** *(Albany) welfare worker [to a woman with a drug addiction]:* Part of eligibility is you have to go to CMU [a substance abuse assessment at the mental health department].... Here's your appointment at CMU to be eligible.

Welfare workers advised or assessed clients regarding an immediate work activity in only 5.1 percent of encounters with applicants. Most advising and assessing occurred in Albany County, where welfare workers had the discretion to select the work activity of applicants and recipients.

In Albany, several workers advised clients they would be referred to the Department of Labor for job search. One worker, after learning that a client had attended a special school and was unable to read and write, referred her for an educational assessment and suggested she apply for disability assistance. Another worker set up an appointment with an employment worker in the welfare agency. The discretion given to welfare workers in Albany led to a less routine pattern of referrals to a work-related activity than in the other welfare agencies.

Only 1.2 percent of encounters with applicants captured welfare workers exempting them from an immediate work activity, a finding consistent with these workers' lack of authority to issue exemptions. In states other than New York, the welfare agencies appeared to rely on documentation furnished by the applicant as evidence of unemployability, such as a letter from a physician. In New York, welfare workers had authority to exempt clients who were pregnant or had infants (under 3 months in Albany County and 12 months in Suffolk County) and were observed doing so. To exempt applicants with other problems that might interfere with work, the welfare agencies required a confirmation of the applicant's statements and letters, which was obtained by referring applicants to other agencies for a physical and mental health assessment of their employability and for an examination of their problems with substance abuse and domestic violence. In Albany, half the discussions with applicants about possible exemptions entailed referrals to the domestic violence liaison.

> *New York (Suffolk) orientation at the workforce agency:* If you are a one-parent family, you have the option of taking off until the child is 12 months of age if you haven't taken an exemption in the past year or so for another child, all right? If you are a two-parent family, then you only have an exemption until the child is three months of age, OK?

> *New York (Suffolk) welfare worker [to a woman with a back injury that required surgery]:* You have an appointment for DOH [Department of Health]. I will definitely send you to DOL. Whether it's as employable or unemployable, DOH will tell.

> *New York (Albany) welfare worker:* You have to make an appointment with a Domestic Violence worker. You can be exempt from some of the requirements.

In Suffolk County, an 18-year-old son was excluded from his family's welfare case because he refused to go to school or the workforce office. In Albany County, one applicant was observed being diverted from welfare by the work mandate.

> **New York** *(Albany) client:* My temporary job ended because I'm going back to school Monday.
>
> *Welfare worker:* Hmm. Are you familiar with welfare reform?
>
> *Client:* No.
>
> *Worker:* You're mandated to work 30 hours a week. You can't be exempted for going to school. We'd put you on a job search. Everyone has to work on welfare, and you have marketable skills. What year are you in?
>
> *Client:* I'm a junior.
>
> *Worker:* Yeah, we can't exempt someone for being in a four-year college.
>
> *Client:* Can I just get Medicaid and food stamps?
>
> *Worker:* You get food stamps now. That will increase, since your income has just dropped. You can still apply for Medicaid. There's no work requirement for Medicaid.
>
> *Client:* Well, that's what I need most.
>
> *Worker:* You're probably better, in my opinion, just getting a little part-time job and going about your business.
>
> *Client:* OK.
>
> *Worker:* So, do you want me to change this to a Medicaid application?
>
> *Client:* Yes, OK.

Texas

Workers discussed the orientation at the workforce agency in 60.0 percent of their encounters with applicants for TANF, food stamps, or Medicaid. In 44.5 percent of the encounters with applicants, they explained the rule that attendance at the orientation was mandatory before cash assistance could be authorized. Workers gave applicants little information about the services available at the workforce agency and sometimes referred applicants to the workforce agency without telling them what would happen there.

Texas *(Grand Prairie) welfare worker:* OK, this is one of the most important documents concerning your case. It shows that I am doing a work
force orientation referral on you, OK?

Client: OK.

Worker: They conduct briefings on Monday to Friday at 8:30. You must attend a briefing before I certify the case, OK?

Client: OK.

Worker: Make sure when you go there that you take this form with you,
OK, make sure they sign it, they put the stamp on there, and put the
date on there, OK?

Texas *(Denton) welfare worker:* TANF is a program where you have to do
a lot of things in order to maintain and keep the program going and we
help you with that. There is certain things that you would need to do
before we can even set you up on TANF or do the actual certification
on it. One of those things is that you would need to attend the
workforce orientation meeting.

Workers advised or assessed clients about Work First in 23.0 percent of encounters with applicants. In these conversations, they were offering routine types of advice rather than assessing the client's need for
workforce services. For example, they advised applicants that the
workforce agencies could help clients get their GED.

Workers were observed discussing exemptions in 16.3 percent of
encounters with applicants, considerably more than in other states. One
large group who were exempt from both the orientation and a work activity were adults who were ineligible for TANF and receiving payments on
behalf of children, like grandparents, disabled adults receiving SSI, and
undocumented aliens. Because the workforce agency's program for
TANF clients served only adults counted in calculating the amount of the
benefit, not these "payee only" adults, ineligible adults were not referred
to the workforce agency. In addition, under a waiver from the federal
AFDC law, Texas exempted from a work activity eligible parents with a
child under three years of age, a group that would have high child care
costs. Eligible adults exempt from a work activity, like pregnant women
and parents with a child under three years of age, were required to attend
the orientation and given the opportunity to volunteer for the program.

Texas *(Grand Prairie) welfare worker:* Each adult member of the household who gets cash assistance must participate in the JOBS program.
You are going to be exempt from that because you're not going to

qualify for cash because of your citizenship status [her residency is undocumented].

Texas *(Grand Prairie) welfare worker:* Who is on SSI?

Client: I am and I'm disabled.

Worker: Since you are on SSI, you don't have to go for that workforce orientation.

Texas *(Denton) welfare worker:* Part of the AFDC program is that you will be required to attend a Texas Workforce orientation and job program. But being as you're four months pregnant, the main requirement is you will attend a workforce orientation.

The observations confirmed that the welfare agencies had abandoned the process designed to "redirect" potential applicants from welfare to employment. No observations of receptionists in the welfare offices captured them telling applicants to visit a resource room for job listings or other employment information. To the contrary, one worker explained to the observer that the welfare office was supposed to redirect applicants from TANF to a resource room, but there was no one to staff it.

Only one encounter captured an applicant being diverted from welfare by the prospect of participation in Work First.

Texas *(Grand Prairie) welfare worker:* OK, tell me again why you want to withdraw [your TANF application]? Because you have to go to the employment office?

Client: Well, yeah. I ain't got no way to get to work 'cause they don't come pick me up and take me.

Worker: How far along are you?

Client: I'm six or seven months now.

Worker: Well, that might exempt you.... But you still will have to go through the orientation class at the Texas Workforce Commission. So it is up to you.

Client: What's that, where you go up there and listen and you fill out all them papers?

Worker: You have to go to class. Even though you're pregnant, you know, you still have to go. Once you bring me that form, then I can put you on the TANF. The TANF is $183 a month, that's all you get. The choice is yours. You have to go and you have to bring us back the paper to show that you have been to classes so I can finish your case.

Client: Let's just not worry about it. I'll find some way to pay my bills. [Client withdraws application.]

More commonly, applicants said they were on the verge of taking a job. Considering the low welfare benefits in Texas, it would be common for welfare applicants to be looking for work. Perhaps Work First further encouraged them to find a job, or perhaps they had a job when they applied for assistance and the requirement to participate in Work First forced them to reveal it.

Texas *(Denton) [first meeting after the orientation] workforce worker:* So it's real important to find a job.

Client: What if you got a job?

Worker: If you got a job, great! For how many hours a week is it?

Client: It's from 9:00 to 4:00 and Monday through Friday.

Worker: OK

Client: I just started it last night.

In summary, the observations show that workers did, in practice, impose a work-related mandate on almost all applicants for TANF. In their conversations with applicants, workers routinely explained the rules about going to the workforce agency, searching for a job, or going to an agency for an assessment of their employability. The only exception was Albany County, where workers had the authority to tailor their referrals to the circumstances of the applicants. In states with a Work First policy — Georgia, Michigan, and Texas — the workers routinely stressed that applicants could not receive welfare unless they complied with these rules. The time frame for compliance with the Work First mandate was short, generally a week to ten days. While workers made exceptions for clients who they judged would eventually be exempt for work, exceptions from the mandate were rare.

In encounters with TANF applicants where staff did not discuss a work mandate, it was generally because a discussion would have been inappropriate or unnecessary. In Georgia, for example, workers did not discuss the job search mandate in 49.1 percent of their encounters with applicants. The text of these encounters shows that a discussion of job search was inappropriate or not needed because these applicants were teen parents required to go to school or training, parents with infants who had taken a one-time exemption from the work requirement, applicants with too much income to qualify for TANF, applicants who were already working or in a full-time training program, and "payee only" adults not applying for assistance for themselves. As explained in Chapter 3, the selection of a sample of encounters rather than clients reduces expected frequencies below 100 percent. In Bibb County, where applicants had several encounters with workers during the application process, the initial meeting was with a "screener" who focused on whether the family met the eligibility requirements rather than on behavioral mandates. The work mandate was discussed in a later meeting. Several applicants in Bibb were in the process of job search and came to the welfare office to bring in documents or complete paperwork. One applicant had found a job and came in to apply for child care.

Workers in the welfare agencies did not assess the ability of applicants to work or their need for employment and training services. In states with a Work First policy, workers referred clients to Work First without determining whether the applicant had a physical or mental problem that would interfere with employment. In New York, specialized workers in other agencies assessed applicant's employability, taking the decision out of the hands of the welfare eligibility workers. Welfare workers in all states frequently inquired about the applicant's education and previous employment and, in doing so, learned something about the applicant's skills, but the mandate to participate in an initial activity was not contingent upon an assessment of the client's vocational abilities or needs for education and training. Only after applicants attended an initial activity did welfare agencies play a part in assessing the needs of clients for services. The imposition of a work mandate on applicants without an assessment by the welfare agency meant that welfare workers had limited discretion to exempt applicants from the mandate, making it a routine part of the application process.

Workers exempted applicants from Work First activities for a narrow set of reasons: advanced pregnancy, a newborn child, a well-documented disability of the applicant or a family member in her care, or the ineligibility of the adult in the household for assistance (a "payee only"). Workers in Georgia routinely gave applicants the option to take a one-time exemption while their child was under 12 months of age. Michigan and New York elected to follow the option in TANF to exempt applicants who were threatened by domestic violence.

Significantly, workers never said they were exempting an applicant due to a lack of capacity at the workforce agency. To the contrary, workers sometimes encouraged the applicant to go to the workforce agency by saying the agency had new services to offer them. Nor did workers exempt applicants from Work First because they lacked child care or transportation. Michigan did not allow applicants to bring their children to the orientation but the welfare agencies paid for child care and transportation so they could attend. The welfare workers in Texas told applicants they could bring their children to the orientation at the workforce agency and children were observed attending these orientations. Applicants needed to find their own transportation to the orientation, but lack of transportation was not an excuse for nonattendance. If they had a means of getting to the welfare offices, which were not all accessible by public transportation, presumably they could get to the workforce office. Georgia paid for child care and public transportation during job search.

With welfare no longer an entitlement, states were able to interrupt and stretch out the application process. The four states did not change their formal policy regarding the time frame for approving or denying the application for assistance, which remained the AFDC time frame of 45 days. Yet this 45-day "standard of promptness" for determining eligibility was no longer a federal rule and, in practice, the Work First mandate could delay the opening of a case. In Texas, the application was not considered complete until the applicant returned the form documenting attendance at the workforce orientation, delaying the start of the 45 days. In Michigan, attendance at the first day of a Work First activity was necessary before the case could be opened, while a period of job search was necessary in Georgia. This meant that applicants with young children in Michigan and Georgia needed to arrange child care before they could receive assistance. If this task became lengthy, the case could not be opened within the formal 45-day period. Unlike prior law, the actions of the applicants influenced the time frame for approving or denying the TANF application.

While the observations show that Work First did divert applicants from TANF, the effect of Work First in discouraging welfare use was undoubtedly much greater. Unobserved by the study were applicants who completed their application but did not attend Work First, thereby ending the application process. Workforce administrators in Dallas noted that fewer recipients came to their agencies for mandated services than they had expected, suggesting that significant numbers of applicants were diverted from assistance. In other sites, administrators and workers spoke of "miracle jobs" found by applicants just as they were required to participate in Work First, suggesting applicants had been working without reporting their employment. Some applicants did not comprehend the need to attend Work First and were denied assistance without understanding why. Others were too angry too attend. How many people were diverted could not be measured by the study, but the observations at least indicate some of the clients' feelings and behaviors motivating their response to the mandate.

The Work First approach was not entirely new to welfare. During the 1990s, an increasing number of states obtained the authority to require job search by applicants for AFDC. At the time TANF was enacted, fully half the states had this authority, including Michigan and New York.[3] Failure to comply with a job search requirement was grounds for denying the application for assistance. Yet some states with the authority to require job search by applicants, such as New York, did not use it on a wide scale. With TANF, states adopted Work First processes more extensively, increasing the demands placed on applicants in their effort to qualify for assistance.

Work Mandates for Recipients

After applicants satisfied the eligibility conditions for TANF and became recipients, how aggressively did the welfare system impose the mandate to participate in a work activity? What was the balance between requiring recipients to engage in immediate job search and giving them

---

3   U.S. Department of Health and Human Services, *Characteristics of State Plans for the Job Opportunities and Basic Skills Training (JOBS) Program, 1995-1996 Edition*, 1995.

an opportunity for education and training that would increase their earning capacity? To what extent did workers assign clients to a work-related activity based on an assessment of their needs? How did workers treat teen parents, who are subject to special rules under TANF?

States with Work First programs designed work mandates and programs for recipients that differed substantially from those designed for applicants. To varying degrees across the states, institutional responsibilities for serving recipients differed, the range of services offered to clients became wider, and rules regarding exemptions became more lenient. Institutional responsibilities in Georgia shifted from the Department of Labor, which handled only applicant job search, to the welfare agencies, which had primary responsibility for the work activities of recipients. In Michigan and Texas, exemptions from a work activity were more lenient than exemptions from the workforce orientation and were granted for health, disability, or mental health problems of the client or other family members. Michigan exempted recipients with a child under three months of age from a work activity, while Texas had a federal waiver to exempt recipients with a child under age three. Rules and services varied by the age of the recipient, with separate rules about education and training for teen parents. Welfare offices in Fulton County and Wayne County were starting to give long-term recipients extra attention, which suggests they were not a focus of attention during the initial period of TANF implementation.

Work Mandates for Adults

Insight into the specific work mandates for adult recipients comes from examining the assessments performed by workers in the welfare offices and workforce agencies. It also comes from the workers' discussions of several topics with their clients, particularly job search programs and education and training programs. Additional insight comes from discussions of exemptions, which shed light on the stringency of the mandate to engage in a work activity.

The attention given to assessing clients varied considerably among the states. Encounters for the primary purpose of assessing clients were 15 percent of all encounters in Georgia, 10 percent in Michigan, 5 percent in New York, and 1 percent in Texas (Table 3-2). These encounters include both assessments to determine the client's needs for social and supportive services and assessments to select a work activity. Workers also assessed clients in the course of encounters for other purposes, but the frequency of meetings with clients for the primary purpose of assessing them is still indicative of the resources explicitly devoted to this task.

The welfare offices generally gave more attention to assessing their client's needs for social and supportive services than for education and training. Although welfare workers often inquired in passing about their client's skills and interests, they did not perform a systematic assessment of their reading and math skills, job skills, or vocational abilities. In Georgia and in Albany County, the welfare offices had responsibility for referring recipients to a work activity and workers inquired more often about the skills and interests of their clients, but they did not perform systematic skills assessments. The one exception to this pattern was Fulton County, where long-term recipients received a battery of assessments as they approached the time limit, as discussed below.

All the workforce offices asked clients about their previous employment, vocational abilities, and interests in order to refer them to potential jobs. The workforce offices in Michigan and Texas routinely administered tests of clients' reading and math skills. With few exceptions, the purpose of these assessments appeared to be to identify jobs the client was capable of performing, not to identify clients with poor skills that would justify further education. Where workers used the tests scores to refer clients to programs, it was to decide whether the client was sufficiently prepared to enter a training program funded by the Workforce Investment Act (WIA), but here the worker was looking for high scores on the tests, not low ones.

To summarize the emphasis workers gave to job search compared to education and training among people other than TANF applicants, Table 5-2 compares the workers' activities regarding these two topics in their conversations with this group. In Michigan, New York, and Texas, most types of worker activity occurred more frequently in discussing job search than education and training. The pattern was reversed in Georgia, where every type of worker activity except explaining rules occurred more frequently in discussing education and training than in discussing job search.

Table 5-2. Discussion of Job Readiness/Job Search and
Education and Training
Encounters other than Encounters with Applicants

(Number of Encounters)	MICHIGAN (158)	TEXAS (114)	GEORGIA (130)	NEW YORK (154)
Percent of encounters discussing job readiness/job search — current or future				
Any worker activity	57.6	49.1	26.2	28.6
Explaining rules	42.2	36.6	14.3	13.0
Advising or assessing	39.6	20.6	12.7	15.7
Excepting or exempting	7.6	5.5	1.3	2.0
Percent of encounters discussing education or training — current or future				
Any worker activity	38.0	50.9	46.9	29.2
Explaining rules	14.8	23.2	11.0	10.1
Advising or assessing	26.5	15.8	21.5	13.3
Excepting or exempting	0.9	2.0	2.0	1.2

Georgia

The sites in Georgia created two work programs, a job search program for applicants operated by the Department of Labor and a more as-
sessment-based program for recipients operated by the welfare agencies.
The welfare offices automatically referred applicants to job search at the
Department of Labor, without an assessment of their need for education
and training. Workers at the Department of Labor, whose major function
was job placement, i.e., referring clients to employers with job openings,
did little advising or assessing regarding education and training. They appeared to have the authority to refer clients to education and training
classes and one worker mentioned the Work Opportunity Tax Credit,
saying the employer would pay the worker as she got trained, but most of
their effort was spent asking clients about prior work experience and job
preferences and using this information to refer them to job openings.

If job search failed to divert applicants from welfare, the welfare offices assumed full responsibility for developing the client's work plan, a

formal document listing the work activities expected of the client and the supportive services to be provided by the agency. Workers in the welfare offices arranged all employment-related activities and performed all advising and assessing about education and training. The Bibb County welfare office administered a literacy test to applicants as part of the intake process but, beyond this, the welfare offices did not assess the client's job skills. In practice, the nature of the workers' advising and assessing regarding work activities was informing clients about the activities arranged by the agency and, in many but not all cases, asking clients which of the programs she would prefer.

The county welfare agencies had some discretion in designing work activities for recipients, resulting in differences between Fulton County and Bibb County in the array of employment-related activities used to meet their work participation requirements. Fulton relied primarily upon short-term vocational training, arranging for a supply of short-term training programs followed by job placement. Workers explained the programs available and asked clients which one they preferred. Bibb County relied primarily on a mix of classes at the local technical college and work experience, where recipients work in exchange for their welfare benefit. Neither county required or even permitted a period of job search like that mandated for applicants:

> **Georgia *(SW Fulton) client:*** I don't want any more training. I already went through nine months of training and didn't get the job promised me.
>
> *Welfare worker:* I remember that. Now the problem is that DFCS will only fund job search one time in your life. So other than that, we have to put you in training. We'll give you time for job search after training.
>
> **Georgia *(SW Fulton) worker:*** What do you like to do? You tell me.
>
> *Client:* I like office type jobs. I don't like seeing people like customer service.
>
> *Worker:* I have a training for office assistant, but today is the last day you can register. Would you like that?
>
> *Client:* Yes
>
> **Georgia *(Bibb) client:*** I'm going to Macon Tech [for vocational education].
>
> *Welfare worker:* Are you going to school 30 hours a week? Because if not, we'll have to supplement your hours with work experience.

Although workers in Fulton County most commonly referred clients to short-term training, they had discretion to refer the client to GED preparation. The formal rules permitted GED preparation to count only as a secondary activity for adults, and workers typically steered adults away from GED programs. Several observations captured workers implementing this rule. For example, one worker told a client that supportive services were not available for adults in GED classes without another work activity and another worker told a client she could go to a GED program at night if she went to training during the day. But a worker was also seen ignoring that rule, telling an adult client she could attend the GED program at the welfare office. Bibb appeared to have a similar rule against GED preparation for adult clients.

Most of the exemptions from work were granted at the time of application for assistance, when a period of job search was required as a condition of eligibility. Few additional exemptions were observed in encounters with recipients. However, as discussed below, observations in the Fulton offices indicate that sizable numbers of long-term recipients were not engaged in a work activity. They were in limbo, neither working nor exempt.

Michigan

Work First programs for adult TANF recipients focused on immediate employment for all participants, not on education and training. Workers in Wayne County and Hillsdale County explained to clients that their offices were Project Zero sites that had adopted the goal of zero unemployment among their caseload. Workers in Macomb County did not mention Project Zero, but their emphasis on immediate employment was equally strong. The welfare offices were charged with removing "barriers to work" with social and supportive services, while the workforce offices were charged with moving people into jobs quickly through job readiness activities, job search, and job placement.

In the orientations required for all applicants, the goal of immediate employment came through loud and clear in the advice workers gave adults about education and training. Workers advised adult parents they could go to school or training, but only if they were already working a minimum number of hours a week. This arrangement, termed "post-employment training," was explained in the Work First orientations conducted jointly by the welfare agency and the workforce agency:

> **Michigan** *(Macomb) joint orientation by welfare and workforce workers:* Once you are meeting the work requirements, you may be eligible for post-employment training. Even a little training will dramatically increase the number of jobs available to you…. To be eligible for training through Michigan Works!, you must be or become a Work First participant. Also, the training will require you to be employed a certain number of hours, depending on the individual requirement and uh, the type of training you wish to access.

Education also came under the rubric of post-employment training:

> **Michigan** *(Macomb) welfare worker [talking with a woman who lost her job] client:* I have to find another job now. But I'm thinking about going back to school.
>
> *Worker:* We want you to go to a program. It's called Work First. Do you know what that means? You got to work first and then you go to school.
>
> **Michigan** *(Wayne) welfare worker [in sending an applicant to the Work First orientation]:* Like if you work at least 20, I think it's 10 or 20 hours a week, you can be eligible for one of their GED programs.

People who worked their way off welfare were also eligible for post-employment training:

> **Michigan** *(Hillsdale) welfare worker:* What I like to tell people is that right now you're unemployed but through Work First, if you take advantage of everything they have to offer you, it's an opportunity. Say for instance you get a job working 30 hours and you go off cash assistance…. Work First will follow you for 90 days and you can still take advantage of this and get your GED. Through them. When you get a job, it doesn't end. You are still eligible for these services for 90 days.

Workers in all workforce offices administered a test of basic reading and math skills and asked clients about their interests, previous work experience, and skills. These assessments were primarily used to determine what jobs might be appropriate for clients and, very occasionally, whether the client qualified for skills training. Workers advised clients they should get their GED to improve their job prospects, and the workforce offices in Hillsdale and Macomb had GED training on site, but education could not be their sole work-related activity. Some amount of employment was necessary.

> ***Michigan** (Macomb) workforce worker:* Your requirements, like I said, are 30 hours. If you do the GED prep, they will be reduced so you would be working 20 and going to school the other 10.

Referrals to skills training were infrequent and referrals to full time skills training even less frequent. Some of the training opportunities appeared to be funded through programs other than TANF.

> ***Michigan** (Hillsdale) workforce worker:* With JTPA [reauthorized as the Workforce Investment Act], we have what's called pre-employment training, so say if you're interested in a factory job and would like to go down to the training center, we can do that prior to you beginning working there.

> ***Michigan** (Macomb) workforce worker:* What is your required hours to work? It's 20. OK. See, each one of these training programs is a bit different in their requirements. Some of them require you to be employed first. OK? Most of them do. You have to get your employment first and then some of them will allow you to reduce your work hours.

> ***Michigan** (Wayne) workforce worker:* Now with that training, it's like a condensed training, and if it's less than six months, you might not have to work. But you would have to be in class for that length of time. Now if you're interested in any less than class-size training — data entry, nursing, anything along that line — I would have to refer you to _____ and they would evaluate you there. I would send over your TABE [Test of Adult Basic Education] and reading scores. Also what would happen, you gotta be working 20 hours.

As these exchanges indicate, education and training were rarely available on a full-time basis. Like Detroit, workers in Macomb mentioned "condensed vocational training" programs for at least 30 hours a week that did not require work, and workers in Detroit mentioned on-the-job training, but these were the exception. College education, which had been used by the JOBS program to reach the federally mandated participation rate, was no longer an authorized work activity.

Workers granted more lenient exemptions from a work activity than from the orientation to Work First. Workers were observed exempting recipients for disability, health problems, children with health problems, pregnancy, living in a homeless shelter and domestic violence.

New York

In Suffolk County, the Department of Labor was responsible for all employment activities. Like the workforce offices in Texas, the Department of Labor had responsibility for assessing clients' needs for all employment and supportive services and for developing the work plan. Workers did not routinely test clients' basic skills but they did question them about their previous education and training, employment history, career interests and goals, whether they had a driver's license, their children's school schedule and physical and mental health, and whether anyone else was available to care for their children.

Although the Suffolk County Department of Labor gave first priority to job search and job placement, an immediate referral to job search was not automatic. Unlike any of the other sites except Bibb County, Suffolk County operated a work experience program in which recipients worked without pay in exchange for their welfare grant. Referrals to work experience were common. Workers could also refer clients to GED preparation, English-as-a-second-language classes, and vocational training for a subset of people who met the agency's requirements. To some extent, they gave clients a choice among work activities.

> *New York (Suffolk) workforce worker:* Right now I would like to see you trying to get your GED but you don't want to do that.
>
> *Client:* I would rather be working and making money....
>
> *Worker:* OK, so what do you want to do — work site, crew, school, job search, what? [Work site and crew were two forms of work experience.] If you don't like school I'm not going to bother sending you because it's not going to be productive.
>
> *New York (Suffolk) workforce worker:* Well, there are certain training programs. They are basically programs that will give you skills that can get you out into today's job market. They're not long-term like college skills and all that.
>
> *Client:* Right.
>
> *Worker:* They're short-term programs. They usually last anywhere from two to six months, all right? But they entail 30 hours a week; that's how we get that 30-hour participation rate.

One intake worker raised the possibility of letting the client continue with her education, although this would need the approval of a supervisor:

> **New York (Suffolk) workforce worker:** We're not gonna have you go for the job readiness training class because it does conflict with your class times. You're going to a school that we send people to occasionally but, since you need to go through our department, we're gonna have to assess you and see that we can approve this school program and use it for our participation, all right? I'll give you an appointment to come back to see a counselor, all right? ... And then the supervisor will look over your paperwork and we'll be able to see if we can use it.

Workers in Suffolk County appeared to refer people to the widest range of employment and training services of any site in the study. The Department of Labor developed numerous work experience sites around the county for welfare recipients, gave recipients some access to the employment and training programs it provided to the general population, and had a staff willing to call other organizations in the county to ask them to serve TANF clients.

In Albany, where the welfare office retained lead responsibility for referring people to work activities, the workers had wide discretion in referring clients to education and training or permitting clients to continue in self-initiated education and training. When they thought the client might need further education or training, they referred them to a contractor for testing. GED preparation was a common referral, although some clients were referred to training programs. Workers told people explicitly that college was no longer an authorized work activity.

Exemptions from work for recipients were similar to exemptions for applicants: pregnancy and childbearing, physical and mental health problems, substance abuse, and domestic violence. Like applicants, recipients were referred to other agencies for an assessment of their employability and for an examination of their problems with substance abuse and domestic violence, removing the exemption decision from the discretion of the welfare workers.

> **New York (Albany) welfare worker [to a recipient with a newborn]:** Now you're exempt for three months from having to work. You have three months to stay home with your child. Come see me after that and we'll discuss what you have to do.

> **New York (Suffolk) workforce worker:** My supervisor looked at it [a form showing the client's psychiatric assessment], says this will be good and we'll see how you're doing in six months. We'll put you on follow-up for six months.

> **New York (Suffolk) workforce worker:** You went for the physical and they said you are employable even though you have carpel tunnel syndrome. That's what they said. What I'm going to do is get you into a work activity.

Texas

The programs for TANF clients at the Texas workforce agencies were geared to job search but also gave some adult recipients an opportunity for education or training. Because local workforce agencies had some discretion to create their program, named Choices, the relative emphasis on these activities differed between Dallas and Denton. None of the welfare offices had responsibility for work activities or supportive services beyond referring people to the workforce agency.

The workforce agencies assessed clients' needs for both supportive services and employment services and, after doing so, developed the work plan. To assess the needs for employment services, all workforce offices administered a basic skills test to all recipients. All offices also asked everyone to indicate their employment experience and interests on a special form. Information from this form was then entered into the Texas Workforce System Database, which matched their experience and interests with available jobs. Many encounters show that this database was a source of referrals to jobs.

The workforce offices in Dallas, operated by Lockheed Martin, created the capacity to offer three types of employment-related services to TANF clients: 1) supervised job search, 2) GED classes, and 3) job training through the WIA program. People who had not completed high school could choose between job search and GED classes, which were offered on site in both offices. Workers in both offices frequently advised clients to attend GED classes:

> **Texas (Masters) workforce worker:** You got 18 months, and the reason that's good to know is that you can kind of pace yourself as to what you want to do with those 18 months. Like get your GED.

Yet they told clients they were free to choose between job search and GED classes:

> ***Texas*** *(Masters) workforce worker:* You can come in for job search Monday through Friday every day until you get a job. Or you decide to go to GED.... We have a GED classroom on site here at this office. So it's up to you. Now if you want to try and find your job first and you decide, well, I want to go to school, just let me know.

> ***Texas*** *(Grand Prairie) workforce worker:* You can do whatever you want to do with your remaining time. You can look for work, or go to school — whatever.

Some workers used job search and GED in combination as a way for people to complete their 30 hours of work:

> ***Texas*** *(Masters) workforce worker:* You attend GED classes in the A.M. and then go to Work First. If you have no interviews on that day, you will return to GED classes. But look for jobs too, OK. You've got to look for jobs if you don't go back to GED.

The staff working with TANF clients did not control access to WIA training and recommended WIA only to people who had a high school diploma or GED. Compared to job search and GED, they recommended training less frequently.

> ***Texas*** *(Grand Prairie) workforce agency:* Once you finish your GED, if you are still eligible, there is the WIA program. If you're eligible for some training, you can go over there to get the training, OK?... But you have to get your GED before you can even discuss that.

The workforce office in Denton emphasized job search and job readiness activities over education. The Denton workforce office did not operate a GED program on site, and none of the observations captured a worker urging someone to study for a GED. One encounter suggests this may have been due to a temporary lack of GED classes; the worker was willing to refer a client for a GED but could not do so for six months because the GED program was "shut down."

> Like Dallas, Denton sent few people directly to training:

> ***Texas*** *(Denton) workforce agency:* Under WIA, different levels of service require that you do different things. If after two weeks of basic job search on your own and a requirement of four weeks at the intensive level of services and we failed in our attempt to help you find and gain employment, then we'll evaluate you for training. And training under the Work Force Investment Act is really a last-ditch effort to say

> "Look, we've done everything we can do; you've done everything you can do and we're not being successful working together. Maybe we need to look at training as an option."

Recipients with a child under age three were exempt from participation in a work activity but they had the opportunity to volunteer. If they chose to volunteer, they were eligible not only for services at the workforce agency but also for an extra period of transitional child care. In contrast, parents or other relatives who were not receiving assistance on their own behalf, like adults cut off by the time limit, sanctioned or a "payee only," were ineligible to receive any of the services the workforce agencies offered to TANF clients.

> ***Texas*** *(Grand Prairie) workforce worker in a job readiness seminar:* To be exempt, your child must be under three years. But the clock doesn't stop.

> ***Texas*** *(Denton) workforce worker:* DHS [the Department of Human Services] has marked you as being exempt, OK, which means that you're not required at this time to participate in the Choices program but if you wish to volunteer, then you may, OK? And plus you're eligible for extended transitional benefits since you're voluntary.

> ***Texas*** *(Masters) workforce worker:* You have no benefits left on TANF and that $99 you are receiving is for the children. So, you are not eligible for our program. You yourself are not on the program, it is the children that are on it. When did your benefits run out?

> *Client:* What do mean? They just started, I just got the nephews. I haven't had them all along, not even a year.

> *Worker:* Well evidently you're not on it. For some reason they've got you coded ineligible, F, and I don't know why. I just know it's a code.

The rules permitted postsecondary education for recipients who were exempt from work because they had a child under age three and came to the workforce agency as volunteers. In two encounters, workers told volunteers they could attend postsecondary education and receive child care assistance without having to work. In several other encounters, clients who were not volunteers were told they would still have to work 30 hours a week if they attended college. If college attendance prevented them from working 30 hours a week, they would be ineligible for TANF.

In summary, policies set at the state or local level regarding the mix of work-related activities strongly determined the frontline workers' actions in mandating work for adult recipients, leaving little discretion to individual workers. Policies in Georgia emphasized education and short-term training over job search for recipients, who had already searched for jobs when they applied for welfare. Michigan's policies emphasized immediate employment, permitting education and training only for people who were already employed. In Texas, the workforce agencies focused their primary attention on immediate employment, although the Dallas agencies gave recipients the option to attend the GED programs they had created for TANF clients. Only the New York sites had a variety of options for recipients and relied on the discretion of workers to refer recipients to job search, education, training, or, in Suffolk, work experience.

Work Mandates for Long-Term Recipients

Observations in two large urban areas, Fulton County (Atlanta) and Wayne County (Detroit), suggest that nonparticipation in a work activity was sufficiently widespread to warrant a special initiative for long-term recipients. Under pressure from the time limit in Georgia and Project Zero in Wayne County, the welfare agencies called recipients into the office to assess their situation and learn why they were not working. After the assessment, workers either referred recipients to a specific work-related activity or encouraged them to seek an exemption.

The Fulton County welfare offices made extra efforts to assess and advise clients who were approaching the 48-month time limit, efforts that account for the relatively high frequency of encounters for the purpose of assessing clients in Georgia. Recipients who had been on assistance for 30 months or were out of compliance with the work requirement were called in to group meetings at the welfare offices and told they urgently needed to prepare to support themselves. A format observed in both offices was a group meeting with training providers followed immediately by individual short meetings with employment workers. Representatives of the training providers described their programs at the group meeting and the welfare workers then met with clients individually to ask them to choose one of the programs.

> ***Georgia** (SW Fulton) welfare worker:* Have you decided what you want to do?
>
> *Client:* I want to go to CareerWorks.
>
> *Worker:* Could we get you started soon? There's a session starting next week.
>
> *Client:* I have to get child care.
>
> *Worker:* OK, do you think you could find some place for your children this week? I can give you transportation this week, so we can get you started.

Workers referred clients to these programs quickly, asking little about the client's interests or abilities. The observations captured three of these group meetings followed by streams of clients being referred to a work activity. In one office, the worker spent an average of 12 minutes per client; in the other office, the worker spent an average of 25 minutes per client.

The Fulton County welfare offices also held group meetings to assess clients for barriers to employment. At the 30-month point, recipients who were not in a work activity were called in to the welfare office for an assessment by staff of the Department of Rehabilitative Services (DRS).

> ***Georgia** (SW Fulton) welfare worker:* We're at a critical point — every one here's been on TANF for 30 months. Under welfare reform, there's a lifetime cap of 48 months of welfare benefits. So we're collaborating with DRS to help us determine how we can best serve you, remove your barriers. If there's a problem of transportation, day care, and that's why you can't work — we want to help. If it's a physical impairment — we want to help make that a matter of record. If emotional impairment — we want to help make that a matter of record. So I want to encourage everyone here to volunteer these issues, so they can be addressed. We're partnering with other agencies. So if there's a chemical dependence issue — namely crack cocaine, let us know, we can help you. If it's domestic violence, let us know. I bring this up because a University of California Berkeley study showed that 54% of welfare recipients had domestic violence issues. Many of these were coupled with chemical dependencies. So if any of these are issues with you, we need to focus on it and help you through. Otherwise, you'll have to walk off the rolls with these issues. In addition, everyone here received a letter from DFACS [the Department of Family and Children Services] — if you don't comply here, you'll not receive benefits next month.

During a one-day group meeting for the purpose of assessing long-term recipients, participants filled out a battery of assessment instruments designed to identify why they were not working and uncover impediments to employment. The meeting was observed in its entirety and summarized in detail:

> **Georgia** *(NW Fulton) welfare workers and staff from the Department of Rehabilitative Services:* In the morning, clients completed the following instruments: a Barriers to Employment Success Inventory to identify the following types of barriers: personal and financial, emotional and physical, career decision-making, job-seeking knowledge, and training and education; a Job Search Attitude Inventory; a Learning Channel Preference instrument to see whether the client's preference for learning was visual, auditory, or motor; a Lifestyle Inventory; an Inventory of Responses to Stress, and some job applications. In the afternoon, clients took several tests to assess their Employability Skills: preparing a resume, filling out an application, interviewing, being punctual, maintaining regular attendance, presenting appropriate appearances, demonstrating positive attitudes and behavior, exhibiting good interpersonal relations, and completing tasks effectively. Finally, clients completed a typical job application form as a test of their ability to follow directions.

The observer reported attendance of about 20 TANF clients, one employment services worker from the welfare agency, and three workers from the Department of Rehabilitative Services, who answered questions and helped the participants complete the paperwork. The assessment was typically scheduled for two or three days, with time to discuss the results of each handout and how it affects the client's overall prospects for getting off welfare and becoming self-sufficient. At the request of the participants, the group leader shortened the observed assessment to one day and skipped the in-depth discussion, with the assumption that participants would discuss the results with their individual caseworkers at a later date. The observer reported that some of the clients did not take the workshop seriously, saying they were tired and wanted to go home or laughing at the employability tests, but the task of completing the Inventory of Responses to Stress brought many participants to tears.

Observations of individual meetings following these assessments show welfare workers referring clients to the standard work activity, which was short-term training, but they also show workers referring clients to the Department of Rehabilitative Services.

> **Georgia** *(NW Fulton) welfare worker:* Now, I know you're ready to go to work, but I'd rather send you to DRS, because you're going through some trying times right now, with the children, the separation, etc. And to have someone help you emotionally.

> **Georgia** *(SW Fulton) welfare worker:* You know what you wanna do?

> *Client:* No. They told me that I have acute arthritis.

> *Worker:* Have you applied for disability?

> *Client:* Yeah, it was turned down, I'm appealing.

> *Worker:* This is gonna help then. You'll talk to the psychologist, and they're gonna determine if you're physically and mentally able to work. And remember that when you get disability they have to pay from the first day you apply. If Social Security denies you again, call Legal Aid. Tell them you were assessed by a doctor at DRS.

> *Client:* Who's that?

> *Worker:* That's who you'll see here. Like I was telling them over there, Social Security gonna want you to see their own doctor. This person's independent.

> *Client:* So I ought to go back to Social Security and reapply?

> *Worker:* You should. It don't take but a minute, but come December — you won't get any check. At least get them working on it.

These meetings with the DRS are evidence that the welfare offices were not able to maintain clients in a continuous work activity. Although some clients suffered from physical or mental problems, the observations show clients who were capable of working but not engaged in a work activity. In the following example, the client had not been enrolled in a work activity for five months:

> **Georgia** *(SW Fulton) welfare worker:* How you doing, Ms. _____? Are you participating in anything right now [May]?

> *Client:* I finished training in December.

> *Worker:* Were you able to find a job?

> *Client:* No, I'm looking, but child care stopped.

Michigan appeared to be keeping some recipients engaged in a work activity by continuous job search. In addition, Wayne County made extra efforts to assess long-term recipients and either move them into a work activity or exempt them from work participation. For these long-term recipients, Project Zero's goal of employing everyone drove an exception to the policy of restricting training to people who were already employed.

> ***Michigan (Wayne) welfare worker [in recertifying a recipient]:*** We're going to be testing everybody here at the office to see if you qualify for training to be a Home Health Aide. We're trying to get you a job so you can get off assistance.... Work First used to be a month or six months or something but people are staying in Work First until they find a job.

The observations recorded the first stage of a new Summer Enrichment Program in the Wayne County welfare office that engaged clients en masse in a work activity, similar to the effort in Fulton County to move nonparticipating long-term recipients into work. The program began with a call-in to the welfare office of all nonexempt recipients with zero income for an "assessment of barriers to employment, skills and interests." If the assessment indicated the recipient was capable of working, she and her children were required to attend the Summer Enrichment Program all day during the children's school vacation. To facilitate attendance, the program provided transportation, child care, and meals. The program had not been completely designed at the time of the observations, but the workers mentioned it would offer GED preparation and computer training. The assessments used a list of questions to identify problems that could be interfering with employment:

> ***Michigan (Wayne) welfare worker:*** Is the shelter/housing that you are living in suitable and affordable. Is it in good repair?
>
> How is transportation over there? Do your girls take the bus to school?
>
> What about your physical health? The girl's health?
>
> What about nutrition? Are you eating OK? Are you able to prepare the meals? Get any fruits and vegetables in your diet?
>
> What about physical fitness? Are you and your children able to exercise? What type of exercise?
>
> What about the reading skills for you and your children? Did you graduate from high school? What was the last grade you completed? What grades are your children in? What about your math skills? How are they? What about the girls' performance in school? How do they interact with the children as well as the teachers?
>
> Do you speak pretty well?
>
> Do you and the children have suitable clothing? For all types of weather? If you were to get a job, would you have the right type of clothing?

What about spirituality? Do you attend church? Do the girls? Is that an interest?

What about personal hygiene? Do you guys keep up appearance and do all that?

How's the family function? How do you all get along? What are some of the things you do as a family?

What about the absent parent? How's the father? What about the other relatives? Are there family members that live close by that can help you out?

What about your household management? Are you able to keep things up at the house?

What about keeping up with appointments?

What about legal issues, child support, your landlord?

What about keeping up with your finances? Are you able to pay your bills on time? Are you able to save some money? Are you interested in taking some classes on that? Household financing?

How do you feel about interacting with the children? How are your parenting skills?

Any domestic violence or substance abuse?

What do you do outside as far as do you have any hobbies? [The client said she earned money doing hairdressing in her home.]

Do the girls have any interests as far as education? Do you belong to any clubs or anything like that or do anything outside of the home besides hair?

Now, we've got some challenges here: math, child support, employment. What steps are you going to take to possibly dissolve some of these challenges?

In the seven assessments observed, workers spent an average of 24 minutes per client administering these questions. The broad array of questions elicited numerous descriptions of difficulties facing the clients, but few of their responses stopped the worker from continuing down the list of questions. The workers discovered one client had just started a job but had not reported it to the welfare office, two had very young infants, one was a victim of domestic violence, and one client had unreported earnings from doing hair in her home. All except the woman facing domestic violence were referred to the summer program, including the mothers with an infant. The client with unreported earnings was reprimanded:

> **Michigan** *(Wayne) welfare worker:* You're going to have to report that income and it's going to have to be budgeted. You also had the issue of the license? What are you going to do about that?... I looked in your case; you've been referred a lot.
>
> *Client:* I was being lazy.
>
> *Worker:* But why, that's the thing, why?
>
> *Client:* You get used to doing things like that after a while, no push, no edge.
>
> *Worker:* You should be pushing yourself. You've got two girls sitting there.
>
> *Client:* This might be the wake up call.
>
> *Worker:* You got two girls. If you don't sit up here and make a difference in their lives you gonna have another generation of young girls getting pregnant early and not finishing school. Or you're going to have a young lady that's going to think OK, I don't have to do anything. You don't want that. You've got to realize if you do not push them now, you're going to end up with problems that you never thought you'd have. So push them, but you gotta push yourself too. When they're studying, you can be studying. And there's nothing out here. Ain't no man.
>
> *Client:* I know that.
>
> *Worker:* It ain't gonna be no man for when your child gets older. There are no man, OK? You know that as well as I do. You not going to find nobody that's going to come in here, help you out, work. You work, you all achieve something together. Those days is over with. So this, right now, you're in the Summer Project Program.

The creation of the summer program and the mass processing of recipients into the program are evidence that not all recipients in the state's largest county were engaged in a reported work activity. Sufficient recipients were not engaged to warrant spending resources on a project providing parents and their children with everything they would need to participate: buses to pick them up and bring them home, child care, and lunch. The program itself had not been fully designed other than identifying the supportive services needed to ensure that all recipients assessed as capable of participating would be able to do so.

In Fulton County, the practice of workers in assessing recipients appeared to fall short of the process designed by the agency. An assessment process designed to extend over two or three days was compressed into one day at the request of clients. According to the observer, the workers had sufficient time to administer the assessment instruments to identify barriers to employment but not to discuss the results with clients individually. In Wayne, most workers administered the assessment as a check list, simply asking the client whether she faced a problem but not asking her to describe her situation. Yet despite a pro forma manner in performing the seven assessments observed, the workers in Wayne were able to identify one client subject to domestic violence and another with a job.

Education and Training for Teen Parents

In explaining rules regarding education and training to teen parents, workers gave the most attention to the special rules for this group. Following TANF's mandate for school attendance or training by unmarried parents under age 18 who do not have a high school diploma or GED, all states treated teen parents differently from adults at some point in the process of implementing work-related activities. Different treatment of teen parents and adults began during the application process in Georgia, which did not require teen parents to search for work. In Michigan and Texas, teen parents applying for TANF were required to attend the orientation at the workforce agency like adults. Only after they became recipients were they subject to a different set of rules regarding employment, education, and training.

Georgia

Because Georgia mandated education or training for unmarried parents under age 20, teen parents applying for TANF were exempt from job search. Typically, workers referred teen parents to education rather than training. The Bibb and Northwest Fulton welfare offices offered GED classes on site, while the Southwest Fulton office sent clients to the Northwest office for GED classes. Workers in all sites could refer teens to GED classes with the assurance that capacity was available and attendance at classes would be monitored.

> ***Georgia (NW Fulton) welfare worker [to an 18-year old applicant]:*** Did you finish high school?
>
> *Client:* No.
>
> *Worker:* Are you working on your GED?
>
> *Client:* No. I want to, but I can't because of child care.
>
> *Worker:* Well you'll have to, because it's mandatory if you're applying for TANF.
>
> ***Georgia (Bibb) welfare worker [during a conciliation meeting with an 18-year old]:*** So what was your reason for not going [to GED classes]?
>
> *Client:* I was going, then school got out for everyone else, so I stopped going.
>
> *Worker:* That's understandable. You have to go year round, though. You get a little break at Christmas, that's about it. So I have to sign you back up.

Although workers referred most teen parents to GED classes, they took advantage of TANF's rule allowing certain types of training for teen parents:

> ***Georgia (NW Fulton) welfare worker [to an 18-year old applicant]:*** Any time you apply for a TANF check, you have to fulfill either training, education, or work requirement. Because of your age [18], you'll have to do GED or something like that.
>
> *Client:* I wanna do Job Corps.
>
> *Worker:* OK, I'll ask our Employment Service person if we have anything with Job Corps, or who our GED things are with now.... She says she wants Job Corps.
>
> *Employment Services worker:* You want Job Corps? OK, I can refer you there.

Teen parents could also combine school and work:

> ***Georgia (NW Fulton) welfare worker [to a teen parent]:*** So you'll have to go to the GED class and send us attendance sheets. If you don't do this, your benefits can be cut off or reduced.
>
> *Client:* So what if I go for a GED and get a job, will I be cut off?
>
> *Worker:* So long as you're getting your GED, no. You have to do GED.

Client: How often is that?

Worker: Every day, 20 hours a week, I think it's in the afternoon. Your primary activity has to be GED, but so long as you do that, you can have a job.

Michigan

State policy in Michigan required school attendance for teen parents under age 18. The sites did not create special GED classes for TANF clients and, based on a small number of observations of teen parents, it appears that workers were telling teens they must go to high school:

Michigan *(Macomb) joint orientation by welfare and workforce workers:* Parents under 18 who don't have a high school diploma or a GED must stay in school to be eligible for cash assistance. For those with a baby less than three months old, this is a good time to be working on your resume and deciding what child day care arrangement you can arrange.

Michigan *(Wayne) welfare worker [reading from a manual regarding benefits for minor parents]:* It says right here you must complete high school or must be attending a secondary school, full-time participation of at least 20 hours a week.

Consistent with the goal of Project Zero to employ all TANF recipients, teen parents in Hillsdale were permitted to combine work and school:

Michigan *(Hillsdale) welfare worker [to a 17-year old parent]:* You are attending high school, OK. And you need to continue to do that and you also need to continue to work on developing some employment.

Client: OK.

Worker: So you need to attend school. That's number one. And then you do need to do 20 hours, we said between school and work. OK?

New York

State policy in New York required teen parents to attend school, but few of the clients observed were teen parents without a high school or GED degree. Only in Albany did the encounters show workers explaining the rule about school attendance:

> *New York (Albany) welfare worker:* Your sister [a teen parent] is required
> to be in high school. She's between 16 and 19 — she has to get a high
> school diploma.

Texas

This state had a formal policy of requiring school attendance by teen
parents without a high school diploma or GED if they were under age 19,
and the welfare offices informed clients of the rule by printing it in the
Personal Responsibility Agreement to be signed by all clients. The state
also had a formal policy of exempting parents with children under age
three from the work requirement. In practice, this exemption negated the
school attendance rule for all teen parents except those who had borne
their last child before they were age 16. No workers were observed telling
a teen parent that school attendance was required.

> *Texas (Grand Prairie) welfare worker [reading the Personal Responsibil-*
> *ity Agreement to a couple with a child under age three]:* The next
> thing says that if you have anybody receiving AFDC who is younger
> than 18, or is a teen parent younger than 19, they must attend school on
> a regular basis. Since she's not attending school, I'll code her as having
> a child under three years old. OK. So she won't have to follow that.

As these conversations indicate, workers in Georgia, Michigan, and
Texas paid considerable attention to explaining the states' rules about
school attendance or training to teen parents without a high school diploma or GED. They implemented a policy of mandating education, a
mix of education and training, or a mix of education and employment for
teen parents in all states except Texas. In Texas, a liberal exemption from
the work requirement in effect negated the formal school attendance policy.

Variations in Work Mandates

In most sites, frontline staff mandated work-related activities more
consistently on applicants than on recipients. Attendance at Work First
became a routine feature of the application process. Staff in the welfare

agencies rarely exercised discretion to exempt applicants from Work First or, in New York, another immediate work activity. Referral to the workforce agencies was the norm for all applicants except those most obviously unable to work. Sites had focused resources on developing the capacity to operate a Work First program and, assured of this capacity, workers in the welfare agencies implemented the formal policies as designed at higher levels.

Although the study did not observe applicants after leaving the welfare office and cannot estimate their response to Work First, a few encounters show the work-related mandate diverting applicants from TANF. In Georgia, New York, and Texas, one encounter in each state showed an applicant who had been diverted or was withdrawing her TANF application. An encounter in Michigan showed an applicant being denied assistance because she had voluntarily quit her job, and an encounter in New York showed a teenager being excluded from his family's case because he refused to go to school or the workforce office.

Once families had passed through the ordeal of the application process and were receiving assistance, workers gave more scrutiny to problems that interfered with their ability to work and exempted some of the recipients who had gone through the Work First process. Compared to the routinized referral of TANF applicants to the workforce agencies, workers gave adult TANF recipients more individualized treatment in discussing their work options. Every site had arranged two or more work activities to enable the site to impose the work mandate on its caseload. Workers asked clients about their educational background, prior work experience, vocational skills, and interests before making a decision about the work activity, or choice of work activities, to offer the client.

Although staff gave adult recipients individualized treatment in referring them to a work activity, the array of work activities was quite limited everywhere except New York. In the other states, state policies and the services arranged by the workforce agencies or, in Georgia, the welfare agencies, constrained staff in choosing among immediate job search, education, and training. For this reason, the balance between mandating immediate job search and giving recipients an opportunity for education and training depended primarily on state or local policy and less on the discretion of the individual worker. Workers exercised even less discretion in dealing with teen parents, consistently giving priority to education in response to the TANF mandate for school attendance.

The balance between mandating immediate job search and giving recipients an opportunity for education and training was influenced by the time limit policy. Georgia sought to divert applicants from welfare by requiring a period of job search, but once people were on assistance, the welfare agency sought to give them job skills training or vocational education to prepare for self-sufficiency. The time limit itself would move them off assistance. Similarly in Dallas, the workforce agencies did not pressure recipients without a high school diploma to search for work but gave them the opportunity to prepare for the GED exam during their limited time on assistance. Michigan, without the pressure of a time limit, emphasized immediate job search to reduce client's need for assistance.

Lodging responsibility for recipients' work activities in workforce agencies was not equivalent to giving TANF clients access to the full range of services offered by these agencies. In Michigan and Texas, where the state gave the workforce system responsibility for serving TANF clients, the workforce system contracted with service providers to deliver a narrow set of work activities to TANF clients. These service providers dedicated separate staff to work with TANF clients and, except in Grand Prairie and Denton, located the staff in a location separate from the office serving the general population. Workers could refer clients to the broader array of services offered by the workforce system, but acceptance into these activities was not guaranteed. Although workers in both Michigan and Texas informed some clients about the WIA program, they indicated that TANF clients had to compete with others for access to them and made few referrals.

These service patterns are reflected in federal reports on the work activities of TANF clients (Table 5-3). In Michigan and Texas, few of the adult recipients reported to be engaged in a work activity were participating in a training program, while many more were in job search. In Georgia, in contrast, over a quarter of adults in a work activity were in a training program, reflecting the welfare agencies' efforts to arrange training programs specifically for adult recipients. In Georgia and Texas, where time limits motivated some sites to allow education, a higher percent of recipients were in education than in Michigan and New York. In

Michigan and New York, where benefit levels were relatively high and recipients could become employed without losing all their TANF benefits, the majority of adults in a work activity were in unsubsidized employment.

Table 5-3. Work Activities and Participation of
TANF Recipients in 2000

	GEORGIA	*MICHIGAN*	*NEW YORK*	*TEXAS*
Adult recipients with some work activity[1]	6,446	24,684	76,842	13,327
Work-related activity[2]	*Percent of adults in work activity*			
Education	7.8	2.7	1.5	10.9
Training	26.5	2.2	5.0	6.3
Job search	4.6	11.6	3.5	42.1
Subsidized employment, work experience, community service	17.7	1.2	33.9	4.8
Other	13.7	0.0	0.0	30.4
Unsubsidized employment	41.3	88.2	59.2	43.0
Families counted as participating in work	3,074	15,995	54,684	8,334
Families in denominator of participation rate	25,291	43,602	164,983	76,406
Participation rate (percent)	12.2	36.4	33.2	25.6 (7.8 without waiver)
Total TANF families	53,269	74,709	258,702	127,880

[1] Adults engaged in more than one activity are included once in this total. They may not be working for a sufficient number of hours for the family to count toward the participation rate.
[2] Adults may be engaged in more than one activity.
Source: U.S. Department of Health and Human Services, *TANF Program Information Memorandum* TANF-ACF-IM- 2002-1, February 14, 2002.

Federal reports on the work activities of TANF clients also support the conclusion that frontline staff mandated work-related activities more consistently on applicants than on recipients. In the year of the observations, federal law required states to meet a minimum work participation rate of 40 percent among families receiving TANF. All states in the study, like the majority of states in the nation, met this rate by applying the caseload reduction credit against the minimum participation rate, subtracting the percentage point decline in the caseload from 40 percent. Applying the credit reduced the minimum work participation rate standard to 5.2 percent in New York and to zero in the other states. In addition, TANF permitted states to ignore certain families in calculating the participation rate, including payee-only cases where no adults received assistance, single parents exempt from work after the birth of a child, and families under a sanction. The waiver in Texas exempting parents with a child under age three also removed these families from the participation rate. As a result (Table 5-3), states met the federal standard with participation rates below 40 percent: 12.2 percent in Georgia, 36.4 percent in Michigan, 33.2 percent in New York, and 25.6 in Texas (or 7.8 percent without the waiver exemptions).[4]

This means that a large share of the TANF families who were subject to the work requirement were not working enough hours to count as participating in a work activity. Additional adults had some work activity, as shown in the first line of Table 5-3, but even counting them, only in Michigan did a majority of the families subject to the work requirement actually engage in a work-related activity. As shown by encounters in Fulton County and Wayne County, the welfare agencies in these sites began to engage long-term recipients in a work activity only after Work First was operating to discourage applicants from welfare. On average, long-term recipients undoubtedly had more barriers to employment than welfare applicants, making them a more costly group to serve. When the caseload reduction credit reduced the participation rate standard, states had little immediate incentive to spend resources on these harder to serve clients.

---

4   U.S. Department of Health and Human Services, *Temporary Assistance for Needy Families Program Information Memorandum*, TANF-ACF-IM-2002-1, February 14, 2002.

6

Financial Inducements to Work

By limiting TANF benefits to welfare applicants who were willing and able to comply with the Work First mandate, welfare agencies created a financial inducement for them to attend the activities of the workforce agencies. Additional financial inducements for clients to seek work were the wages paid by the available jobs and the supplement to wages provided by the Earned Income Tax Credit (EITC). Disregarding a portion of earnings in calculating the amount of the TANF benefit meant that the welfare benefit could also supplement a recipient's wages. In addition to these positive inducements was the negative inducement of sanctions, which reduced welfare benefits for failure to comply with program rules.

The behavior of staff in discussing and implementing these positive and negative inducements with their clients influenced the stringency of the work requirement. Staff responsible for making job referrals could refer clients to minimum wage jobs or could use their discretion, however limited, to allow clients to hold out for jobs paying higher wages. Staff could discuss the EITC and the earnings disregards, taking a positive approach to motivating clients to work, or they could neglect to explain these complicated rules. TANF permitted states to increase the severity of sanctions on people refusing to work without good cause, enabling staff to impose tougher sanctions but also giving them reason to help their clients avoid the harsher penalties.

This chapter examines the behavior of frontline workers to understand how they used these positive and negative inducements to encourage work. First, it examines their conversations in referring clients to jobs to learn what jobs were available and the wage levels paid by these jobs. It then examines the frequency and accuracy with which workers explained the financial incentives to work provided by the earnings disregards and the Earned Income Tax Credit. Finally, it analyzes the workers' conversations to learn how they allocated their attention to the various TANF mandates and administered sanctions to enforce them.

Referring Clients to Jobs:
Job Availability and Wage Rates

Doubts about the capacity of the regular labor market to generate enough jobs for welfare recipients have long been an impediment to implementing a stringent work requirement. To increase job availability, the WIN and JOBS programs permitted states to use various mechanisms to create or subsidize jobs for welfare recipients, as outlined in Chapter 1, and TANF permitted states to subsidize public and private jobs. In the view of some social critics, the welfare system itself contributed to the lack of good jobs, with its low benefits serving to maintain a pool of low-wage labor.[1] The observations of workers discussing job opportunities with their clients give some insight into the labor market for people in the welfare system, particularly the availability of jobs and the wages paid for these jobs. To what extent were jobs available for the people required to work? What kinds of jobs were most common? Did workers require their clients to accept any job, regardless of its wage rate, or did they allow job seekers to hold out for a job more commensurate with their skills, experience, and interests? This perspective on the labor market

---

1   Piven and Cloward, *Regulating the Poor.*

does not give a full picture of the job search process of welfare clients, but even a partial view offers some evidence for answering these questions.

Staff in the workforce agencies were generally upbeat about the availability of jobs for their clients. They made a strong pitch that job seekers could find some sort of a job if they made sufficient effort.

> *Georgia (Bibb) workforce worker:* In this workshop, we pretty much cover just about everything that you will need to know on how to get a job. You know we want you to succeed. And you will.

> *New York (Suffolk) workforce worker:* You would have to come here once a week for four weeks and they'd give you like 30 job contacts and you have to go contact them and see how it goes. They're usually pretty effective.

> *Michigan (Wayne joint orientation):* The papers are full of jobs that all of you can do.

> *Texas (Masters) workforce worker:* We have a lot of clerical and warehouse.... We've got everything that you need here to find work.... It's just a matter of how much you put into it. It's like anything else. The amount you're gonna get out of it is what you put into it.

The staff of the workforce agencies, which had responsibility for job search, used several sources of information about job openings to assist clients. These sources of information varied from state to state depending on institutional arrangements. Where the workforce agency serving TANF clients also served the general population — the Georgia Department of Labor, the Suffolk County Department of Labor, and the Texas Workforce Centers — workers relied primarily on listings of job openings coming from employers. These offices also engaged in some job development, where staff take the initiative in contacting employers to learn about available jobs. The workforce offices in Michigan, which did not serve the general population, relied more upon jobs located by job developers or by the clients themselves. Regardless of the technology, the workers in all offices conveyed the impression that job openings were sufficient to sustain the job search activity of their clients.

The types of jobs discussed most frequently were those requiring low-level skills. Workforce workers often mentioned openings in food service such as fast food restaurants, hospitals, and schools; housekeeping in hotels, office buildings, nursing homes, and so forth; warehousing in factories, direct marketing firms, and warehouses; clerical work; data entry; cashier work; customer service such as retail sales; and security in buildings and airports. Many clients mentioned they had job experience in these areas, although workers also referred clients to these jobs without any experience. In Georgia, workers routinely justified referrals to these jobs by telling clients they had "transferable skills," skills they had used in previous jobs or the home. These jobs typically paid wages in the range of $5.50 to $8.50 per hour, with some paying $10-$12 for workers who had more skills, like secretarial skills or the ability to operate a fork lift in a warehouse. Workers advised clients to apply quickly for jobs paying the higher wages, since they were filled rapidly.

With an ample number of low-wage job openings, an important question is whether workers pressured their clients to accept just any job regardless of its wage rate or whether they allowed clients to hold out for higher wage jobs for which they were qualified. All offices asked their clients about their skills, experience, and interests and, to a greater or lesser degree, sought to match them with a job they were capable of doing and that met their interests. In general, the offices in Georgia and New York made greater efforts than others to avoid referring clients to the lowest paying jobs.

> *Georgia (SW Fulton) client:* I have a lot of experience in cashier.

> *Workforce worker:* You're not gonna want the ones we have — they're like $5-6/hour. When you were an operator — what kind?

> *Client:* Operated machines on the line.

> *Worker:* OK. Let me see what we have. So your first choice would be something like production.

> *Georgia (Bibb) workforce worker:* So you got seven months at a nursery school and 16 months in fast food. My recommendation, and it's strictly a recommendation, I would put down one of them, something you got experience in. See, that's the name of the game. What's the best way to get a job? If you already have experience at a job.

> *Client:* But I put down that my employment goal is to be a legal office assistant.

> *Worker:* You could leave it like that. If that's what you want to be, go for it. It's strictly up to you.

> **New York** *(Suffolk) client:* I worked at Kinney's [sales] and now I work at Blimpy's [fast food] but they're not giving that many hours. Pays $5.60 an hour.

> *Workforce worker:* I have a really good job but it's not sales. Or are you dead set on sales?

> *Client:* Anything.

> *Worker:* It's with a company that maintains a big office building. They have porter positions open where you'd be polishing furniture and other different tasks. They usually start you at about $8.00 an hour. There's a good opportunity for advancement, and they're very flexible in their hours.

In the Texas workforce agencies, the job search process made heavy use of computers to match clients with jobs. A statewide job bank contained information about available jobs and information about clients' qualifications, interests, and salary requirements. Clients first looked through the job bank to select jobs to pursue. If this approach was unsuccessful, job developers gave them referrals to employers generated by the computer. The mention of salary requirements suggests they were relevant, although workers in one office cautioned against setting their salary requirement too high or told clients to leave the salary field blank in searching through the job bank.

> **Texas** *(Denton) workforce worker [sitting at a computer with a client]:* We'll go in and look at clerical/sales jobs so I'm gonna type in a "2." And then it takes you down here; it says enter an "x" for jobs requiring no experience. We're gonna leave that blank, OK, 'cause we want any jobs to pull up. And you can actually enter in a monthly salary if you want to; we're going to leave that blank too, OK? And hit enter.

Although workers in Texas tried to avoid placing people in minimum wage jobs, few workers were observed trying to find jobs with high wage levels. In Dallas, workers often gave clients the opportunity to prepare for the GED instead of taking a minimum wage job. Workers in Denton pointed out that the low unemployment rate was encouraging employers to pay more than the minimum wage. And, they argued, because benefit levels were low, even a minimum wage job paying $5.15 an hour provided a higher income than the TANF monthly benefit.

> **Texas** *(Denton) workforce worker:* Page three shows the amount of money you could receive from TANF in comparison with the amount of money you could earn from working full-time. For one child in the

household, you're only going to get $174 for the entire month. That is nothing. That barely even pays a utility bill. If you're making minimum wage, you're going to earn at least $886 for the entire month. Good news is most of the time, right now, employers are having such a hard time finding people, they're paying more than minimum wage.

The message was mixed in Michigan, where the goal of Project Zero was employment for the entire caseload. Workers valued good jobs, but they also valued employment in itself.

> **Michigan** *(Hillsdale) [joint orientation] worker:* We want to help you get that first job, but we also want to see you get a better job. We want you to be able to become self-sufficient. Our goal is not to stick you in some minimum wage job for 20 hours a week where you never get ahead. Another thing, and this happens periodically, let's say you are working 20 hours and you are making $5.50 an hour and you have an offer for another job that is going to pay you $7.00 an hour. However, that new job will only be 18 hours. If you accept that job you are also going to have to look for another job. You have to work those minimum hours. We are not looking just at monetary value.

> **Michigan** *(Operation Help) workforce worker:* You cannot refuse a job. OK, that's final. But let me tell you all how to get around refusing a job. You talk to your job developer, say, "I went to school and I'm able to do so-and-so. Help me find a job in that area."

Personal characteristics of the clients, such as a learning disability, a physical disability, or a family member with a disability, interfered with employment.

> **Texas** *(Denton) client at workforce agency:* A lot of people want cashiers but that's another problem I got, I can't count money. It's embarrassing to say that. It just takes me forever, like with the change. I just can't do the change.

> **Georgia** *(SW Fulton welfare agency) client:* I try to find a job but when they hear that I received Workman's Compensation, they change their mind.

Prison records also interfered with employment. In talking to clients with a prison record, several workers in Georgia, New York, and Texas mentioned the availability of funds to bond ex-offenders to encourage employers to hire them.

> **Texas** *(Masters) workforce worker:* Do you think you have any turndowns based on your record?

> *Client:* Yeah. I've had a couple, yeah.

> *Worker:* Remember I told you I was going to give you that list of businesses that will hire ex-offenders? I found that list so I am going to give you that and just kind of work it against your interviews.

> **Georgia (SW Fulton) workforce worker:** Any questions, concerns?

> *Client:* My criminal background got in the way of the job I was telling you about.

> *Worker:* Let me explain the federal bonding program. It's designed because we know that for folks with this kind of background it's virtually impossible to get a job. What they do is bond for $5,000 for the first six months, after that they decide if they want to renew it.

This evidence suggests that the labor market generated sufficient jobs for the welfare population seeking employment, although at wage levels likely to leave many families in poverty. Overall unemployment rates were unusually low during the period of the observations, and the availability of jobs for TANF clients is consistent with the findings of Blank and others that job opportunities for low-skilled women were growing during the 1990s.[2] The infrequent referral to unpaid work experience, used only in Bibb and Suffolk, is another indication of an overall sufficiency of jobs. Rather, the primary impediments to employment were the cost of child care and transportation required to accept these jobs. In addition, welfare clients lacking a high school diploma or GED often faced very low wages and a limited range of jobs.

Increasing the Financial Incentive to Work

Considering the attention frontline staff gave to the mandate to work, they gave surprisingly little attention to two policies that increased the financial incentive to work, the earnings disregard and the Earned Income Tax Credit (EITC). Disregarding a portion of earnings in calculating the amount of the welfare grant gives recipients an incentive to work because their earnings do not cause a dollar-for-dollar cut in their grant. The EITC supplements the earnings of low-income families through the income tax system. Both policies have the effect of increasing the finan-

---

2 Rebecca M. Blank and Lucie Schmidt, "Work, Wages, and Welfare," in Rebecca M. Blank and Ron Haskins, eds., *The New World of Welfare* (Washington, DC: The Brookings Institution, 2001).

cial reward from working at the low wage jobs typically available to welfare clients.

Under AFDC, federal law required states to disregard a portion of monthly earnings in calculating a family's benefit: $90 for work expenses and, to encourage work, $30 of earnings for 12 months plus one-third of earnings above $30 for four months. In addition, a disregard could be taken for child care expenses up to $200 for each child under age two and $175 for each older child. TANF gave states authority to design their own disregards. At the time of the observations, the monthly earnings disregard in Michigan was $200 plus 20 percent of remaining earnings and in New York was $90 plus 42 percent of remaining earnings. Administrators in Texas reported that the disregard was being increased to $120 plus 90 percent of remaining earnings for four months. The disregards in Georgia had not changed.

Workers explained the earnings disregard in 4 percent of encounters in Michigan, 1 percent in New York, and in no encounters in Georgia and Texas (Table 3-3a). In Michigan, two observations captured workers explaining the disregard correctly, both in interviews with applicants. Only one of the orientations observed included a full explanation of the disregard and the worker made an arithmetic error in describing it. The other encounter where the worker explained the disregard was in a job club, where the worker also made an error.

In New York, the percentage of earnings disregarded was mentioned in only one encounter. In another, the worker explained the disregard only by saying the welfare agency "budgets" their income.

> *New York (Albany) client:* Social Services don't help anybody. They take your money when you work.

> *Welfare worker:* No. You got it wrong. If you work, they budget your income. Nobody takes your money. If you are employed, they don't give you full assistance. Nobody takes your money except child support.

A worker in Georgia said that a recipient could be employed and still receive assistance but did not explain the disregard explicitly.

> *Georgia (NW Fulton) welfare worker:* The standard of need for a household of three is $424. You can only make that to get a partial check. Over that you won't get any check at all. For food stamps the limit is $1,304. So you'll still be eligible for food stamps.

In Texas, workers never mentioned the earnings disregard or the possibility of combining work and welfare. The following example was typical:

> **Texas** *(Grand Prairie) workforce agency client:* As soon as I started working I reported it and they cut my AFDC back.
>
> *Worker:* Well, you can't work and get the TANF.

The EITC is not a component of TANF and is not administered by the welfare system, but it complements the employment goals in TANF by helping to "make work pay." In 2000, a family with one child was eligible for a refundable credit against its federal tax liability of 34 percent of yearly earnings up to $6,920, or a maximum credit of $2,353; a family with two or more children was eligible for a refundable credit of 40 percent of earnings up to $9,720, or a maximum credit of $3,888. New York supplemented this with a credit against state income taxes.

Workers mentioned the EITC in every state, although it was a topic in few encounters: 1 percent in Georgia, Michigan, and New York, and 2 percent in Texas (Table 3-3a). Workers in Albany and Denton gave the most attention to the tax credit. Workers in Albany urged their clients who were working or starting a job to ask their employer about the credit. In Denton, the workforce agency handed out printed information about the EITC during all their orientations.

> **Texas** *(Denton) workforce orientation:* The next page here says the government may owe you money; this is the earned income tax credit. Do you know what this is? You do, OK. For some of you that don't, I don't know a lot about it but I know that you will qualify for it. If you get a job you can talk to your employer about maybe getting this on your paychecks during the year or you can wait until the end of the year when you file your income tax and you can get one lump sum.

The observer who had seen the handouts in Denton asked the worker in Dallas why she did not use them. The worker admitted that she had handouts but did not distribute them because the clients just left them lying around and she "would rather be a social worker than a housekeeper." She said it was better to communicate the information only verbally to make sure it was understood fully.

In summary, these financial incentives to work received little attention in the welfare and workforce offices. Except in Michigan, workers gave clients virtually no information about the amount of the earnings disregard and, even in Michigan, several workers had difficulty explaining its details. Fortunately for recipients, benefit calculations are computerized and do not depend on the worker's understanding of the disregards. After receiving a benefit reflecting the disregard, a client should realize that her benefit did not fall by the amount of her earnings and understand she increased her income by working. However, because the observations show that clients do not always fully understand why their benefits change, they may not be able to decipher the relationship between benefits and earnings.[3] In Texas, the workers' statements about work eliminating TANF benefits raises the question of whether the computer system had been programmed to implement the state's new disregard policy.

Workers did not need to understand the complex details of the EITC in order to urge their clients to take advantage of it and could help their clients just by informing them of its availability. Unlike the earnings disregard, which was implemented automatically by the welfare system, the income tax system did not automatically implement the EITC. Earners needed to file a tax return in order to claim the EITC and to indicate on the return that they might qualify for the credit. Nationally in 1999, about two-thirds of families had heard about the EITC and former welfare recipients were even more likely to have heard about it. Knowledge of the EITC was lower, however, among parents in very poor families, parents who had not completed high school, Hispanic parents, and immigrants.[4]

Sanctioning for Noncompliance with Mandates

One of the more controversial reforms in TANF was the authority it gave states to increase the severity of the financial sanctions imposed on recipients who failed to comply with state mandates. While federal law

---

3   An ethnographic study of welfare recipients in four large urban areas found that recipients had a clear understanding of the earnings disregards in only one of the areas. Janet Quint et al., *Big Cities and Welfare Reform* (New York: Manpower Research Demonstration Corporation, 1999).

4   Katherin Ross Phillips, *Who Knows about the Earned Income Tax Credit?* Assessing the New Federalism Series B, No. B-27 (Washington, DC: The Urban Institute, 2001).

had required states to sanction adults who failed to comply with the mandates regarding work and child support enforcement, TANF allowed states to sanction families for additional reasons and to increase the amount of the sanction. The sanction could be a portion of the welfare grant or, if a state chose, a full family sanction in which the family's entire grant was withheld. Additionally, states had permission to impose sanctions for failure to comply with other behavioral mandates, like children's immunizations and school attendance. Both Michigan and Georgia adopted the full family sanction for failure to comply with mandates to work and cooperate with child support requirements, and Georgia chose to extend the full family sanction for failure to comply with the work requirement over the client's lifetime. All states except New York elected to impose sanctions on additional grounds (Table 6-1).

Explaining mandates and asking clients to sign forms agreeing to comply with them does not guarantee that mandates are actually enforced. Enforcing mandates requires resources. At a minimum, resources must be devoted to monitoring the behavior of clients for compliance. In the case of applicants who are not complying, the agency can enforce the mandate by the simple process of denying the application. In the case of recipients, mandates can be enforced by reducing or eliminating the client's benefit, but this is a more complex process. Imposing a financial sanction requires the agency to operate an appeals process for clients requesting a hearing to contest the sanction. Although no longer mandated by federal law, welfare agencies can also devote resources to operating a conciliation process to resolve disputes before the sanction is imposed. Did workers in practice enforce all the mandates in state TANF policies, enforce them selectively, or not enforce them at all?

During the application process, all the welfare agencies in Michigan and Texas paid attention to monitoring compliance with the Work First mandate. The workforce agencies in Michigan communicated with the welfare agency electronically, entering information about applicants' attendance at Work First activities into a database shared with the welfare agency. The Texas workforce agency gave applicants attending its orientation a form to take back to the welfare agency as proof of attendance. Conversations between workers and clients referred to these processes for monitoring attendance, indicating they were used in practice.

Table 6-1. Discussion of Sanctions
All Encounters

MICHIGAN	TEXAS	GEORGIA	NEW YORK
State Policy Regarding Reduction in Benefits			
*First Instance of Noncompliance With Work Requirements**			
25% deducted for at least 1 month	$78 deducted for at least 1 month	25% deducted for at least 1 month	Adult portion deducted until compliance
*Most Stringent Sanction for Noncompliance With Work Requirements**			
Full family sanction (100% deducted) for at least one month	$78 deducted for at least 6 months	Full family sanction (100% deducted) for lifetime	Adult portion deducted for 6 months and until compliance
*First Instance of Noncompliance With Child Support Requirements**			
Adult portion deducted until compliance	$78 deducted until compliance	Full family sanction (100% deducted) until compliance	Reduced 25% until compliance
*Prolonged Noncompliance With Child Support Requirements**			
Full family sanction (100% deducted) until compliance	$78 deducted until compliance	Full family sanction (100% deducted) until compliance	Reduced 25% for 6 months and until compliance
*Other Grounds for Sanctions***			
School attendance of children; immunization of children	School attendance of children; immunization of children; health screening of children	School attendance of children; immunization of children	None
Percent of encounters discussing sanctions			
(Number of Encounters)	*(269)*	*(229)*	*(202)*	*(264)*
Any worker activity	13.5	14.8	11.4	13.6
Explaining rules	7.6	9.2	7.1	5.6
Advising or assessing	6.8	1.7	0.8	3.1
Excepting or exempting	1.3	1.0	0	0.1

* Sources: U.S. General Accounting Office, *Welfare Reform: State Sanction Policies and Number of Families Affected*, March 2000, GAO/HEHS-00-44.
** Gretchen Rowe, *Welfare Rules Databook: State TANF Policies as of July 1999* (The Urban Institute, November 2000).

Monitoring job search, which required more resources than monitoring attendance at an orientation, was less rigorous. The welfare agencies in Georgia asked applicants to keep a log of the employers contacted during their job search. Applicants in Bibb were required to bring a list of the previous day's job search contacts to the welfare office every morning. The offices in Fulton checked the logs less frequently or not at all, as discussed in Chapter 9.

How many applicants were denied assistance because they failed to comply with this and other mandates is unknown. For example, because Texas did not consider the application for assistance to be complete until applicants attended the workforce orientation, people who did not attend the orientation were not formally denied assistance. Closing the application without an official eligibility determination did not count as a denial of assistance. Without data on informal denials, it is impossible to know their frequency.

Sanctions for failure to comply with program rules without good cause were mentioned in 11 to 15 percent of all encounters (Table 6-1). Most frequently in these conversations, workers were explaining the rules about sanctions. The observations also revealed another tool for enforcing compliance — closing the case. One difference between a sanction and a case closure was the length of the penalty. A sanction could be imposed for a specified time period, while a closure ended whenever the client came into compliance. The conversations indicated that formal sanctions occurred less frequently than case closures, which were used by workers to enforce rules or to prompt clients to come to the welfare office.

Georgia

The state's sanction policy for noncompliance with work requirements was so severe that administrators, under political pressures, were reluctant to implement it fully. The policy called for a "strike one" sanction cutting benefits by 25 percent and a "strike two and you're out" sanction eliminating the family's full benefit for the client's lifetime. Before imposing a permanent full family sanction, the state required a review of the case by administrators and staff, including a visit to the client's home to learn whether the agency could bring the client into compliance and whether the sanction would place the children at risk. Instead of routinely engaging in this resource-intensive process, all the welfare offices called noncomplying clients into the office for a conciliation discussion in an attempt to bring them into compliance and remove the first strike. None of the offices in the study had imposed a "strike two" sanction, although a few full family sanctions had been imposed by other offices in the state. Instead, as many staff explained, they were doing a lot of conciliation.

All the conciliations observed were in response to the client's failure to comply with work requirements, none for failure to comply with the other TANF mandates. In every instance, the worker gave the client another chance to satisfy the mandate to work. Workers urged clients to continue their current program or begin a new program, or they referred clients to the rehabilitation agency for an assessment. One client who was caring for an ill grandmother was permitted to count this activity as "community service" and asked to complete an attendance sheet showing the hours she spent taking care of her grandmother.

In addition to imposing sanctions, the agencies had the power to close the case for noncompliance. Unlike a full family sanction, which barred clients from welfare for life, a client whose case was closed could reapply for assistance. These administrative case closings were less resource-intensive than a full family sanction and more common. In an encounter in Fulton County, a child care worker was interviewing a client whose case had been closed because she had not given the agency her children's birth certificates and immunization records. In Bibb County, a client had not been attending her GED program or working because, she explained, her child had been sick. The worker had attempted to contact the client for conciliation but the client had moved without leaving an address, leading the worker to close the case. When the client returned to the welfare agency, the worker was willing to reinstate her TANF benefits but imposed a strict work mandate: full time attendance at the work experience facility operated by the agency. A van would pick her up in the morning to make sure she got there.

The welfare agency's authority to close cases was also observed during the assessments of long-term recipients discussed earlier:

> **Georgia** *(SW Fulton) welfare worker:* We are asking you to come in today because each of you has been on TANF for at least 30 months. You

may not believe it, but I can pull it up and show you. The new rule is 48 months lifetime limit. So today we need to see where you are — who has a GED, who needs what training. I want to thank you again for coming, because the second half of my day will be closing out the 45 cases of people who didn't come today.

Michigan

State policy in Michigan also called for a full family sanction but, unlike Georgia, the sanction was temporary and the observations indicate it was actually imposed. State policy called for an initial sanction of 25 percent of the family's grant for up to four months followed by a full family sanction for at least 30 days. State policy required a home visit every three months for a complying client, but every month for families under a 25 percent sanction. Monthly home visits were designed to provide multiple opportunities for conciliation.

All the clients under a sanction were being penalized for failure to comply with work requirements, none for failure to comply with the other TANF mandates. Observations captured workers in Wayne and Hillsdale telling clients they would receive no assistance for 30 days because they had failed to work or attend school. After the 30 day penalty, they could reapply for assistance.

Administrative case closings also occurred in Michigan. In one instance, a worker conducting a routine home visit was unable to find the client because she had moved without leaving a forwarding address. The client said she had telephoned the welfare office about her move but the worker had not received the message, making it impossible to conduct the home visit or notify the client about the impending closure. When the client returned to the welfare office, she was able to reapply for assistance.

The observations in Wayne County captured particularly recalcitrant clients and impatient workers.

> **Michigan** *[Wayne] welfare worker:* You are going to be required to go back to Work First because you do have to participate or stay employed. It's just not something that we can play with.
>
> *Client:* Well, I'm going to have to because I need the medical.
>
> *Worker:* And you have to participate because if you do not, there will be repercussions and I will not be able to process your case open either.

Client: OK. Now what if someone call me for a job and I can't attend the Work First?

Worker: You need to contact the worker coordinator and let them know what's going on and if they tell you that you still must report to them, then you still must report. You know when you're going to be going to Work First because the orientations are always on Wednesdays. OK?

Client: Right.

Worker: So when you go to make this appointment to interview for a job, make sure that you don't set it up for that time period so that you don't have to call back saying, "Oh, I can't make it." Because, see, it's already down on the records with Work First that you haven't complied. So if you don't comply, you're going to be sanctioned. Your case is just going to be denied.

We always get people calling, and I don't like to view people that way, but we get people all the time saying, "Oh, I didn't go because I had a job interview."

Client: OK, what I'm saying...

Worker: "I didn't go because I got this job." They go to the job, they work two days. Bam, they're back. They don't go anymore.

Client: OK. Now what if someone calls...

Worker: So they're playing the game and maneuvering everything around, manipulating things. So now it's cut and dry. You must attend.

Client: No matter what.

Worker: You must attend. If you want to apply for a money grant, you must attend.

The observations of the assessments of long-term recipients in Wayne also suggests that the welfare agency had not been enforcing the work requirement on all its clients. Only two of the seven long-term clients were under a sanction, including the following:

Worker: Miss ___ has documentation that she has been trying to get in touch with you and also your case has been sanctioned for not complying with the work requirements for the State of Michigan. You haven't even been to orientation. You haven't gone to any of the training programs. If you decide that you're not going to comply at all, this case is going to close completely. Welfare Reform is really now and they're going to close cases the way they did general assistance. That's it, they're not playing. Right now they have you enrolled in a summer project program. You and your two children.

Client: You say summer program?

Worker: The summer program deals with job training skills, computers. It also deals with day care assistance and there will be transportation provided. So, if you decide you're not going to participate in that, it's going to close and there will be no coming back. This is it and you've got to find a job.

Client: So when did that start?

Worker: We're Project Zero. All the district offices are Project Zero. If you decide I'm not going to comply over here, we code it on the computer. It's coded that you refused to participate, so you can't even walk into another office and get assistance. What a lot of people have been doing is finding a job.

The other six clients, however, were not under a sanction when they were called in for the assessment even though they were not complying with the work requirement. Apparently, under the pressure of Project Zero, the welfare agency was paying attention to clients it had not been monitoring closely.

New York

New York's sanction policy called for eliminating the parent's share of the benefit while maintaining benefits for other family members. In Albany, the three conciliation meetings observed were conducted by eligibility workers. In one case, where the client was being sanctioned because she quit her job, the worker agreed to lift the sanction when she found another job. The other two clients had recently been fired from their job, but because the workers believed the clients were responsible for the termination, they imposed a 90-day sanction.

In Suffolk, workers from the welfare agency were located in a special unit at the Department of Labor to handle child care, transportation expenses and sanctions. The study oversampled conciliation interviews, observing 34 discussions about impending sanctions.[5] The observations show two workers from this unit participating in each conciliation inter-

---

5   As explained in Chapter 2, all observations were weighted to reflect the distribution of time of workers in that position. Because these observations were over-observed, their weight was reduced in tabulating the data.

view, one with the title of "mediator." Almost all the discussions about sanctions involved poor attendance at the activities and programs operated by the Department of Labor, such as appointments with employment counselors and participation in job readiness training and work experience. Only one observation captured a client who was being sanctioned for failure to cooperate with child support enforcement and no clients were being sanctioned for poor attendance at other work activities. The predominance of cases involving poor attendance at the activities and programs of the Department of Labor suggests that the workforce agency monitored compliance with its own programs more vigilantly than others, perhaps because it was procedurally easier.

In the encounters, clients explained they had failed to attend because they or a family member were ill, they didn't have transportation, they didn't receive the letter notifying them of the meeting, they forgot the appointment or thought it was another day, they were in court or attending a funeral or at church for Good Friday, they didn't understand they needed to report to the agency, or they were on a job interview or employed. Workers imposed a sanction in about half the interviews and, in the others, either rescinded the sanction order or delayed it pending additional information.

Texas

The observations in Texas did not capture any workers imposing sanctions. The state welfare agency had recently transferred this function from the local welfare offices to a separate centralized sanction unit, so the local staff no longer had a role in sanctioning clients. According to the welfare administrator for the Dallas/Denton region, this reorganization was at the urging of the workforce agency, which argued that local welfare offices were sanctioning insufficiently and too slowly. The workforce agency had responsibility for meeting the work participation rate, which excluded from the denominator for three months those families sanctioned for failure to work. A process that increased short-term sanctions would lower the denominator and thereby increase the measured rate of participation.

The sanctioning process began when workforce agency staff identified clients who were not complying with the work requirement and sent this information electronically to the welfare agency's central sanction unit. Staff in the central sanction unit did not meet with clients for conciliation, nor did staff in the welfare offices any longer routinely see clients threatened with a sanction. Clients who could not satisfy the rules of the workforce agency could only appeal the sanction and be heard by a traveling appeals officer. Because this officer was not on the roster of welfare staff used to select the sample of encounters, the study did not observe any appeals.

In explaining the sanction rules, workers in both agencies were rarely explicit about the dollar amounts of the sanctions and they often were uncertain or incorrect when they did specify them. The Personal Responsibility Agreements, which welfare workers routinely read and asked clients to sign, did not contain information about the amount of the sanctions for failure to comply with the work requirement, child support enforcement, and the child health and school attendance mandates. At the bottom of the form where clients signed, it simply stated that penalties might be applied for failure to meet the responsibilities. One of the few observations in a welfare office of a client who had been sanctioned was a meeting for recertification, at which the client said her benefit had been reduced by $50 but she did not know why. The worker informed her that the benefit cut was a sanction for failure to meet the school attendance requirements for her two children, a $25 sanction for each child.

Local administrators and staff noted that sanctioning had increased following TANF implementation. Administrators in the Dallas workforce offices reported that a substantial number of recipients never appeared at the workforce agency after the initial orientation, which was necessary to complete the application process, and were sanctioned for noncompliance. Even after the sanction, many did not come to the workforce office. Apparently the sanction of $78 a month was not large enough to enforce compliance with the mandate to attend the activities of the workforce office.

The observations are consistent with information from the U.S. Department of Health and Human Services about sanctions imposed on families receiving TANF and families whose TANF case had closed. Of families receiving assistance in 2000, 13.6 percent in Texas were sanctioned, over half of them for failure to comply with the work requirement, and 8.8 percent New York were sanctioned, almost all for failure to comply with the work requirement. Only 2.7 percent in Michigan were sanctioned, few due to the work requirement, and only .7 percent in Georgia were sanctioned, none due to the work requirement. Of families whose cases were closed, 10.6 percent in Michigan were closed by sanctions, almost all for work-related reasons, 1.1 percent in New York were closed by sanctions, all for work-related reasons, 1.9 percent in Georgia were closed by sanctions, none for work-related reasons, and no cases in Texas were closed by sanctions.[6] Looking at sanctions in the form of both benefit reductions and case closures, all the states except Georgia imposed them primarily for failure to comply with the work requirement.

Several factors could explain the high rate of sanctioning in Texas. Without a conciliation process, workers no longer met with clients to discuss the reason for the sanction and, potentially, use their discretion to intervene on behalf of the client. If workers had more sympathy for their clients than a traveling appeals officer, taking the sanctioning function away from workers would increase the rate of sanctioning. This hypothesis is suggested by an observation of a welfare worker explaining to a client that she could no longer help the client avoid a sanction. A second explanation for the high rate of sanctioning is the small size of the sanctions in absolute dollar terms. Recipients could decide to accept the sanction and continue to receive assistance for their children.

The severity of the states' sanctioning rules was tempered by the conciliation process. Michigan and Georgia, the states with the harshest sanction policy, put more effort into conciliation and had a lower rate of sanctioning than Texas, a state with a less stringent sanction policy but with no conciliation process and with procedures that isolated clients from the workers who knew them. The most severe sanction — a "full family" sanction that cut all cash benefits for the client's lifetime — was not being implemented at all in the offices observed in Georgia.

---

6   U.S. Department of Health and Human Services, *TANF Fourth Annual Report to Congress*, May 2002, Tables 10:14 and 10:44.

Policymakers had designed a rule that the welfare system was reluctant to implement, producing slippage between the policy designed at the top and its realization at the bottom.

Summary and Conclusion

Overall, the frontline staff observed in the welfare and workforce offices devoted more effort to moving clients into jobs than to sanctioning them for failure to comply with the work requirements. Welfare agency staff followed routine procedures to refer applicants to the workforce agencies, and workforce agency staff focused their attention on their primary task of referring clients to jobs. While all the states created new arrangements for providing employment services, only in Texas did the welfare agency create a new process for imposing sanctions. This new process bypassed the frontline staff, eliminating the opportunity for them to use their discretion to prevent or lift a sanction. The observations in the other states indicate that the welfare offices continued to operate a conciliation process, giving staff the opportunity to resolve problems leading to sanctions.

In exhorting clients to work, staff frequently discussed the availability of jobs but rarely explained the financial inducements to work provided by the earnings disregard or the EITC. Working recipients received the earnings disregard automatically, whether they understood it or not, but they needed to take the initiative to claim the tax credit. Fortunately, people may have had other sources of information about the tax credit, like acquaintances and the media, and other research shows that the majority of former welfare recipients knew about the EITC.

7

Financing Child Care and Transportation to Support Work

To support TANF's goal of promoting work, the Personal Responsibility Act contained several provisions to increase the availability of child care for low-income families. It consolidated the existing funding streams for child care assistance into the Child Care and Development Block Grant (CCDBG), increased funding levels for the CCDBG, and permitted states to use TANF funds to provide assistance with child care, thereby expanding funding and giving states flexibility in designing their child care assistance programs. It also encouraged states to give parents their choice in selecting a child care provider. The law did not require states to limit parents' choice to a licensed or regulated provider, which enabled them to choose child care of any quality. TANF did not contain specific provisions for transportation assistance or asset rules limiting ownership of a vehicle, giving states flexibility in designing their transportation policies.

The need for child care assistance was evident at the front lines. When workers asked clients why they were not working, clients frequently said they could not afford child care. Lack of money to pay for child care, not a lack of jobs or an inability to work, was the most common reason they offered for being out of the workforce. Some clients said their inability to pay for child care made them hesitant to enter the workforce or reluctant to continue working in a low-wage job. Some said they came to the welfare office in order to request child care assistance. A request for child care assistance was often the first response of applicants and recipients after being told they must work in order to receive welfare. Assistance with child care, then, was necessary for meeting the work goals of welfare reform. Fewer clients said they were out of the workforce because they lacked transportation, but the welfare agencies recognized that assistance with transportation would increase the likelihood that clients would participate in work-related activities.

All sites developed a process for assessing clients' needs for child care and transportation. Depending on the mandates imposed on welfare applicants and the generosity of the state in providing these supportive services, the sites did one, two, or even three assessments of a client's needs for child care and transportation as they moved from being applicants to being participants in a work activity. These assessments were generally short and routinized, with workers collecting just enough information to ascertain the client's need for services and complete the paperwork to provide services. In some sites, workers performed these assessments as a separate activity, in others as they determined eligibility for assistance or referred clients to a work activity.

The child care assessment was generally little more than questions about the age and school attendance of the children and whether the client needed child care to participate in the upcoming work activity. The assessment for transportation generally included a question about car ownership and whether the client needed a voucher for gasoline or, more commonly, tokens or a swipe card for public transportation. Michigan devoted more funds than other states to removing transportation as a barrier to employment, enabling workers to be liberal in offering clients funds to repair a vehicle and even purchase a car. Assessing needs for transportation assistance in Macomb and Hillsdale Counties entailed numerous questions about car ownership, car problems, repair estimates, insurance coverage, drivers' licenses, and traffic violations, as well as explanations of the rules governing car repairs and purchases.

Child Care to Support Work Activities

The states' eligibility policies for child care assistance were complex, with separate rules for four categories of clients: applicants, recipients, former recipients who worked their way off welfare,[1] and low-income families not receiving welfare. How much attention did frontline workers give to the child care needs of families? Did workers appear to have adequate funds to implement the policies as designed, or did they engage in informal practices for rationing inadequate resources? Did workers give parents their choice of child care provider, as required by federal law?[2] Did the supply of child care slots appear sufficient to meet the demand, or did families express difficulty in finding child care providers? Were single parents exempt from work due to an inability to obtain child care for a child under six years of age, as required by federal law?[3]

Workers discussed child care in 67 percent of all encounters in Georgia, in slightly over 50 percent in Michigan and Texas, and in one-third in New York (Table 7-1). Child care was discussed more frequently than any other topic in Georgia, ranked fifth in frequency of discussion in Michigan and New York, and tenth in Texas (Table 3-3a). Clearly, workers gave attention to child care in their conversations with applicants and recipients.

The workers' activities regarding child care generally consisted of gathering information about the age and school hours of the children and explaining rules about eligibility for child care subsidies, the amount of the subsidy, the types of providers clients could use, and the procedures for choosing a provider and informing the agency of the choice. None of the clients were exempt from the work mandates due to lack of child care; in the conversation coded "excepting or exempting," workers explained that clients who were exempt from the work mandates because they had infants would be eligible for child care once they began working. The worker activities coded as "assessing" and "advising" were broadly simi-

---

1   Prior law called this "transitional child care."
2   42 U.S.C. 9858c(c)(2)(A).
3   42 U.S.C. 607(e)(2).

Table 7-1. Discussion of Child Care
All Encounters

	MICHIGAN	TEXAS	GEORGIA	NEW YORK
State Policy Regarding Eligibility for Child Care Assistance				
Applicants attending orientation or job search	Yes	No	Yes	NA
Recipients in work activity	Yes	Yes	Yes	Yes
Welfare leavers (transitional child care)	Yes, with sliding fee schedule	Yes, with sliding fee schedule	Yes, with sliding fee schedule	Yes
Low income families (not welfare related)	Universal, with sliding fee schedule	Subject to funding	Subject to funding	Subject to funding
Percent of encounters discussing child care				
(Number of Encounters)	*(269)*	*(229)*	*(202)*	*(264)*
Any worker activity	54.1	52.4	67.0	33.0
Explaining rules	28.0	21.0	32.3	15.1
Advising or assessing	28.9	18.0	24.6	13.0
Excepting or exempting	1.6	0.5	0.6	1.0

Source of policy information: management interviews.

lar to the activities coded "collecting information" and "explaining rules." For this reason, this section does not distinguish among the workers' activities and instead is organized by the topics discussed in the encounters.

Georgia

Local welfare administrators explained that the state had created four "pots" of funding for child care, with separate allocations of funds for 1) TANF applicants doing job search, 2) TANF recipients in a work activity, 3) people who worked their way off TANF (transitional child care), and 4) the working poor. They considered the allocations of funds for applicants and recipients to be sufficient to meet the demand and reported that everyone in job search or on TANF could receive child care assistance. Funding was adequate because the state had given priority to TANF applicants and recipients in allocating child care funds. But funds for the working poor were far from sufficient to meet the demand and long waiting lists existed in both counties, leading some low-income people to apply for welfare solely to receive help with child care. Transitional child care was available to recipients who applied for it as soon as they went to work and before their TANF case closed. If the case closed before transitional child care was in place, explained the administrators, the former recipient could lose her child care and go on the waiting list for low-income child care.

Both Fulton County and Bibb County had adopted a policy of parental choice, which left the choice of a child care provider to parents. The increase in funds for child care had encouraged an expansion of child care providers, particularly those offering care during weekdays. Administrators acknowledged that child care during nontraditional hours — evenings, nights, weekends, and before and after school — was still in short supply. The Bibb welfare agency was so intent on eliminating child care as a barrier that it operated its own child care center on site, next door to the welfare office, and five centers offsite in the community. Administrators reported that other child care providers in Bibb had complained of competition from the welfare agency's centers, suggesting that the supply of child care slots was generally adequate.

All three welfare offices gave responsibility for administering child care to specialized workers who authorized child care and monitored its use. These specialized child care workers — four in Bibb County, six in Northwest Fulton, and six in Southwest Fulton — handled the paperwork for subsidizing child care but, in keeping with the policy of parental choice, did not make referrals to specific providers. The Department of Labor had no responsibilities related to child care.

Eligibility for child care assistance. The allocation of child care funds into four "pots" was evident in the rules explained to clients. Workers consistently assured welfare applicants and recipients of the availability of child care payments for everyone engaged in applicant job search or in a work activity listed on their employment plan. Because work was expected, the agency would finance child care.

> ***Georgia (SW Fulton)*** *welfare worker during an orientation:* The President signed a bill in 1996. Everyone who's been receiving since 1997, as of December 2000, checks will end.... So if there's a problem of transportation, day care, and that's why you can't work — we want to help.

> ***Georgia (NW Fulton)*** *welfare worker [to an 18-year old]:* Now did you finish high school?

> *Client:* No.

> *Worker:* Are you working on your GED?

> *Client:* No. I want to, but I can't because of child care.

> *Worker:* Well, you'll have to, because it's mandatory if you're applying for TANF.

> *Client:* I don't have money....

> *Worker:* We'll supply you with support services, including child care.

> ***Georgia (Bibb)*** *welfare worker [to an applicant]:* For 30 of your 45 days, you'll be involved in intensive job search. After that, if you don't have a job, you'll be placed in work experience. In order to do job search, do you need day care?

> *Client:* Yes

> *Worker:* I'll give you Ms. ___'s name to arrange that.... We offer day care and transportation so they can't be used as reasons not to do job search.

Bibb County was sufficiently committed to eliminating child care as a reason for not participating in work or work-related activities that when a client refused an offer of child care, the worker asked her to sign a form stating that child care was not needed.

Although all applicants and recipients qualified for child care assistance, workers mentioned limits on the amount of child care assistance per child. Charges above these limits, which varied with age, were the responsibility of parents. To learn the amounts charged by child care centers, parents were required to visit the centers to get a "quote sheet" showing current availability and the amount charged. Workers then explained that parents would need to pay any charges above the limit.

Georgia *(NW Fulton) welfare worker:* You have four children, ages 7, 5, 3, 18 months. They're charging a $50 registration fee; we'll pay $50 for each child for registration. They're charging $95 for Trina; max we'll pay is $85 — a $10 difference. Charging $80 for your three year old; we'll pay $75. So for a $15 difference. The five year old they charge $65; we'll pay that. $47 for after school program, we'll pay that. Will you need transportation services for them?

Client: Yes.

Worker: We don't pay transportation services. So you'll have to pay $15 weekly, and transportation.

Client: Maybe I'll find another day care, because I don't have the $15. And I need transportation.

Worker: You might want to see if they'll waive the transportation — sometimes they do. How much they say it was?

Client: $10 for one child, $5 each additional child.

Worker: That's $25 per week. And $15. $40 per week. That's a lot. You want to call them? They might waive it, or maybe they give you a set amount.

Client: I'll call and ask. [uses phone] She said she'll give me free transportation for two of them. That'll be $30 per week.

Worker: That gonna work for you?

Client: I guess so. I'll see if their daddy can give that to me.

The cost of child care summed to $302 per week, $272 to be paid by the welfare agency and $30 by the client. The welfare agency also paid the initial $200 registration fee. In the case of this family, mandating work and paying for child care was considerably more costly to the state than just paying welfare. If the mother did not work, she would have received the welfare benefit for a five-person family with no income, $378 per month.[4]

To encourage recipients to meet the 30-hour participation requirement, all the offices told clients they could only receive child care if they worked a minimum number of hours per week, usually 30 hours but sometimes 25 hours. For example:

Georgia *(NW Fulton) welfare worker:* Well, you need to work at least 30 hours a week to get child care.

---

4   U.S. House, Committee on Ways and Means, *2000 Green Book*, 385.

Although the encounters did not observe any workers in the welfare agencies making exceptions to this 30-hour rule, an encounter at the Department of Labor suggested this might occur:

> **Georgia** *(SW Fulton) workforce worker:* You were saying you have to work 30 hours to get child care.
>
> *Client:* If I don't take child care, can I work part time? I take medications that make me drowsy.
>
> *Worker:* Talk to whoever referred you to Work First, to ask if you can have an exemption.

Only a few encounters captured discussions of transitional child care assistance, which was paid on a sliding fee schedule basis. In the encounters where workers mentioned transitional child care, they explained it briefly:

> **Georgia** *(Bibb) welfare worker:* Once you find a job, your case will be transferred to another worker. More than likely you'll be eligible for what we call TCC, for when you need child care and you're not receiving TANF. If you exceed that, there's another program.
>
> **Georgia** *(SW Fulton) welfare worker [during a quarterly review when the client is referred to training]:* You will be eligible for TCC, Transitional Child Care.

Only one encounter witnessed the actual authorization of transitional child care.

> **Georgia** *(NW Fulton) welfare worker [looking on her computer]:* You no longer receive TANF?
>
> *Client:* No, I received it for a month, but only a month.
>
> *Worker:* Your TANF was closed due to employment?
>
> *Client:* I think. She sent me a check for May—
>
> *Worker:* And then nothing for June. Yeah, your TANF stopped due to employment. Since you're no longer receiving TANF, we'll assess your fee based on your income. Let's see. [calculates fee] Your weekly assessed fee will be $5. We'll pay $85 to the center, you'll pay $5, plus transportation. OK?

Funds for low-income families not on welfare were exhausted in Fulton County, as reported by administrators, resulting in a waiting list that was mentioned by the frontline workers. In Bibb County, they made no references to a waiting list.

Georgia (SW Fulton) welfare worker [to an applicant]: If you get a job, call me and we'll talk about income and see if you're still eligible for TANF. If not, you can get on the list for child care for non-TANF.

Georgia (NW Fulton) a friend of the client: What's the length on the waiting list if you don't get TANF?

Worker: Here's the story with the waiting list. We have opened it, but we're dealing with the backlog first, before dealing with the new waiting list.

As administrators suggested, some families in Fulton County applied for TANF in order to receive child care. While the welfare administrator in Bibb County explained that workers sometimes told clients to apply for TANF so they could qualify for child care, the only encounters capturing this behavior were in Fulton:

Georgia (NW Fulton) welfare worker: So you're applying for TANF so you can get child care.

Client: Yes ma'am. I don't want the check cause it's barely enough to get by, but I need the child care....

Worker: What happened with your last job?

Client: Child care. I couldn't afford it....

Worker: OK, you know you have to do three weeks of job search and I'll take care of child care and transportation.

Georgia (NW Fulton) welfare worker [to an applicant for child care]: How many hours you worked last week?

Client: 15 hours.

Worker: If you could get to 30 hours a week, that would be cool.

Client: I can't, I have to keep my son. [Client explains that she is getting a new job soon.]

Worker: My opinion is, do not apply for TANF. Why waste one or two months if you know that you are getting a new job soon?

Client: I really need child care. When I went to apply for child care, the worker across the hall said that I need to apply for TANF. I really don't need it.

Child Care Providers. The child care workers in the welfare agency showed a preference for center-based child care. They explained that the agency would pay for other forms of child care as well, distinguishing among family care, in-home care, and care by relatives (grandparents, aunts, and uncles) and mentioning the need for licenses and for background checks for unauthorized providers. While mentioning center-based care more often than other forms, workers generally followed the policy giving parents the choice of child care provider.

> **Georgia** *(NW Fulton) welfare worker [during an orientation]:* Be very careful when you're selecting. We're paying child care so you don't have to miss activities, participation. If you have a relative doing it, and they have something else to do, it may put you in a bind.... Now we know emergencies happen, so it may be worth looking at a place with more than one person to look after them.

> **Georgia** *(SW Fulton) client:* What if my sister keeps my baby?

> *Welfare worker:* It'll take much longer to get her paid. She'll have to come up here for a class, fill out papers, etc. Much harder now, but that's your choice if that's what you want to do. I know some people don't want to let anybody else watch their children.

The agency's policy of parental choice generally took priority over parents' requests for help in locating providers. The encounters indicate that child care workers possessed lists of providers who were authorized vendors in the county but did not share the lists with parents:

> **Georgia** *(NW Fulton) client:* Do you know a day care center nearby?

> *Welfare worker:* There are some, but I can't name any — because then if something happened, we'd be liable — "they told me to take my babies there." So you're gonna have to look around.

> **Georgia** *(Bibb) welfare worker:* School is out in two weeks, you need to start looking for day care. Who kept them before?

> *Client:* My brother.

> *Worker:* I would suggest that you sit down with the phone book. We can't suggest who to go to. It's up to you.

In some instances, however, the Bibb County workers did refer clients to providers. In addition, the welfare agency operated its own day care center on site and offered it to clients as a last resort:

> **Georgia** *(Bibb) client:* I don't know anyone here. I just moved from Illinois.

> *Welfare worker:* Let me call the day care on my list to see if I can get some openings for your children.

Georgia (Bibb) welfare worker: Do you have a day care in mind?

Client: Yeah.

Worker: So, since you have a day care in mind, we'll call and see if they have room, and you may need to get a second choice. If all else fails, you can use our day care center — they'll pick them up in the morning and drop off in the afternoon.

Michigan

With the focus on removing barriers to employment, Michigan made financing child care a high priority. Responsibility for authorizing child care funding was given to the workers in the welfare agency who determined eligibility for cash assistance, Medicaid, and food stamps. Administrators in every site agreed that funds were sufficient to finance child care for TANF clients and for low-income families meeting the income-eligibility rules for subsidized child care. Families applying for TANF or receiving TANF were eligible for child care funding without incurring a copayment, while low-income families who were income-eligible paid for child care according to a sliding fee schedule. Because eligibility for child care subsidies was broad, state expenditures for child care increased substantially in the implementation of TANF, becoming almost as high as expenditures for cash assistance.

While administrators reported no waiting lists for child care assistance, they did mention a lack of child care providers, particularly during the evening, nights, and weekends. They also mentioned the apprehension some parents felt about leaving their children in the care of others. To expand the supply of child care providers and ease parents' concern about leaving their children with strangers, the state permitted families to use a wide range of licensed and unlicensed providers, including relatives.

Eligibility for child care assistance. The encounters confirm the sufficiency of child care funding for TANF clients who were searching for work or engaged in a work activity. No families were told they could not receive a child care subsidy because funds were unavailable. Workers routinely offered child care as a necessity for employment:

Michigan (Hillsdale) [joint orientation]: One of things that we are going to be doing here is removing any roadblocks that we possibly can. If you don't have a car, how can you look for a job, how can you get to a job? If you don't have day care, then what do you do with your kids? So those two things are the major things that we tackle.

Michigan (Macomb) [joint orientation]: We are here to help you achieve your goals and remove barriers. Now, is anybody here going to need day care while they are at the Work First program or while they are working?

Michigan (Wayne) [joint orientation]: We have services such as we can help you achieve your goals and remove some of your roadblocks by offering you day care, transportation.

Workers at the joint orientation in Macomb explained the welfare agency could provide an "early cash payment" for child care for people beginning a new job. Parents could put their children in day care quickly, with little paperwork, and then have 28 days to turn in all the necessary documents.

As an inducement for TANF clients to get a job, workers held out the promise of child care funding even if they earned their way off welfare. Workers never used the term "transitional" child care, perhaps because child care subsidies were available to low-income families on a sliding scale whether or not they had received welfare.

Michigan (Hillsdale) [joint orientation]: You can make quite a bit of money and still be eligible for a lot of your day care to be paid. If you have two, three, four kids, sometimes over half your paycheck can be going out to day care. Don't just let your day care close because you are tired of dealing with the system or something like that. If you need the day care, make sure you let the worker know and they will keep that part of it open for you.

Michigan (Macomb) welfare worker: Don't ever just call and say, hey, close the case, because there are benefits to just sort of letting me know what's going on and to gradually just get off. And then, depending on your income, you might still be eligible for food stamps and day care. No guarantees. I mean, if you're out there making $22 an hour, I'll be honest, you probably won't be eligible for those items. But until you get to that point, there's still probably some day care and food stamps and the one year of Medicaid.

Michigan (Operation Help) workforce worker: After you've gotten a job, they might not pay for it [child care] anymore. If, if you're making over X amount of dollars.

Client: Which is over $6 an hour?

Worker: No, that's too low. You'd have to be making about $9-$10 an hour before they would cut it out.

Workers were also observed offering child care subsidies to low-income working families not receiving welfare:

> **Michigan** *(Hillsdale) welfare worker [to a client not on TANF]:* So based on your income, your gross monthly income, that determines what percentage we're going to pay. My guess is you're going to be probably in the 95 percent, so that we pay $0.95 out every $1.00 that Jean charges. And I think she charges $2.00 an hour, right?

> **Michigan** *(Macomb) welfare worker:* You aren't eligible for cash assistance because you have an income of $1,400 or more. Now the day care is a different story. OK. So I brought a day care application.... We pay on a sliding scale. We pay between 30 percent and 95 percent of the day care costs and for a family of two, it says here that if you make between $1,497 and $1,533 we can pay 90 percent. So that's kind of an estimate, I haven't put it into the computer yet, but it looks like we can pay, you know, quite a bit.

> **Michigan** *(Wayne) client:* I'm just really applying for food stamps and day care.

> *Welfare worker:* Oh, OK. Well, I gotta go get you a whole other set of applications. I'll be right back.

Child Care Providers. Michigan permitted families to use both licensed and unlicensed child care providers, a policy that facilitated an increase in child care slots to meet the demand generated by the increase in child care funding. In all orientations for TANF applicants, workers explained the four types of providers eligible for subsidies. The welfare agency subsidized 1) licensed day care centers, 2) licensed day care homes, 3) unlicensed care by a relative (child's grandparent, great-grandparent, aunt, uncle, niece, nephew, or cousin), and 4) unlicensed care by nonrelative. Unlicensed care could be given in the child care provider's home or in the home of the child. Before the agency authorized payment to unlicensed providers, they were subject to a background check only to learn of any history of abuse or neglect. Although the welfare agency could pay relatives, it apparently did not offer to pay them if they were already providing free child care.

All welfare agencies relied on child care coordinating councils (4-C agencies) to give clients information about the names and locations of licensed providers. Representatives from the local 4-C agency attended the Work First orientations to explain their database of licensed centers and day care homes and how clients could contact them when they needed help locating a provider. Workers stressed that locating a child care provider was the responsibility of the client, who could select the provider of her choice. In Macomb County, "enhanced referrals" by the 4-C agency were mentioned to people having difficulty finding child care.

Although there were no waiting lists for funding, parents talked about waiting lists at particular child care centers.

> **Michigan** *(Macomb welfare agency) client [regarding a mentally ill child who attends a special program]:* Well I could do that if I got him in latchkey, but I think there is a waiting list for latchkey also. I can check that out though. I'll do that today.

Parents of teenagers, who did not qualify for child care assistance, expressed the need for someone to oversee their children:

> **Michigan** *(Macomb workforce agency) client:* Last year I was offered a graveyard shift at this grocery store and I went through the training and whatever, but there was no way I was going to be working until 5:00 in the morning and leaving them all night. And having a 15 and soon to be 16 year old, you know what I'm saying, alone, night after night and therefore, I declined. Really and truly that became an obstacle, that was a barrier in itself. Because at least you know when they're little, they have to be fed and their diapers changed and what have you, but they're not going to get pregnant, they're not going to get in legal trouble and whatever…. But the money is at night, especially in everything I used to work in food, restaurants, liquor sales. Tabs are bigger at night than during the day, therefore, your tips are bigger. That's where the gravy is, nights. [The worker arranged daytime work activities for the client.]

The 4-C agency in Wayne County tried to address the lack of child care for teenagers:

> **Michigan** *(Wayne) 4-C worker at an orientation:* Four C's has compiled a youth activities listing and we have some on the back table. The listing was compiled due to the fact that FIA [the Family Independence Agency] does not pay for care of children above 12 years of age. Basically, the activities on here are low or no cost, OK? They consist of after school, evenings, and weekends.

New York

Albany County and Suffolk County, as locally administered welfare systems, had more responsibility for the financing and delivery of child care than the local systems in the other states. The counties financed child care with multiple funding streams, each putting together its own pots of money. Administrators reported having sufficient funds to finance child care for TANF clients and a year of transitional benefits, but only Suffolk reported having enough funds for child care for the working poor. Administrators in Albany implied they had insufficient funds for all low-income families when they discussed how workers could use their discretion in granting child care subsidies on a case-by-case basis and mentioned that families came back on assistance after exhausting their year of transitional child care subsidies.

Administrators in Albany reported an insufficient number of regulated child care providers, a situation present in other sites, but it was the only site where they mentioned that clients refusing unregulated care would be exempt from work activity. Administrators perceived an adequate number of unregulated relatives, friends, and neighbors who could babysit, but they could not require clients to send their children to an unregulated provider against their will. Both counties often required clients to engage in a child care search, similar to a job search, to demonstrate they were looking for a child care provider and referred them to the local 4-C agency for information about available providers.

Both welfare agencies had a specialized child care staff whose primary function was to authorize child care and pay the client or the provider. Unlike Georgia, where the child care staff helped monitor the work activities of the client, the staff in New York had a more clerical job, particularly in Suffolk County. In this county, administrators reported that clients generally contacted child care workers over the phone and mailed in their request for child care. Child care workers generally authorized payment without seeing the client, although they could meet with the client if a problem arose. Because only face-to-face encounters were observed in the study, these telephone contacts were not included in the sample of encounters.

Eligibility for child care assistance. The encounters in New York indicate a sufficiency of child care funding for TANF clients who were searching for work or engaged in a work activity. No encounters captured workers telling TANF clients that child care subsidies were not available while they engaged in a work activity. To the contrary, the encounters show workers routinely urging parents to find child care so they could begin a work activity.

A search for child care was often assigned to clients as a mandated activity in both New York sites. A child care search, generally for a period of two weeks, was frequently the first step toward work for people who did not already have child care arrangements. Other states told clients to find child care before job search but did not make it a formal process or give people as much time.

> *New York (Albany) welfare worker:* I'll put you on a child care search. You need to child care search before you job search. This is a child care search book.

> *New York (Suffolk) workforce worker:* It's very important to have child care arrangements.... Can you say you'd have child care in two weeks, from 9:00-2:30? I will put a notation here to give you two weeks after the interview to find child care. You need to fill out a child care search form.

While workers in both counties offered the child care subsidy as an inducement to participate in a work activity, workers in Suffolk sometimes presented the subsidy as a way to eliminate child care as an excuse for not working.

> *New York (Suffolk) workforce worker:* The Child Care Council will help with finding people. It is very important to document your search because if you really can't find anything they want to know why. They can sanction you, or cut your case off, if you don't document your search.

> *New York (Suffolk) welfare worker [to a client facing a sanction]:* Like I said, do you have a problem with child care? 'Cause they're going to set you up with something, and they won't accept no child care as an excuse.

Workers mentioned transitional child care frequently enough in Albany to suggest it was routinely offered. Workers were observed informing people about the availability of transitional child care and authorizing transitional assistance.

> *New York (Albany) welfare worker:* Everything for March is covered. You are eligible for transitional day care. Your benefits have been stopped, but we'll put in a new request to start in April to switch to federal transitional aid.

In Suffolk, however, none of the workers made an explicit reference to transitional child care. Transitional child care was not mentioned by workers in the welfare agency, or by workers in the workforce agencies during orientations or their individual meetings with clients. The absence of discussion about transitional child care may be due to the sample of encounters observed, which included only face-to-face interactions. Phone contacts and mailed-in requests for child care, as reported by local administrators, would not be captured by the encounters. Still, the encounters did not illustrate how clients would learn to make these phone contacts and mail in their child care request.

The encounters did not observe workers discussing the availability of low-income child care or offering it to clients in either county. Workers in Albany County could authorize transitional child care, but it appeared they could not automatically authorize low-income child care. For this reason, as indicated by the following encounter, the worker saw an advantage to labeling the client's termination from assistance as a closing due to employment rather than a sanction.

> **New York** *(Albany) welfare worker [to a client who is working but is under a sanction for failure to report information to the welfare agency]:* We're going to close you for too much money. It's not automatic to get day care.... I'll do everything I can to make the transition off for income. Closing for making too much money is a great reason for closing, because we can do transitional child care.

Workers in Suffolk County mentioned "employment-related child care," but it was not clear whether this was for people receiving assistance or other low-income families:

> **New York** *(Suffolk) workforce worker:* This child care package I'm giving you today is for job search. When you get a new job, you'll need to call the number for employment-related care.

Again, because child care funding was authorized over the phone or through the mail, the observations may have missed the interactions where workers discussed low-income child care.

Child Care Providers. Workers permitted all types of child care, including both licensed and unlicensed providers, and gave parents their choice of provider.

> **New York** *(Albany) client:* What about day care for weekends?

Worker: Tell them you need informal day care, so you can get it on the weekend.

New York *(Suffolk) workforce worker [during an orientation]:* While you're in class, child care is reimbursed. So if you have a child care provider, it doesn't matter who it is — it can be a friend or relative or anything — and we would reimburse you as you're in one of our activities.

More than in other states, clients had difficulty finding child care providers. Parents mentioned the difficulty of finding convenient child care in the rural areas of Albany County and in suburban and rural areas of Suffolk. Recent immigrants mentioned their reluctance to leave their children with people who did not speak their language. Parents and workers acknowledged the difficulty of finding child care for infants and child care at night. Workers in the Suffolk workforce agency nonetheless discussed jobs during the 11 to 7 graveyard shift and double shifts of 16 hours, making demands on clients.

New York *(Suffolk) workforce worker:* What shift can you work? Everyone can do the first.... There are some places, you would have to call, that'll watch them overnight. Yep. Some people do it, do it out of their homes, will do it overnight. I used to do day care for six months and there were people who worked an 11 to 7 shift. The kids slept. To me it's the greatest thing in the world.... But second and third shift's kinda tough. Uh, are you able to work overtime?

To help parents search for child care, Albany County contracted with the Capital District Child Care Coordinating Council, which stationed staff at the welfare agency to give clients information about providers. Suffolk County gave clients the telephone numbers of two organizations they could call for referrals.

New York *(Suffolk) workforce workers:* Normally what we do is give you the numbers of Little Flower and the Child Care Council and then they would contact the providers in your area and see if they had any openings and then let you know whether or not they had openings.

Texas

As in Georgia, administrators referred to pots of money for child care: 1) child care for TANF clients, 2) transitional child care for people who worked their way off TANF, and 3) low-income child care unrelated to TANF. They reported that more money was available for child care than prior to TANF, but it was still not enough to meet the demand. Funds for TANF clients and transitional child care were adequate, but funds for low-income child care were routinely insufficient and waiting lists were common. To reduce waiting lists, some funds allocated for TANF child care had been used for low-income child care. Nonetheless, many low-income families could only receive child care assistance if they received welfare.

Access to child care was largely outside the control of the welfare agency, which was responsible only for authorizing transitional child care. Because TANF applicants did not receive child care assistance to attend the orientation at the workforce agency, parents brought their children along. Authorizing child care assistance for TANF recipients was the responsibility of the workforce agency. Once the agency scheduled TANF recipients in a work activity, it authorized child care assistance and referred them to an innovative Texas institution, the Child Care Management System (CCMS). The CCMS served as a source of information about providers, reimbursed providers, and handled payments for transitional child care after authorization by the welfare agency. The CCMS also authorized assistance for low-income families not on welfare.

The observers in the workforce offices captured an additional category of child care assistance. Its explicit purpose was to divert applicants from welfare. During the workforce orientation, workers described "applicant child care" for applicants who found a job immediately and did not continue with their TANF application. The availability of applicant child care during a narrow window of time added to the extreme complexity of the rules governing eligibility for child care.

Eligibility for child care assistance. As in the other states, the encounters indicate sufficient child care funding for TANF clients who were searching for work or participating in a work activity. Workers viewed the increase in funding as one of the important features of welfare reform.

> **Texas** *(Denton) [during a workforce orientation] client:* They [CCMS] have a huge waiting list.
>
> *Worker:* Yeah, but not if you come through the Choices program, they don't.

Client: I had to sit on the waiting list for over a year and then I just said, "Oh, forget it."

Worker: Right. The Choices program, you have a job, I fax over the information, you call and set it up, you're in, just like that, OK? You can't believe that, huh?

Texas *(Grand Prairie) welfare worker:* When you find employment, you can get child care now. That's always been the real holdup in a lotta this.... Now, they [the workforce agency] have an onsite CCMS person. It is really nice; they're really working, trying to get it up here because that's always been one of the drawbacks in trying to get off of the welfare system is the child care. And that's available now and it's really been good. They have a person down there now, I think she told us they can get it approved within 24 hours, the child care.

Client: 24 hours?

Worker: So if you get a job, you can get immediate child care.

Texas *(Masters) welfare worker:* The advantage to going through them [the workforce agency] is that they do offer you child care. If you go out and find a job on your own, you have to go on a waiting list. So if you could just call them, they do give you guys priority over the people that just go out and find a job.

Transitional child care also appeared to be funded adequately relative to the demand for it. Staff at the workforce agency presented transitional child care as a routine benefit to clients who worked their way off welfare, and CCMS staff located at the workforce agency explained it when they arranged child care for TANF recipients:

Texas *(Masters) CCMS staff:* Right now your child care is free of cost, but after you get your GED and you get a job and you report that to the caseworker, your TANF will be denied [i.e., closed] and your case goes from TANF to transitional and we will continue to help with your child care. However, it will not be free of cost anymore. You will have to pay 11 percent of your gross income towards the child care and we will help you with the rest.

Although workers did not mention a lack of funds for transitional child care, the path of access to this benefit was narrow. Workers observed at the welfare agency rarely mentioned transitional child care. The workforce agency's orientation for all TANF applicants was an opportunity to mention transitional child care for people who might not return to the workforce agency for services, but only the workforce agency in Denton mentioned transitional child care during the orientation. Access appeared to be solely through the workforce agency, so that a recipient finding a job on her own might not learn of her eligibility.

> **Texas** *(Masters) workforce worker [to a client who just found a job and needs assistance with child care]:* Now let me tell you how to play this out on benefits with the Department of Human Services. You say you've reported your job to them.

> *Client:* Right.

> *Worker:* OK in about 30 or more days you will become transitional. You'll become TP07 and what that means is you've reported to them [the welfare agency] on everything they've asked you, you've returned all forms to them, if you move you give your address change to them, and you report to me monthly. We make it transitional, which means that Medicaid and food stamps if you're on them could be transitional for up to a year and your child care could be. You may have to pay a portion of the child care depending on what you make and that will be between you and CCMS at that time. By reporting and keeping these cases active, like they are supposed to be, you will have transitional benefits for approximately a year. Any questions specifically on those would go to DHS because they do issue them. I do my report on my end and they do theirs on theirs. If you just dribble the ball on this stuff, then you'll be in great shape.

Not everyone dribbled the ball well, clients or workers. The encounters observed people who had earned their way off welfare but were not receiving transitional benefits because they had failed to report their earnings to the workforce and welfare agencies or the workforce agency had not processed the necessary paperwork.

> **Texas** *(Masters) workforce worker:* I spent the morning trying to salvage child care for a lady who didn't report to me for three months. I stopped the child care, immediately she called me, she had to go back and get her case reactivated at DHS, we tried to reactivate her child care, it's all transitional, she's having to go to CCMS headquarters all because she just didn't report. So, it's important that you report to me and to DHS so that we know to keep it.

Texas policy gave "extended" transitional child care benefits to recipients who were exempt from work but volunteered to participate. However, only the workers in Denton explained them clearly and completely. Workers in the other offices referred to extended transitional benefits for volunteers but did not explain that child care was one of them.

> **Texas** *(Denton) workforce worker [during an orientation]:* Right now you
> all are mandatory, um but you. So everybody in here but Candice.
> Candice, you're exempt, that means if you don't want to participate in
> the program, you don't have to, but if you volunteer, you can get ex-
> tra, like transitional benefits with your child care and all that.

The inability of the welfare agency to refer anyone directly to child
care meant that none of the encounters in the welfare agencies observed
workers offering child care benefits to low-income people not receiving
TANF. Instead, the welfare agency referred low-income people to the
workforce agency for child care.

> **Texas** *(Denton welfare agency) client:* Day care is what I'm having a prob-
> lem with. If I don't qualify for the AFDC thing, do I have to wait for
> CCMS? Is there any other way to get around it?
>
> *Welfare worker:* Ask them over at the TWC [Texas Workforce Center],
> cause you've got to go there for the Work First Orientation anyway,
> and ask them what all types of things are available. Tell them you
> started working, there's a possibility you might be over income and
> what else can you do cause you want to continue to keep the job.

Workers in the workforce agency, however, were observed telling
clients they could only provide child care to people on welfare. They did
not have child care funds for people not on TANF.

> **Texas** *(Denton) workforce worker [at an orientation for applicants]:* If
> you don't get certified for TANF, then no child care assistance is
> available. This is just for people that are on TANF. I get so many calls
> daily, I heard you help with day care. Well, are you on TANF? No. I
> don't help. I'm sorry.

As stated above, the one exception was a category of child care assistance for TANF applicants available during a narrow window in the
application process. At the workforce orientation required of all applicants, the encounters showed workers discussing "applicant child care."
Workers told applicants they could qualify for applicant child care if they
did not continue with their TANF application. If an applicant found a job
before the welfare agency authorized assistance, the workforce agency
would authorize child care. In effect, applicant child care was a form of
diversion assistance that counteracted the incentive for low-income people to receive welfare in order to receive child care assistance. Workers
explained it could last for up to one year.

> ***Texas** (Masters) workforce worker [at an orientation for applicants]:* Some applicants may be able to avoid the necessity of receiving cash assistance altogether since we can offer child care assistance, which is subject to availability of funding, if you go to work. This is considered the applicant child care. We can offer child care assistance after verifying you're starting to work before becoming certified for TANF benefits. So, for example, if one of you guys said that you had a job today, you would go through the steps to verify your employment and you may receive a subsidy as the applicant child care. That just means that you will not receive TANF at all.

> ***Texas** (Denton) workforce worker [at an orientation for applicants]:* If any of you leave today and have a job offer, call me. Because I can help you with daycare; it's called the Applicant Day Care because you are an applicant.

While the workforce agencies could offer child care to applicants who found work immediately after the orientation, they did not permit applicants to enter their work program for TANF recipients. This was a subtle distinction, one not fully understood by all applicants. Some applicants returned to the workforce agency after completing their welfare application and, because welfare was not yet authorized, were turned away.

> ***Texas** (Grand Prairie) workforce worker:* I will look at the computer and see which of you are eligible to be here. If you are not receiving a check then there is nothing I can do for you.... Four of you can stay and two must leave. Please understand that until they get your case done, there is nothing I can do for you.

> ***Texas** (Masters) workforce worker [to an applicant who is not yet certified for assistance]:* You're not eligible for our benefits which would be a job search, going to some kind of school, transportation, and child care. As soon as you are on the computer that you're getting AFDC....

> *Client:* That's what I signed for, AFDC and food stamps.

> *Worker:* Right. As soon as it comes up here, money, see where over here it says money grant, zero. Whenever that changes, come on back.

Child Care Providers. The CCMS was responsible for providing information about child care providers and managing payments to providers. CCMS staff explained that clients could use several types of providers, including child care centers, group homes, and smaller day homes. They could use self-arranged care by a child's grandparent, aunt, or uncle, but not by a child's cousin or a great aunt or uncle. Within these constraints, the choice of provider was the client's.

> **Texas** *(Masters) CCMS worker at an orientation:* This is a parent's choice program. And what that does, it empowers you to get out and find your own child care facility that meets all your child care needs. There are about 800 throughout Dallas County that you have to choose from.... Now, we do not ever recommend day care centers. Because it's up to you to find what you feel is a good day care center.

> **Texas** *(Grand Prairie) orientation:* As soon as you get on the system, participating with the Work First class, we will find child care for you. It will be your choice as to where you want your kids to go.

While not recommending providers, the CCMS was able to assist clients in searching for them. The CCMS could do a computerized vendor search based on the client's address and ZIP code that picked child care facilities randomly and printed out these options for the client. Perhaps because only authorized vendors were in the system, clients were not observed choosing informal child care.

In summary, the encounters document that child care funding and the availability of child care slots, a prerequisite to requiring parents to seek and accept employment, expanded with TANF implementation. The increased funding for child care resulting from the Personal Responsibility Act was evident in the workers' conversations with TANF applicants and recipients. Workers assured TANF applicants and recipients that they would receive assistance in paying their child care expenses if they worked or searched for work. Lack of money for child care was no longer a reason, or an excuse, for not working. Second only to the emphasis on work participation, the increased availability of child care funds was the change due to welfare reform most frequently mentioned by frontline workers.

For the working poor who were not applying for TANF, however, child care subsidies were widely available only in Michigan, Georgia, and Texas allocated insufficient funds for low-income child care to meet the demand, as indicated by waiting lists for assistance. New York offered low-income child care but the encounters observed few workers discussing child care subsidies outside the welfare system, perhaps because the workers authorizing these subsidies were not in the sample or they authorized low-income child care over the telephone.

In general, the supply of child care slots appeared to be sufficient to meet the demand, particularly during standard business hours. The rules in Michigan and New York permitted parents to use both regulated and unregulated child care providers, giving parents the ability to leave their children not only with licensed child care centers and homes but also with neighbors, friends, and relatives. Workers in Georgia often told clients they could not use unregulated care unless the provider was a relative, although exceptions to this rule were observed. The CCMS system in Texas led parents to regulated care, which appeared to be in ample supply. With liberal rules about the type of child care used, clients rarely reported they were unable to find a child care provider. Workers required clients to find child care quickly, within a few days in all states except New York, again suggesting that finding child care was feasible. Child care providers willing to take children during the evening, night, and weekend were less plentiful, as were providers willing to take children with physical or mental problems. Providers willing to take infants were also less numerous. In suburban and rural areas, clients mentioned difficulties finding child care convenient to their home or workplace.

Policy in all states gave parents their choice of child care provider. With few exceptions, the encounters did not observe workers recommending specific providers. In Michigan, New York, and Texas, the task of disseminating information about providers was contracted out to specialized child care agencies, leaving workers in the welfare and workforce agencies no role in making referrals to providers. When parents asked workers for help in locating child care, workers told them to contact the child care agencies.

Although child care funding and availability expanded, the encounters also show that child care continued to be a weak link in the process of moving clients into employment. Parents continued to face difficulties finding child care, suffered from unreliable providers, were not always satisfied with their providers, and had difficulty transporting themselves and their children to child care.

> *Georgia client:* My day care — my baby has chronic asthma and they don't really want to keep him.

> *Michigan client:* My child care worker went to jail.

> ***Texas*** *client:* I kinda figured they were grabbin' my son in the wrong places and then I found, I ended up finding like real bad nail marks in his back and I mean that was the last time my son was in day care.

> ***New York*** *client:* I was fired on Friday for being late too many times. I depend on the bus. I have to drop my baby off. It makes it hard for me to get to work on time.

> ***Texas*** *client:* On November 7th the apartment right next to mine caught on fire and the Fire Department had to knock my ceiling out and so we weren't able to live there and they didn't get it fixed until like the middle of December. So we were living out to my mom's and I had no way to get them back and forth.

Workers in all states urged parents to find a backup:

> ***Wayne*** *[joint orientation]:* Even if you have someone to watch your child, you should always, always have a backup plan. You never know when you have to go to work and someone calls you and states "Well, I can't watch your child today." What are you gonna do? You have to go to work, OK. So you should always have a backup plan and we at 4-C's can help you with that backup plan.

The encounters also show errors by the agencies in determining the client's eligibility for child care assistance and in processing payments to child care providers, causing providers to refuse caring for a client's child. Parents who did not submit the correct paperwork or attend a required meeting with their worker lost child care and with it, their job. In Michigan, where the workforce agency placed people in jobs while the welfare agency authorized child care, information about the client's employment did not always reach the welfare worker in a timely manner. Similarly in Texas, where the workforce agency placed people in jobs while the welfare agency authorized transitional child care, failure to report earnings to the welfare agency, either by the workforce agency or the parents, resulted in failure to receive transitional child care.

While parents had a choice of child care providers, the agencies generally told people to find child care very quickly, allowing them little time for gathering information about available providers and comparing the alternatives. In New York, the welfare agencies gave parents two weeks, but the observations showed workers in other states giving parents less time.

> ***Georgia*** *(Bibb) welfare worker:* I have you starting job search on Monday, to give you two days to get day care set up.

> ***Georgia** (NW Fulton) welfare worker:* That gives you all week to get child care together.

> ***Michigan** (Hillsdale) joint orientation by welfare and workforce workers:* You know you are going to be here on Tuesday with Sarah so get your day care set up before that.... You have from now until then to get a babysitter set up so make sure that you do it.

This time frame for finding child care is short by the standards of middle-income parents. Workers urged parents to search for a provider they felt comfortable using, but they gave them little time to do so.

Transportation Assistance to Support Work Activities

The mandate to attend Work First and participate in a work-related activity required applicants and recipients to travel to places such as the welfare and workforce offices, employers, education and training providers, and child care providers. Which employment-related activities were supported with transportation assistance? What types of assistance did workers give clients to travel to work-related activities? Did workers consider transportation to be a constraint in making job referrals, sending clients only to jobs accessible by public transportation?

Transportation was a topic of conversation in half or more of all encounters in Michigan, Texas, and Georgia and in a quarter of encounters in New York (Table 7-2). Part of this conversation was about transportation as a means to support work, but conversation about vehicle ownership also had to do with determining eligibility for assistance. In Texas, because the population was widely dispersed and public transportation was limited, applicants were more likely to own automobiles than in other states. Eligibility workers in all states routinely asked TANF applicants about vehicle ownership, but eligibility workers in Texas focused their attention on this asset. They had access to computerized records from the Department of Motor Vehicles, which they scrutinized for unreported automobiles and trucks. The information in these records also prompted workers to ask about family relationships and unreported income that might affect an applicant's eligibility for assistance. Because workers gave so much attention to vehicles during the eligibility interviews, transportation was the most frequently mentioned topic in the Texas encounters (Table 3-3a).

Table 7-2. Discussion of Transportation
All Encounters

	MICHIGAN	TEXAS	GEORGIA	NEW YORK
	Percent of Encounters Discussing Transportation			
(Number of Encounters)	*(269)*	*(229)*	*(202)*	*(264)*
Any worker activity	56.0	69.4	50.2	25.4
Explaining rules	25.4	16.4	13.1	7.1
Advising or assessing	23.6	7.8	19.6	8.3
Excepting or exempting	0.5	0	0.6	0

In Georgia, welfare staff used the disbursement of transportation assistance as a means of monitoring the work activities of clients. Workers in Fulton County monitored job search by requiring clients to come to the welfare office weekly to pick up their swipe card for public transportation, giving workers the opportunity to ask them about their contacts with employers. Workers in Bibb County monitored job search by giving applicants only a one-day supply of bus tokens for job search and requiring them to report the job search contacts made the previous day when they came to pick up their tokens.

Discussions regarding transportation as a service to support work revealed wide differences among the states in their generosity with transportation assistance. Michigan had the most benefits to offer clients and, compared with other states, workers in Michigan more frequently explained rules and advised clients regarding transportation (Table 7-2). Workers often explained the workforce agency was able to finance vehicle ownership for people who found employment and advised clients to take advantage of this benefit. Benefits were more limited in the other states, yet the observations captured no instances where clients were exempted from work due to a lack of transportation. The text behind the percentages for Georgia and Michigan in Table 7-2 do not show workers excepting or exempting clients from an activity due to a lack of transportation.

Georgia

The welfare offices in Georgia assisted TANF applicants with public transportation while they searched for work. Fulton County gave applicants a weekly swipe card to use the Metropolitan Atlanta Rapid Transit Authority (MARTA) and Bibb County gave applicants bus tokens. The welfare offices also assisted recipients with transportation while they participated in education and training programs. Fulton gave recipients a monthly MARTA card and Bibb reimbursed up to $3.00 a day for transportation. In general, workers were clear and consistent in explaining the availability of transportation assistance during job search and during participation in education and training programs.

The Bibb County welfare agency operated a van to transport clients, particularly clients with poor attendance at mandated work activities. Observations captured workers telling clients threatened with a sanction for failure to attend mandated activities that they and their children would be picked up by the van and taken to child care and the agency's Work Experience Building behind the welfare office.

Workers were less clear and consistent in explaining the availability of transportation for recipients who became employed. Several observations captured workers telling clients they would pay their transportation if they worked 30 hours a week, but others told clients they would pay their transportation until they received their first paycheck. Only one observation captured a worker telling a client the welfare agency might be able to help with car repairs. Compared to the attention given to child care for people who worked 30 hours a week, workers gave less attention to transportation.

Public transportation did not serve the entire Atlanta region, particularly many of the high growth areas in the suburban ring. In making job referrals, workers at the Department of Labor asked applicants if they had a car and, if they did not, referred them to jobs accessible by the MARTA.

Georgia (SW Fulton): workforce worker: You have a car?

Client: No.

Worker: OK [searching on computer] I'm trying to narrow it down. Oh, here's a clerk. Is Marietta too far?

Client: I don't know where that is.

Worker: Oh — it's not on the bus line. [reads position] But we need to find you something on the bus.

Michigan

Removing transportation as a barrier to employment was a high priority in all the Michigan sites. With discretionary funds from Project Zero, Work First offices offered assistance with transportation that was far more extensive than the transportation assistance offered by the other three states. What distinguished Michigan was the ability of the Work First offices to assist their clients with expenses incurred for automobile transportation. Work First offices were even able to offer TANF clients and other low-income families assistance to purchase an automobile, with one proviso — they must be employed.

In Hillsdale, a rural area with no public transportation, clients were more likely to own vehicles than clients in the other sites and were reimbursed at $.15 per mile during participation in Work First. To eliminate transportation as a barrier to employment for clients without vehicles, the site engaged a transportation services company. Company vans could drive children to child care and drive clients to all types of employment-related activities, including the Work First orientation, Work First programs, and employers any place in the county. During the Work First orientation, workers explained these benefits and the other transportation assistance financed through Project Zero.

> *Michigan (Hillsdale) [joint orientation]:* If you have a problem with transportation and you do not have a car or you are depending on someone else, we can be that transportation for you. If you have children that need to go to daycare we can drop your children off and pick them back up at the end of your shifts. If you are working third shift you can also have a ride. We have 24 hour transportation, 7 days a week in Hillsdale County now. You do have to schedule in advance, preferably 24 hours notice in advance.... Our drivers carry cell phones, so in

the event that you get ill or your child gets ill or something like that at work, you won't be stranded. They even do emergency transportation or if your car is going to be in shop for a couple days.... If your car is broken, we can help you repair it. We can do a one-time insurance; we can help you with plates; we can help get you a driver's license if you don't have it. However, we won't cover any fines, if that is the reason you don't have a license. Once you start working and you don't have transportation at all, we may be able to even help you purchase a car.

In Macomb, a suburban area with some public transportation, the welfare office did not appear to offer transportation to the Work First orientation, which was held in the welfare agency. But it did offer transportation assistance for participants in Work First programs, including bus tickets, van service, and a transportation allowance of $5.00 for each day of attendance at the Work First site. At the orientation, workers mentioned the availability of assistance for car repairs and car purchases.

In Detroit, the welfare office did not appear to offer transportation to the Work First orientation, but it did offer bus tickets to participate in all Work First programs. The conditions for assisting with car purchases were explained at the Work First orientation:

> **Michigan** *(Wayne) [joint orientation]:* If you're working a job, it might be necessary that you have a car. If you can't get a bus at a certain time or buses don't run that late in the evening. Maybe you're too far away from home too long. There are a lot of considerations that we use in helping a person to get a car.

Observations in the Hillsdale and Macomb workforce offices captured workers and clients discussing car problems that necessitated repairs and discussing car purchases, indicating that workers were in fact implementing these forms of transportation assistance. Workers in Detroit explained the rules about car purchases as an inducement to work but were not observed actually offering to buy a car for a client. In all the sites, the maximum payment for car repairs was $900, while the maximum payment for a car purchase was $1,200.

> **Michigan** *(Macomb) workforce worker:* There's funds up to $1,200 to purchase the vehicle. If you came to me with an estimate for a car that's going to cost you $5,000 and we're going to give you $1,200, we're going to wonder, well, where is she coming up with all this extra money? So it has to be something that you're going to be able to handle. OK? What I would do if I were you is I would start looking for your vehicle. You have to be employed two weeks before we can put

it through. It's going to take you a while to find the car. So if you start looking now, hopefully by that point, when you're ready, when you have your two weeks of employment, we can put the paperwork through real fast.

Because public transportation did not exist in Hillsdale and was limited in Macomb, the workforce agencies gave high priority to assisting clients in repairing their cars and purchasing new ones so they could take jobs accessible only by car. Workers in Detroit, relying on the city's denser network of public transportation, tended to refer clients to jobs accessible by public transportation. Yet not all these jobs were close to home or perceived by clients as easy to reach by public transportation:

> **Michigan** *(Wayne) client at the welfare office:* I did that [participate in Work First] and half the jobs that they sent you on was either way out, you didn't have no transportation to get there, and then they didn't want to give you enough bus tickets, it's way out in the boondocks.

New York

Welfare agency staff had authority to exercise discretion in providing transportation assistance to clients in a range of situations. In most of the observations dealing with transportation, workers were distributing bus tokens. In Albany County, workers gave bus tokens to applicants in job search, applicants who were employed, and recipients who were participating in a work activity. They also gave bus passes to recipients who were employed or participating in a work activity. In Suffolk County, workers were observed discussing the availability of reimbursement for travel expenses to clients who were employed or were participating in a work activity, telling them they should request reimbursement over the phone or by mail.

According to welfare administrators, workers also had the authority to pay for car repairs, car insurance, and car purchases. One encounter in Albany captured a worker offering to help an employed recipient with car repairs or a car purchase, saying she could spend up to $500 dollars for this purpose. Suffolk operated four vans, which were used to drive clients to work experience and training programs. Like Bibb County, the van was used to drive clients who were out of compliance with the work requirements to a work experience site:

> **New York** *(Suffolk) welfare worker at workforce agency:* I don't know if you're familiar with the Suffolk County work crew. What that is, is it's a work van that picks up at several designated locations. It picks up at 9:00 in the morning and lets out at 3:00.

Workers at the Suffolk County Department of Labor made an effort to refer clients to education and jobs that were accessible, noting that multiple transfers were difficult for clients. Yet observations in both Albany and Suffolk captured clients who had taken jobs or started programs they could not maintain due to difficulties with transportation.

> **New York** *(Suffolk) welfare worker at a conciliation meeting talking to a client through an interpreter:* We asked her to come in because she didn't go to the job readiness training program.... Now what I was wondering when they discussed assigning her there, did she discuss any transportation problems?
>
> *Interpreter:* No.
>
> *Worker:* I'm just wondering why she would agree to go somewhere [when she knew she might have problems getting there].
>
> *Interpreter:* Because she said that lady over there was very strong in talking and she didn't know what to do.
>
> **New York** *(Albany) welfare worker [to a client who had been off welfare for six months]:* Why are you here?
>
> *Client:* I was fired on Friday. I was late too many times. I depend on the bus. I have to drop my baby off. It makes it hard for me to get to work on time.

Texas

Applicants for TANF in Texas received no assistance with transportation to the Work First orientation at the workforce office. Once their applications were approved and they began participating in activities at the workforce offices, the workforce offices gave clients vouchers for either gasoline or the bus while they searched for work or attended education and training activities. Workforce workers explained that if they found a job, the workforce office could help with transportation until the client received their first paycheck. The first paycheck would disqualify the client from TANF and thereby the services of the workforce agency, including transportation assistance.

Public transportation served the Masters and Denton welfare and workforce offices and parts of the areas around them, but there was no public transportation in Grand Prairie. Clients in Grand Prairie needed private vehicles to reach the welfare and workforce offices, often relying on rides from relatives and friends. Funds for car repairs were available through another program, Welfare-to-Work, but workers explained that qualifying for this program was difficult. Despite the dependence of Texas residents on the automobile, the work program for TANF clients did not pay for car repairs or purchases.

> **Texas** *(Grand Prairie) workforce worker:* I do need to tell you that the State of Texas does not recognize the fact that you don't have a car.

> *Client:* I don't even have a driver's license; it wouldn't matter.

> *Worker:* It's not something that the State of Texas recognizes.

In making job referrals, workers were somewhat constrained by the client's access to transportation. More clients owned vehicles in Texas than in the other states, enabling workers to refer some clients to jobs without regard to public transportation. In talking to clients who did not own a vehicle, workers advised them to get familiar with the bus schedule, arrange for a car pool, or find a job close to home.

> **Texas** *(Denton) client:* My car is not in good shape right now.

> *Workforce worker:* So you will need to find something close to your house.

A bright spot in Texas was the government's willingness to pay for children's transportation to child care. If the child care facility provided transportation to and from the child's home or school, it could provide transportation to TANF children. Workers mentioned this option frequently, suggesting many child care facilities offered transportation to their clients.

In summary, the sites varied considerably in offering applicants and recipients assistance with transportation. Michigan made assistance for transportation a centerpiece of its efforts to reach the goal of Project Zero, particularly in the suburban and rural counties where public transportation was limited or nonexistent. Macomb County and Hillsdale County arranged for vans to transport clients to Work First activities. Staff there routinely explained the availability of funds for car repairs and purchases for employed clients and followed through with the procedures for disbursing these funds to people who found jobs. In all the sites, workers held out the possibility of an automobile for people who became employed.

Workers also assisted employed clients with automobiles in Albany County, although the assistance was limited to repairs. Bibb County and Suffolk County used vans to transport clients to work experience sites. In the remaining sites, workers offered tokens and swipe cards for public transportation or vouchers and reimbursement for gasoline.

All sites offered transportation assistance to participants in job search, education, training, or other activities satisfying the participation mandate. Workers in Michigan and New York routinely offered transportation assistance to recipients who became employed in regular jobs. Some workers in Georgia explained that transportation assistance was available to recipients who worked 30 hours a week while others implied that assistance was not available to employed recipients. Workers in Texas did not mention transportation assistance for employed recipients.

Observations captured workers limiting their referrals of TANF clients to employers accessible via public transportation. Such referrals were a reasonable strategy if funds were not available to repair or purchase private vehicles, but they were not best for clients. To the extent the constrained range of employers affected the quality of the jobs in terms of wage rates and other characteristics, it lowered their quality relative to the jobs clients could secure with their own vehicles. Reliance on public transportation also led workers to refer clients to jobs requiring infeasible travel arrangements. Several observations captured clients who had been referred to jobs in places they could not easily reach with public transportation, resulting in failure to accept or retain the job. With pressure on workers to make job placements, they may have developed overly optimistic expectations about the ability of clients to navigate to the job with public transportation.

Implications for Meeting
the Work Goals of TANF

Administrators, workers, and clients all agreed that the needs for child care and transportation raised the most common barriers to work among welfare applicants and recipients. In order to mandate work, welfare systems gave clients greater access to these supportive services. Although their efforts to build capacity varied considerably, all welfare systems developed policies and processes to deliver these supportive services and devoted funds to increasing their availability. With these supportive services lowering the most common barriers to work, the workforce agencies enforced the work mandate more widely. In response, applicants for welfare could decide either to participate in the work activities of the workforce agencies or to withdraw their application, while recipients could either participate in work activities or be sanctioned. All responses contributed to the decline in caseloads.

In some ways, child care was a more tractable problem than transportation. Child care was provided by individuals or small firms who could enter the market easily, enabling the supply of child care slots to increase in response to demand. As shown by the observations, few clients said they were unable to find someone to care for their children. Similarly, welfare clients who were given money for car repairs or car purchases were able to find a supplier. But when welfare clients were dependent on public transportation, money to ride the bus or rapid transit system did not always enable them to travel to the best jobs they were capable of taking. Michigan's decision to devote resources to car repairs and purchases, while expensive, was an attempt to give its welfare clients the opportunity to enter the mainstream labor market.

8

Explaining Eligibility Rules for Medicaid and Food Stamps

When Congress created TANF, the Medicaid and food stamps programs were recognized as supplements to earnings that could help families reduce their reliance on welfare. As welfare use declined, eligibility for these programs would help cushion families against a decline in income. But while eligibility for the federal food stamp program has never been limited to families on welfare, eligibility for Medicaid prior to TANF had typically been linked to eligibility for welfare. Linking the programs had created incentives for families to apply for welfare in order to receive Medicaid and had discouraged families from leaving welfare. Continued linking would also mean that families diverted from TANF would be diverted from Medicaid as well. To reduce these incentives and to prevent the restrictions in access to TANF from limiting access to Medicaid, the 1996 reforms "delinked" Medicaid from cash assistance.

Contrary to plan, both Medicaid and food stamp caseloads initially declined with the decline in welfare caseloads. Medicaid enrollment fell by 4.5 percent among children and 10 percent among nondisabled adults from a peak in 1995 to a low in 1998, while food stamp participation fell by 37 percent from a peak in 1994 to a low in 2000. Estimates vary of the relative strength of the factors explaining these declines, including the strong economy during this period, changes in eligibility rules, and a decline in program participation among eligible individuals. Yet studies using several methodologies attribute a portion of these declines to the practices of welfare offices. Practices designed to discourage applications for welfare served to discourage applications for food stamps and Medicaid, while families leaving welfare ceased to participate in the food stamp and Medicaid programs as well.[1]

Although eligibility for TANF, Medicaid, and food stamps were separate in federal law, the programs remained linked administratively in the welfare offices examined in this study. All the welfare offices used a single application form for TANF, food stamps, and Medicaid, with space on the form where applicants indicated the program or programs they were applying for. Much of the information requested on the form was common to the three programs and was entered into a single integrated information system, enabling workers to determine eligibility for all three programs together. A joint application was administratively efficient and promoted program coverage among families who applied for only one program and automatically became eligible for others. But a joint application also meant that the Work First process and other behavioral demands that diverted applicants from TANF could interfere with applications for food stamps and Medicaid. Without knowing the programs were independent, people diverted from TANF could conclude they were ineligible for food stamps and Medicaid, while people leaving TANF could conclude they were no longer eligible for these in-kind benefits.[2]

---

1   Courtney E. Burke and Craig W. Abbey, *Managing Medicaid Take-Up, Medicaid Enroll-ment Trends: 1995-2000* (Albany, NY: Rockefeller Institute of Government, August 2002); Alan Weil and John Holahan, "Health Insurance, Welfare, and Work," *Welfare Reform and Beyond: The Future of the Safety Net*, Isabel V. Sawhill et al., eds. (Washington, DC: Brookings Institution, 2002); and U.S. Department of Agriculture, July 2001, *The Decline in Food Stamp Participation: A Report to Congress*, Report No. FSP-01-WEL.

2   Many states were slow to build the new rules into their information system or use manual processes to override the system. Until states changed their procedures, Medicaid was not delinked from welfare in practice. See Mark Ragan, *Managing Medicaid Take-Up, Medicaid and Information Systems: Delays in Modifying Infor-mation Systems Contributed to the Decline in Medicaid Enrollment after Welfare Reform* (Albany, NY: Rockefeller Institute of Government, January 2003).

How much attention did the frontline workers observed give to Medicaid and food stamps? Did they explain that Medicaid and food stamps might be available to families without getting on TANF? Did they explain that families might be eligible for these benefits after they left TANF?

Discussion of Medicaid and Food Stamps with TANF Applicants

Eligibility rules for Medicaid varied among the states, particularly for adults who were not eligible for TANF. In the four states, adults and children who were eligible for TANF were automatically eligible for Medicaid. Transitional Medicaid, or Medicaid for families leaving welfare because their earnings increased, was available for 12 months in Michigan, Texas, and New York, and for 24 months in Georgia (Table 8-1). Low-income children and pregnant women without a connection to TANF were eligible for Medicaid in all states, but the rules for other adults were complex and varied among the states. Eligibility rules for food stamps did not depend on the composition or behavior of the family and were more liberal in most respects than eligibility rules for welfare.

Workers frequently discussed Medicaid and food stamps during their conversations with applicants. Workers in Texas mentioned Medicaid in 90.6 percent of encounters with applicants, while workers in Michigan mentioned it in 70.3 percent of these encounters. In Georgia and New York, where the conversation was not recorded on tape, workers discussed Medicaid in more than 40 percent of the encounters with applicants (Table 8-1). Workers in Michigan and Texas mentioned food stamps in over 80 percent of their encounters with applicants, while workers in Georgia and New York discussed food stamps in about half of these encounters (Table 8-2).

Although workers mentioned these in-kind programs frequently, they were generally not the focus of attention and consumed only a small part of the conversation. Most of the conversation about these programs consisted of explaining the rules, even conversation coded as "advising." In a common situation, where a parent came to the welfare office to apply for all three programs, the worker engaged in little conversation with the client to establish her specific eligibility for Medicaid and food stamps.

Table 8-1. Discussion of Medicaid
Encounters with Applicants for TANF, Food Stamps, or Medicaid

	MICHIGAN	TEXAS	GEORGIA	NEW YORK
		State Policy		
Eligibility for Transitional Medicaid*				
	12 months	12 months	24 months	12 months
Eligibility If Not Applying for TANF (Income and Asset Limits Vary)*				
Children and pregnant women	Yes	Yes	Yes	Yes
Parents and other caretaker relatives — not medically needy	Yes	No	Yes	Yes
Parents and other caretaker relatives — medically needy	Yes	Yes	No	Yes
Eligibility If Lose TANF Due to Time Limit or Failure to Work*				
	Adult ineligible if loses TANF for failure to work	Adult ineligible if loses TANF due to time limit	Eligible	Eligible
Percent of Encounters Discussing Medicaid				
(Number of Encounters)	*(111)*	*(115)*	*(72)*	*(110)*
Any worker activity	70.3	90.6	43.5	45.4
Explaining rules	34.7	64.5	22.3	20.0
Advising or assessing	26.8	34.6	10.0	12.3

* Source: Broaddus, Matthew et al., February 13, 2002. *Expanding Family Coverage: States' Medicaid Eligibility Policies for Working Families in the Year 2000.* Washington, DC: Center on Budget and Policy Priorities.

Table 8-2. Discussion of Food Stamps
Encounters with Applicants for TANF, Food Stamps, or Medicaid

	MICHIGAN	*TEXAS*	*GEORGIA*	*NEW YORK*
	Percent of encounters discussing food stamps			
(Number of Encounters)	*(111)*	*(115)*	*(72)*	*(110)*
Any worker activity	84.5	89.6	53.6	48.6
Explaining rules	60.5	60.6	22.8	22.5
Advising or assessing	31.5	37.8	17.3	10.6

Most of the conversation was devoted to collecting financial and demographic information needed for all three programs and administering the rules regarding TANF. Because this family would be eligible for food stamps and Medicaid if eligible for TANF, few questions about the family's eligibility for the in-kind programs were necessary.

A noteworthy share of TANF applicants said they were already receiving Medicaid and food stamps. Among the encounters with applicants, the share in which someone in the family received Medicaid was 39 percent in Michigan, 21 percent in Georgia, and 16 percent in New York and Texas. The share of applicants receiving food stamps was 22 percent in Georgia, 15 percent in Michigan, 14 percent in New York, and 9 percent in Texas.

Workers generally did not need to gather additional information to determine a family's eligibility for food stamps and they seldom gave explicit attention to this program. When lengthy conversations about food stamp eligibility occurred, they were most often about the composition of the applicant's household. The definition of a household for purposes of food stamps differed from the definition under TANF and Medicaid, requiring the worker to apply two sets of rules.[3]

> **Michigan** *(Hillsdale) welfare worker:* So your friends, do you eat together with them as a family or do you have your own food separately?

---

3   Federal law defines a food stamp household as a group that purchases food and prepares meals together, which may live within a larger group that does not share food. An exception to this rule is a parent age 21 or younger living with her parents, who are all considered to be a single food stamp household even if they do not purchase food and prepare meals together.

Client: Yeah. We have our own food separately but we eat together.

Worker: OK. So when you say you have your food separately...

Client: I buy our food and they buy theirs.

Worker: OK, but you sit down at the same table?

Client: Yes.

Worker: And that's OK. We're talking about do you share a gallon of milk, do you share a loaf of bread, and I'm hearing no. That tells us they have their own food group, you and your daughter have your own, and that's the way we will do that.

Georgia *(NW Fulton) welfare worker:* How old are you Ms. ____?

Client: 18.

Worker: Who do you live with?

Client: My mother.

Worker: What I can do is, because you're 18, I can't let you apply for food stamps, your mother'd have to apply. But I can apply you for TANF and Medicaid.

When workers interviewed families whose income was low enough to make eligibility for TANF likely, they typically devoted little attention to Medicaid, which came with it. Workers sometimes asked whether the family was already receiving Medicaid or whether the family wished to apply. The application forms included a question about unpaid medical bills, a question workers asked most frequently in Texas. When a client reported unpaid bills, the workers often recorded the information without a verbal response although the worker occasionally explained that Medicaid would pay the bills. Unpaid medical bills sometimes triggered a question about the health insurance coverage of the absent parent. Discussions of child support enforcement also triggered discussion about the absent parent's insurance and its coordination with Medicaid. When a worker learned a low-income applicant was pregnant, this information often prompted an explanation of her eligibility for Medicaid and, less uniformly, expedited her enrollment in the program.

Workers were more likely to give explicit attention to food stamps and Medicaid when they judged the applicant to be ineligible for TANF or when the applicant decided to withdraw the TANF application:

Michigan *(Hillsdale) welfare worker:* Do you want to bother with the cash assistance at this point for a few bucks?

Client: No, there's no point, no.

Worker: OK. What I will do is run a budget officially, send you the letter saying you withdrew your application for the cash assistance.

Client: But is that gonna hurt us for anything else?

Worker: It does not affect your eligibility for anything else. We look at each different program on its each individual situation, OK? Like we said, cash assistance is one thing. Then we look at the food stamps and then we look at Medicaid. So we have basically three different programs at this particular point, OK? So we're not gonna deal with one but we still have the other two. We still have the Medicaid and the food stamps. So we're not, we're not saying "no" all the way, OK? That's the important part.

Texas *(Grand Prairie) Client:* I'm working, but I cannot pay the $700 rent and all the utility bills. He's not giving me any money.

Welfare worker at the reception desk: Well, if you're working, then you wouldn't be eligible for TANF. But you could fill this application out for food stamps and for Medicaid.

In Albany County, the welfare office was in the process of enrolling all Medicaid clients into a managed care plan. Enrolling them in managed care appeared to be a high priority of the office, receiving attention from several workers during the intake process. Workers at the reception counters who did a "prescreening" (reviewing the client's application, copying documents, and entering the application into the information system) routinely gave applicants a packet of information about their choice of a managed care plan. Observations of eligibility interviews captured workers asking whether the applicant received the packet and telling them they needed to choose a plan.

New York *(Albany) [in the reception area of the welfare agency] client:* Will I be eligible for benefits?

Worker: I do the clerical work. You'll see an eligibility worker. Are you familiar with your managed care options?

Client: No.

Worker: When you pick a plan you fill out this paper. They'll send you a list of doctors you can go to. Fill this out and hand it to the eligibility worker. I'll copy your documents.

In summary, workers generally gave more attention to TANF policies than policies relevant only to Medicaid and food stamps. In order to become eligible for TANF and continue to receive benefits, clients were told they must conform to numerous behavioral mandates: pursue a work activity, cooperate in child support enforcement, and meet additional requirements imposed by the states. Discussion of these mandates gave rise to a considerable amount of conversation. Talking about the supportive services needed to conform to these mandates, particularly the child care and transportation needed to work, also generated conversation. Eligibility for Medicaid and food stamps for families with children was not similarly conditioned on the behavior of parents but depended primarily on the family's income, assets, and medical expenses. Because information about income and assets was collected in the process of determining eligibility for TANF, in many cases workers could determine eligibility for Medicaid and food stamps without additional questions, enabling them to give these programs little explicit attention.

Discussion of Medicaid and Food Stamps for Families without TANF

The observations captured interviews with applicants where workers explained that TANF, Medicaid, and food stamps were independent, but the explanations were prompted by the client's situation, not offered as a routine part of the interview. Workers generally began the interview by collecting information about the client that was relevant for all three programs. When workers concluded the client was not eligible for TANF, they often told applicants they might still be eligible for Medicaid and food stamps. People withdrawing their applications during the interview were also often told they might still be eligible for Medicaid and food stamps. But if the applicant appeared to be eligible for TANF and interested in applying, the worker generally did not tell them they might be eligible for Medicaid and food stamps even if the Work First process ultimately diverted them from TANF. Discussion of this important contingency was not routine during eligibility interviews, where Medicaid and food stamps were typically only a small part of a conversation focused on TANF.

Group orientations for applicants gave workers another opportunity to explain the rules about eligibility for Medicaid and food stamp benefits without receiving TANF. By far the clearest explanations were given during the orientations in the workforce office in Denton, where workers told clients exactly how to communicate with the welfare agency if they wanted these benefits:

> **Texas** *(Denton) workforce orientation:* This next page, do you all know that you can get food stamps and Medicaid without being on TANF? (General assent). You do know that, OK. Sometimes I have people come through this orientation, they realize all of the hoops they're gonna have to jump through to keep their TANF and they think it's not worth it. This is a way that you word it to DHS if you want to withdraw your TANF application, OK? A lotta times people do want to withdraw their applications but they want to keep their food stamps and Medicaid and I've had people in the past that have gone to DHS to do this and didn't word it just, just right to DHS and they cut everything off. So if this is something that you're interested in, this tells you how to word it. You need to write it out on a piece of paper to DHS that you want to withdraw your TANF application, that you want to continue to apply for Medicaid and food stamps, OK? So the reason we put this in here is because it was becoming a problem.

In the other two Texas workforce offices, the orientations observed did not mention the availability of food stamps and Medicaid without receiving TANF.

The orientations in Michigan, run jointly by the welfare and workforce agencies, also varied in the attention given to Medicaid and food stamp benefits without TANF. In Hillsdale County, the scripted orientations mentioned Medicaid and food stamp benefits without TANF:

> **Michigan** *(Hillsdale) joint orientation by welfare and workforce workers:* OK, the purpose of this orientation is so we can explain these services to help you find a job or get a better job if you are currently working but still receiving assistance, so that you become self-sufficient. By self-sufficient we mean that you have enough income and resources needed to support your family without the cash grant. You can still get food stamps, Medicaid, and day care and not have to participate in Work First.

The scripted orientations in Macomb County said individuals could receive Medicaid and food stamps if they were working, but said nothing about these benefits if they were not receiving welfare:

> **Michigan** *(Macomb) joint orientation by welfare and workforce workers:*
> If you are eligible for a cash grant and get a job, your cash grant may
> continue, depending on your income. You may also continue to re-
> ceive Medicaid, food stamps, day care, or other assistance while you
> are working.

The one orientation observed in Wayne County said nothing about eligi-
bility for Medicaid and food stamp benefits without receiving TANF.
However, the workers appeared to believe that many applicants for
TANF were already receiving food stamps and Medicaid:

> **Michigan** *(Wayne) joint orientation by welfare and workforce workers:*
> On March 1, our policy changed. Customers who are in noncompli-
> ance for Work First without good cause are subject to the following
> penalties: On the first disqualification your FIP and food stamp case
> will close for a minimum of one month.... In order for you to get sup-
> portive services [clothes from a thrift shop], you're gonna have to
> have a current Medicaid card [as a form of identification]. How many
> of you have current Medicaid cards? OK. Then raise your hands if
> you don't have a Medicaid card. OK. Do you know why you don't
> have one? C'mon, some answers.

Three orientations were observed in Georgia, one by the Department of Labor and two by the welfare agency for people approaching the
time limit. One orientation by the welfare agency mentioned benefits
without TANF, although only in response to a question by a client:

> **Georgia** *(SW Fulton) client:* If you choose to close TANF, can you still get
> Medicaid?

> *Worker:* If you don't want to be here, don't want to keep TANF, we can
> close you, you can still get Medicaid. It will cause issues in your food
> stamps.

The welfare agencies in New York did not hold group orientations.
The group orientations in the Suffolk County Department of Labor made
no mention of food stamps or Medicaid.

An exception to the scant discussion of Medicaid for nonrecipients
of TANF was when a parent wanted Medicaid to pay for her own medical
expenses. All the states had some provision for extending Medicaid to
parents and other caretaker adults who were not receiving cash assistance. All states except Georgia had a program for medically needy
adults, while all states except Texas had some other arrangement for extending Medicaid to parents and other caretaker adults (Table 8-1). Rules

governing eligibility for these programs were complicated and produced some time-consuming conversations. Considering the complexity of the rules, however, workers devoted a modest amount of time to explaining them and, with some exceptions, did not describe them fully. Unlike the rules governing time limits, work activities, child care, and transportation, where the rules could generally be discerned from the conversation between the worker and the client, the rules governing Medicaid for these parents and caretakers did not emerge clearly. Workers mentioned the spend-down for medically needy adults in only seven encounters, four of them in Hillsdale County. Other rules were not articulated clearly. Workers sometimes discussed Medicaid eligibility without specifying who would be eligible, making it impossible to know whether the adult in the family was eligible or just the children. Imprecision about the eligibility of adults was further increased when workers used the term "Medicaid" to refer to the 1997 expansions to higher income children.

Transitional Medicaid was mentioned in 21 encounters, 10 in welfare offices and 11 in workforce offices. Only two encounters in welfare offices (in Hillsdale County and Macomb County) captured a worker explaining transitional Medicaid to a new applicant; the other encounters were with people who were already receiving transitional benefits or had received them in the past. Four encounters in the Albany welfare office captured workers informing people leaving welfare that they were eligible for transitional Medicaid. No encounters in other welfare offices captured any mention of transitional Medicaid. Three encounters at a workforce office in Wayne County captured a worker explaining that transitional Medicaid could help his client take a job that does not provide health insurance. Seven encounters in the Texas workforce offices and one encounter in the Macomb workforce office mentioned transitional Medicaid but did not explain it in any detail.

Workers mentioned transitional Medicaid less frequently than transitional child care. A possible explanation is that while child care is needed to maintain employment and independence of welfare, motivating workers and clients to discuss it, Medicaid coverage is less essential for employment. Another possibility was mentioned by a worker in Wayne County:

Michigan *(Wayne) workforce worker:* I don't know if you've ever heard of it before, the transitional Medicaid? It's been around for a long time. It's not something that they publicize a lot because they want employers to offer medical insurance.

Summary and Conclusion

Frontline workers frequently mentioned Medicaid and food stamps, but the discussion was primarily in the context of determining eligibility for cash assistance. The attention given to Medicaid and food stamps as a support for work among families not on welfare was modest and uneven. A few offices made a systematic effort to inform TANF applicants they could continue their applications for Medicaid and food stamps regardless of whether or not they attended Work First or found a job, but the majority of offices did not. Workers in most offices delivered the information at their discretion or in response to questions by clients, delivered partial information, or did not deliver any information. Compared to the explicit and routine processes for enforcing the work requirement and assessing parent's needs for child care and transportation to support work, few offices developed a process for informing them about the conditions under which they and their children would be eligible for Medicaid and food stamps if they chose work over welfare. Where applicants did not learn that eligibility for cash and in-kind benefits were determined separately, applicants diverted from TANF by Work First might have been less likely to pursue their applications for the in-kind benefits.

Adults seeking Medicaid who were not receiving TANF were subject to eligibility rules that were more complex than the rules governing Medicaid eligibility for children or adults receiving TANF. Unlike most other rules discussed by workers, the rules regarding Medicaid for adults could not be understood from reading the encounters. The eligibility categories were numerous, subtle, and described in jargon or not at all, leaving the reader and, undoubtedly, the applicant with an incomplete understanding of them. Compared with the rules regarding the TANF mandates, education and training, child care and transportation, explaining the rules regarding Medicaid for adults appeared to be a lower priority of the welfare system.

Although a critic could frame this as a failure of the frontline workers, the criticism belongs with policymakers and managers. When policymakers design complex rules to allocate limited resources, as they did with Medicaid, managers need to devise a process that enables and requires workers to communicate these rules to their clients. After decades of implementation failure, such a process was developed to communicate the work requirement in TANF. Without a well-specified process, workers cannot be expected to deliver the information accurately to everyone who should have it. Their time is too limited and their understanding of the policy often too imperfect for managers to rely on their initiative and style of communication to get the information across.

9

Using Information Systems to Verify Eligibility, Monitor Behavior, and Detect Fraud

A t the front lines of welfare system, along with the workers and their clients, are the computers used to process the volumes of data demanded by assistance programs. Computerized management information systems (MIS) for administering welfare have become increasingly sophisticated over the years, a trend that continued with the implementation of TANF. State welfare agencies, on their own initiative and in response to federal mandates and funds, introduced more powerful computer technology in their welfare systems and strengthened the links between these systems and others at the local, state, and national levels. Workforce agencies also developed more powerful computerized MIS systems to deliver services, particularly job search and job placement. Because MIS systems were used to verify eligibility for assistance, monitor the behavior of clients, and detect fraud, they could play an important role in reducing welfare use and encouraging work.

These systems gave workers a remarkable capacity to gather, record, and verify information about their clients. The observations captured workers determining welfare eligibility by entering detailed information about the client into one or more MIS system and using one or more MIS system to verify the information provided by the client or obtain additional information about the client. The computer then processed this information to generate the decision to authorize or deny assistance. The computers in the welfare agencies were increasingly linked to those of other agencies, most commonly the workforce agencies, giving welfare workers the ability to gather and verify even more extensive information about the client.

At the same time that computers were increasing the quantity of information pulled into the welfare system, welfare and workforce staff continued to use the old paper forms and the telephone to gather and verify information about the client and monitor their behavior. Workers also observed the client directly, noting attendance in the agency at appointments, orientations, meetings, and training sessions. Finally, to varying degrees among the sites, workers verified information and monitored behavior by visiting the client's home.

Determining Eligibility

Although all states developed increasingly sophisticated computer systems, the pace of development varied from state to state. In Georgia and Texas, a computer sat on the desks of the workers who had primary responsibility for determining eligibility and was used instead of a paper form to record information about the applicant. The process in Texas is illustrative. Workers in Texas entered information onto a "screen" as they conducted eligibility interviews, moving from one screen to the next as the interview progressed. Many screens had subscreens for clients in particular situations. The screens prompted the worker to collect specific pieces of information, obtain answers to questions, obtain applicant signatures, and verify information before the screen could be "cleared." Incomplete screens were "pended" until all items of information were entered and the client fulfilled all requirements. Because all screens had to be cleared in order to certify eligibility, the screens structured the eligibility interview and controlled access to benefits. Importantly, the application was "pended" until applicants provided paper documentation of attendance at the orientation at the workforce agency. In effect, the process for determining eligibility and benefits was dictated by the MIS screens.

By clicking on a menu, the eligibility workers in Texas could also access the information systems of other government agencies. By connecting to the system of the Texas Workforce Commission, they could inquire about the client's employment and earnings history and unemployment insurance claims. By connecting to the Social Security Administration, they could verify Social Security and SSI benefits. By connecting to an Interagency Database Network containing Health Department information, they could learn whether children had been immunized (physicians were required to notify the Health Department when they immunized children). This database also contained birth certificate information for everyone born in Texas, providing the name of the father acknowledging paternity. By connecting to the Attorney General's Office, workers could inquire about and verify receipt of child support payments. Moreover, if child support for the applicant was not being enforced, the welfare agency's system generated a referral of the applicant's child support case to the Attorney General's Office with the relevant information from the welfare systems database. Workers could also connect with a database to verify an applicant's immigration status.

In addition to these government systems, the Texas welfare agency purchased data from a private data broker. By connecting to the database of the data broker, a worker could learn about the client's credit card charges and payments, vehicle ownership, driver's license, criminal history in the state, previous employment, and neighbors' names and addresses. The primary motivation for introducing the data broker was to detect fraud in the food stamp program, as the federal government's Quality Control program was threatening the state with penalties for excess rates of error, but it was also used in determining eligibility for TANF. For example, owning an expensive car or recent payments on a credit card was evidence that the applicant might have unreported income.

Texas (Grand Prairie) welfare worker: So as far as monthly payments on your credit cards, I see one that's being paid and that's $20 a month.

Client: So what does that have to do with anything?

Worker: Well, if a person comes in and tells me that they have no money coming in, and I see they have $3,000 worth of bills and everything is paid up to date…

Client: Oh, OK, that tells you something.

Worker: Yeah, it tells me something.

The process of verifying information was interactive. Workers verified information while the applicant was sitting at the desk, asking questions and trying to get answers by looking through the information on the screens. Comparing information from the client with information on the screen, workers looked for unreported income and assets as well as misreported information about family members. Workers made phone calls at the moment to verify residency and other information.

The Texas Workforce Commission also upgraded its information system by creating a single system for all its programs, including TANF and child care as well as programs for unemployed workers, disadvantaged groups, veterans, migrants, food stamps recipients, and so forth. Staff in the workforce agencies could also view some items in the welfare agency's database such as the amount of the TANF benefit and the reason for a sanction. The encounters captured workforce staff using this information to deny service to people who were not receiving TANF benefits and to help others resolve sanctions.

In Georgia, the site visits observed the Fulton County welfare offices as they were introducing a new computerized system that, for the first time, required eligibility workers to enter information while they were conducting their interviews. Training to use the new computer system took workers away from regular duties, requiring more time than they had spent when they were in training to implement TANF. The menu of links to databases of other agencies was shorter than in Texas, so that workers had access only to the client's employment and earnings history and unemployment insurance claims, Social Security and SSI benefits, and child protective services. Even this more limited range of information surprised at least one client.

Georgia (NW Fulton) welfare worker: [typing on computer]

Client: Hey, all my information you getting off that computer, huh?

Worker: Yeah. Our computer tells us a lot these days. They want to make sure you don't forget to tell us something.

Georgia (Bibb) welfare worker: It's showing you have earned income when we run an interface [with DOL and Social Security]. Looks like you worked at the ————. What happened with that?

In Michigan and New York, workers at the reception desk used computers but most eligibility workers entered information onto paper forms while they met with their clients. Data entry was a separate step, often performed by specialized workers, as was verification of the information provided by the client, often done while the client was not present. Only in Suffolk County, where fraud workers routinely met with applicants as discussed below, did the observations capture the verification process.

Without the constraints of the computer screens, eligibility workers in Michigan and New York had more flexibility over the order of topics discussed with clients and spent more time looking directly at the client when they talked. Because a computer was still needed to determine eligibility and the amount of the benefit, separation from the computer meant that workers could not immediately give an applicant a definitive statement about whether or not income was low enough to qualify for assistance. Nonetheless, workers did tell applicants they would be unlikely to qualify for assistance and turned the discussion to other options.

Another technological innovation, adopted by the welfare agencies in New York and Texas, was finger-imaging. New York welfare agencies began using electronic fingerprinting and photographs to deter fraud before TANF was enacted. Texas, seeing New York's success in identifying multiple welfare applications and other fraud, mandated statewide electronic fingerprinting just before the period of the observations.

Texas (Grand Prairie) welfare worker: You must be finger-imaged prior to your case being certified, OK?

Client: How long does it take to do the finger.... I mean you just put your finger in ink and....

Worker: No, you don't even do that, it's all on the computer. She'll tell you to put your left finger first and then your right finger, just the index fingers is all it takes and then they take your picture and that's it.

While computers were central to the eligibility process, workers also used other methods to verify information about clients. Collecting documents and sending clients to obtain verification of information were commonly used methods, as discussed in Chapter 3. Another common method was telephoning people who could verify the information provided by clients, such as landlords, employers, schools, child care centers, other government agencies, and so forth. Because the observations were limited to the time workers spent in face-to-face contact with clients, it is likely that many phone calls were not observed.

Monitoring Compliance With Mandates

The process of monitoring compliance with the behavioral mandates was generally low-tech, relying primarily on paper, telephone and faxes, and direct observations. Of all the behavioral mandates, the greatest attention went to monitoring work activity. Clients brought in logs listing the employers they had contacted during their job search and attendance sheets listing dates of attendance at education or training programs. Education and training providers also faxed attendance sheets to the workers responsible for monitoring work activity. In Fulton County, workers reviewed bills from child care providers with dates of the children's attendance for evidence that the client was participating in a work activity. Workers responsible for placing clients in jobs telephoned employers to track their employment. Direct observations of clients as they attended orientations, individual meetings, job readiness and job search programs, and other programs operated by the welfare and workforce agencies were a particularly accurate way of monitoring compliance. In Michigan, welfare workers observed clients directly by making routine visits to clients' homes.

How assiduously the workers actually monitored work activities varied from site to site. The effort to monitor applicant job search in Georgia, for example, varied from one office to another. According to managers in Bibb County, the welfare office monitored the job search of applicants daily, stationing a worker near the building entrance each morning to take the names and addresses of employers that applicants had contacted the previous day and hand out bus tokens for job search that day. The worker then spot-checked the validity of the contacts by calling some of the employers. At the other extreme, the managers of one office in Fulton County acknowledged that the office needed "a better handle" on monitoring. The office did not check the logs kept by applicants during their three weeks of job search because, with so many cases, it was hard to stay on top of it. Also, the office was reluctant to call employers to check the validity of the contacts for fear of alienating them. The managers of the other Fulton office reported that a sample of employers were contacted to validate the job search logs.

In Michigan and Texas, the state specified a process for monitoring the applicant's attendance at the Work First orientations that appeared to be followed strictly by the local sites. The agencies in Texas used a paper process, a form stamped at the workforce orientation that applicants carried back to the welfare agency. Michigan used a computerized process based on the state workforce agency's computer system. Workers in the welfare agency could view computer screens from this system to learn when someone attended an orientation, a Work First activity, or was placed in a job. They authorized assistance only after learning the applicant had attended the orientation and the first day of Work First. To inform the workforce agency about the status of clients, they could enter the names of applicants expected to attend the orientation and the names of case closings and sanctions into this system.

The monitoring of participation in a subsequent work activity also varied from one site to another. Monitoring participation was the responsibility of the workforce agencies in Michigan, Texas, and Suffolk County and the responsibility of the welfare agencies in Georgia and Albany County. Two approaches to monitoring participation were most commonly observed, both involving frequent direct worker contact with the client. In one approach, monitoring was paired with disbursing financial assistance for child care or transportation to a work activity. In Texas, the workforce agencies gave clients bus passes or gas vouchers to last only a few weeks, which prompted frequent returns to the agency. When they returned, the workers reviewed their activities and gave them further suggestions for job search, education, or training. In Fulton County, the welfare workers did some verification of work activity when clients came in to receive assistance with transportation and child care. In these offices, face-to-face encounters were the impetus for reviewing job search logs and attendance sheets, and making phone calls to verify this or other information about the client's participation. Workers gave a one-week pass for public transportation to clients who they judged to need strict monitoring and a monthly pass to clients who needed less strict monitoring.

The participation of clients was most easily monitored when they were placed in work activities on site at the agency responsible for monitoring, enabling their participation to be observed directly. Four of these agencies offered GED preparation on site, and eight of them offered job readiness and job search programs on site. The failure of clients to attend these on site activities or missed appointments at these agencies accounted for a majority of the encounters taking place for the primary purpose of discussing attendance problems and sanctions.

The encounters with clients and the interviews with managers do not give a clear picture of the process for monitoring new employment. If clients found the job themselves, the rules called for them to report it to the welfare agency. Welfare workers routinely told clients to report any changes in their situation quickly and the walls of many welfare offices were posted with signs "Report Changes." The encounters captured clients telling their workers about their new job, often in the context of needing child care assistance, but also captured clients who had not reported their jobs to the welfare agency. The workforce agencies operated under performance standards for job placement, giving them an incentive to track their placements, yet it is not clear how this was done. Managers reported that job developers might call employers to follow up on their referrals or the employer might send a form indicating a hire. Managers also said the client was a major source of information about job placements. Neither of these methods guaranteed the workforce agencies would learn about the placement.

Detecting Fraud

All the welfare offices had procedures for referring cases of suspected fraud to a specialized worker or unit located either on site or in a centralized location. For example, Bibb County had one Intake Eligibility Investigator on site, while Suffolk County and Albany County had several Front End Detection System (FEDS) workers on site. The welfare offices in Texas sent cases suspected of fraud to a centralized Quality Assurance Division that sent out their Q.A. technicians to investigate the case. These workers and their counterparts in the other sites visited homes, sometimes unannounced, or called clients into the office for further questioning.

Although the study did not routinely ask managers about the extent of welfare fraud among their clients, two managers spontaneously expressed the opinion that fraud was common. A manager in Dallas, in response to a question about what had happened to clients who left welfare, said:

> We don't really know. I think that a lot of them were fraud cases, and we made it harder for them. Because we can access information through Data Broker and TWC. Food stamp cases, especially single men, just stopped coming in. The TANF cases, I think a lot of them were living with the other parent. And lots were already working and supplementing their income with AFDC.

In Suffolk County, a manager said:

> I have to tell you — there is a substantial number of instances in which a person doesn't tell us they are working. One way we know this is through the FEDS unit. This is an exceedingly effective system. When someone applies, their case gets sent to the FEDS unit. They do a home visit to verify the information. I went out with two of our FEDS units. It was a real eye opener. They went out on ten cases in one morning and got three case closures out of it. Blatant lying — about who was living there and so on. And they verify whether someone is working. If they ask for so-and-so at the door and someone says, "no, he's at work," then you smell a rat.

In Michigan, the managers and workers who discussed fraud said they did not always pursue fraud aggressively. Macomb County welfare workers noted a drawback to aggressive pursuit in response to a question about following up suspected fraud.

> Some workers follow up. Some don't. Anything that's questionable — you can ask for more documentation. God forbid you deny someone benefits when they are eligible — that's almost worse than giving them benefits they aren't eligible for. Because they'll do a fair hearing and that will come back at you.

Yet managers in Macomb also noted that routine home visits uncovered fraud and deterred welfare use.

We may see a nice house and suspect the client is over income. They can be referred to a recoupment specialist if blatant fraud is suspected. The goal of home visits is to identify barriers to employment and remove them. What has really happened is that clients don't want you in their home and so they get a job and leave welfare. Workers who make more home calls have fewer cases. Other times you go and see that they are really struggling.

The encounters showed the workers in New York and Texas pursuing welfare fraud more aggressively than the other states. Workers in the welfare agencies in these states routinely took finger-images and photographs of applicants. In every site, many encounters captured workers informing applicants they must go to finger-imaging before their application was complete. Moreover, the eligibility processes included an explicit antifraud component. The eligibility interviews in Texas followed a common pattern driven by a "management screen" on the computer. Workers asked applicants for a detailed list of income and expenditures and entered them onto the management screen. They entered additional financial information from the database of the private data broker. Workers then questioned applicants about possible inconsistencies between the totals on the screen that might indicate unreported income, like actual expenditures in excess of reported income.

> ***Texas*** *(Masters) welfare worker [communicating through an interpreter]:* How much do you spend for shelter?
>
> *Interpreter:* $462 for apartment rent.
>
> *Worker:* What about utilities?
>
> *Interpreter:* Just telephone, $31 a month.
>
> *Worker:* How much on food per month?
>
> *Interpreter:* $70 a week.
>
> *Worker:* Car payment?
>
> *Interpreter:* No.
>
> *Worker:* How much do you spend on gas?
>
> *Interpreter:* $50 dollars a week.
>
> *Worker:* Child care?
>
> *Interpreter:* No.
>
> *Worker:* Personal items for the household?

Interpreter: $15 a week.

Worker: Tell her she's a negative. She's got a negative management with the money they're spending. Her husband brings in about $800 a month. The income and the management is way off.

Interpreter: She says no, that the husband's job is the only money coming in.

In New York, the antifraud FEDS process was observed in detail in Suffolk County. Workers there told almost all the applicants observed that they must return to the welfare office for an appointment with a FEDS worker. At these appointments, the FEDS worker asked applicants for additional information to verify their family situation, residence, credit, motor vehicles, and so forth, much like the rigorous eligibility interviews in Texas. In one of the seven observed FEDS appointments, the client was deterred from continuing her application for assistance. When the worker told the applicant that the office had visited her home and found her away, the client explained she had been offered two jobs and her husband promised to send her money. Citing these possible sources of income, the worker encouraged the client to withdraw her application. When the client did so, the worker said she could reapply for assistance if things didn't work out and told her to apply for the Child Health Plus program for low-income children. For more intensive fraud investigations, Suffolk had a Special Investigation Unit (SIU), mentioned in only one encounter.

Although antifraud activities were less conspicuous in Georgia and Michigan, the observations captured workers warning clients against fraudulent behavior. In Georgia, most of the instances of suspected fraud stemmed from unusually large expenditures by the client and from unreported changes in the client's circumstances, particularly changes in employment and residence. In Michigan, workers mentioned fraud in connection with unreported income, lost benefit checks, and discrepancies between the family members reported to be living at home and those discovered during the workers' home visits.

In addition to welfare fraud, observations in every state revealed several clients with a history of employment in the underground economy. Applicants admitted to previous earnings under the table when asked how they had been supporting themselves or when asked about their previous employment experience. They also explained that their need for assistance arose because their boyfriend or husband had recently lost a "side job" or a job that paid in cash. Recipients in job search, when asked about their prior work experience, mentioned employment off the books. Staff expressed neither surprise nor disapproval when told about previous employment in the underground economy, and a few inquired about it explicitly. Work in the underground economy was acceptable provided the earnings were reported to the welfare agency.

Conclusion

The attention that welfare offices gave to verifying eligibility and pursuing fraud indicates that the new policies in TANF for limiting access to welfare did not reduce the use of these traditional methods. Advances in computer technology strengthened the traditional methods, increasing the information available to workers as they determined whether a client legitimately met the criteria of eligibility for assistance. This access to additional financial and demographic information enabled welfare offices to exclude more applicants from assistance and undoubtedly was a factor contributing to the decline in caseloads.

Additional information about earnings may have been particularly important. With easy access to the databases containing workers' employment and earnings history, the welfare agency could uncover earnings that employers had reported to the unemployment insurance system but clients had not reported to the welfare system. In addition, expansions in the amount of the EITC in 1994-1996 made it more rewarding for people to work for employers who reported their earnings instead of employers in the underground economy. Thus, welfare eligibility and benefits might have declined not only because more people worked, but also because more earnings from the traditional economy were reported to the welfare agency and more workers chose employment in the traditional economy.

10

Managing the Implementation of TANF

In assessing the success of an implementation effort from the perspective of the front lines, the glass can appear as half empty or half full. Assuming the policy goals articulated at the top are clear enough even to permit an assessment, the opportunities for slippage between policy and frontline practice are so numerous that some deviation is inevitable. Any study will identify points at which states, welfare agencies, or workers ignored or deviated from a policy. We can observe many such points and conclude the policy was circumvented, or we can identify a pattern of consistency between policy and practice and declare that, on balance, the implementation of the policy was a success. Ultimately, the conclusion is one of judgment.

In the cases examined in this study, the conversations at the front lines are strong evidence that the practices of workers in these sites conformed to the policy goals regarding employment set forth in TANF. Workers consistently implemented policies designed to discourage families from relying on welfare by mandating employment-related activities and by supporting these activities with child care. Most importantly, they imposed a work-related mandate on applicants as part of a highly routinized process to determine eligibility for assistance. This mandate was imposed with few exceptions, becoming an embodiment of TANF's provision that welfare is no longer an entitlement. The sites discouraged people from using welfare not by explicitly denying them entry to the welfare system but by imposing a behavioral mandate as a condition of entry. Although it is impossible to measure the magnitude of the impact of these practices on caseloads, they certainly contributed to their sharp decline.

In contrast, the conversations at the front lines show that workers in these sites did little or nothing to promote TANF's goals regarding marriage, out-of-wedlock childbearing, and the formation of two-parent families. At the time of the observations during the first half of 2000, states had not incorporated these goals into their TANF programs. With little knowledge about the design of effective programs and little consensus about the appropriate role of government in these areas, states were cautious in articulating policies and designing specific procedures to be followed. Without directives from the states, the local welfare offices took a hands-off approach toward these goals and the observations show that few workers counseled clients about marriage or out-of-wedlock childbearing. The one exception was Georgia, the only state in the study with a family cap, where workers had authority to refer clients to family planning services.

Why did these sites succeed in implementing the work provisions of TANF when repeated reforms of the welfare system had failed to encourage work among welfare recipients? How did the organization and management of the welfare system produce the behavior of workers observed at the front lines? This chapter addresses these questions by examining the political, financial, organizational, managerial, and procedural changes that ultimately resulted in the policies enacted by the frontline workers.

Leadership by Governors and State Welfare Administrators

When President Clinton placed responsibility for implementing TANF on the governors, he was giving them what they had asked for. States leaders were chafing under the mandates in the federal welfare law and regulations, which from their perspective gave them insufficient authority to design and manage their programs. After President Reagan devolved partial authority for welfare employment programs to the states in the early 1980s, several governors and state welfare administrators took the initiative in designing employment programs and claiming credit for innovative solutions to the problem of welfare dependency.[1] When these initiatives proved politically popular, the National Governors Association worked with Congress to craft the Family Support Act of 1988, the final reform of AFDC. But the Act emphasized education and training for welfare clients and, perhaps because it deemphasized immediate employment, was ineffective in reducing caseloads. As caseloads rose, state leaders turned their attention away from implementing the 1988 law and, instead, sought waivers from federal law to design their own programs. The vast majority of states jumped on the waiver bandwagon, which unraveled the federal AFDC law and ultimately led Congress to create the TANF block grant.[2]

Several factors enabled governors and state welfare administrators to generate political capital by taking the lead in welfare policymaking. With a rising share of middle income mothers participating in the labor force, the public was less willing to pay low-income mothers to stay home with their children. The conflict in goals between supporting mothers to care for their children and requiring them to work, an inherent tension in welfare, was resolved in favor of work. As a stream of evaluations of the state-initiated welfare employment programs showed which approaches were most effective, uncertainty about the service technology for moving welfare clients into jobs declined. With growing public support for employment by welfare clients and research support for effective employment programs, state leaders risked little by giving their own support to welfare reform. Finally, welfare has long been a code word for talking about race, adding another dimension to the politics of welfare reform.[3]

---

1   Nathan, *Turning Promises into Performance.*

2   Michael Wiseman, "State Strategies for Welfare Reform: The Wisconsin Story," *Journal of Policy Analysis and Management* 15:4 (1996) and Irene Lurie, "State Welfare Policy," in *The State of the States*, 4th ed, Carl Van Horn, ed. (Washington, DC: CQ Press, 2006).

3   See Mimi Abramovitz's review of *Race and the Politics of Welfare Reform*, Sanford F. Schram, Joe Soss and Richard C. Fording eds., in *Social Service Review* 79:2 (2005).

Among the states in the study, Governor John Engler of Michigan took the highest profile in reforming his state's welfare program. Engler rose to national prominence on the strength of his welfare reform proposals beginning in 1992 and his political success with this issue inspired activism by other governors. By 1996, through the initiative of governors or state welfare administrators, all four states had obtained waivers from the federal law. When the time came to implement TANF, all the governors associated themselves with their state's reforms. As Gais argues in analyzing the governance of welfare reform, "A striking feature of devolution has been the salient and often dominant role played by governors and top state executives."[4]

System-Wide Management Changes

TANF gave state leaders new flexibility to address the management challenges of implementing the law. The Clinton administration and Congress had attributed the failures of previous reforms partially to the management of welfare agencies, which they criticized as being unwilling to make the employment of their clients a driving goal and to alter their procedures and daily routines to emphasize work. To change the management of the welfare system, TANF placed fewer restrictions on the operations of state programs. Of particular importance, states were no longer required to operate welfare programs through a single welfare agency but could decentralize the administration of TANF to other organizations. TANF could be operated through any type of organization, including government, nonprofit, for-profit, and faith-based. In exchange for flexibility in management and program design, TANF held states accountable for meeting a higher work participation rate and rewarded them for performance in meeting other goals.

In response to these pressures and flexibility, state level officials in all four states adopted the policy goal of encouraging and supporting work for their TANF clients. With the exception of New York, state offi-

---

4   Thomas L. Gais, "Concluding Comments: Welfare Reform and Governance," in *Learning from Leaders, Welfare Reform Politics and Policy in Five Midwestern States*, Carol. S. Weissert, ed. (Albany, NY: Rockefeller Institute of Government, 2000), 174.

cials chose to begin pursuing this goal with a Work First process for TANF applicants. To further these work policies, all states designed a package of management changes to signal the new policy goal, to build the capacity to operate the new system, and to hold local agencies accountable for delivering its components.[5]

Organizational Structure and Resource Allocation

To signal the goals of work and economic self-sufficiency, two states changed the name of one or more organizations in their welfare system. Michigan changed the name of its welfare agency from the Department of Social Services to the Family Independence Agency. The local workforce agencies with responsibility for arranging employment services for TANF clients were named Michigan Works! agencies. In New York, the governor dismantled the Department of Social Services into several agencies, giving oversight for TANF to a new Office of Temporary and Disability Assistance. These largely symbolic name changes signaled that assistance was temporary because work was expected.

In addition to changing the name of the welfare agency, three state welfare agencies changed the job title of their eligibility worker. Michigan replaced the job title "Assistance Payment Worker" with the title "Family Independence Specialist," also giving these workers a slightly broader set of duties. The state welfare agency in Georgia created positions known as "Family Independence Case Managers" that combined the responsibilities formerly split among several specialized workers. The Texas welfare agency gave its eligibility workers the title "Texas Works Advisers," a purely symbolic change without any adjustment in duties.

More substantively, the ability of frontline workers to mandate employment for TANF clients depended critically on creating a supply of employment-related services exclusively for TANF clients.

---

5   For a discussion of similar management changes made in other states, see Karin Martinson and Pamela A. Holcomb, *Reforming Welfare, Institutional Change and Challenges*, Occasional Paper Number 60, Assessing the New Federalism (Washington, DC: The Urban Institute, July 2002).

Without an adequate supply of services, workers would simply be unable to mandate participation in employment activities. Creating a pool of services dedicated to TANF clients eliminated the possibility that service providers would reject TANF clients in favor of others perceived to be more attractive candidates. A pool of services offered by specific providers also permitted managers to develop routine procedures for workers to follow in referring clients to these services.

To create a pool of employment-related services, state leaders gave workforce agencies new funds and responsibilities to serve TANF clients. All the four states, to a greater or lesser degree, allocated TANF funds for employment activities directly to workforce organizations rather than welfare agencies. As described in Chapter 2, Michigan and Texas allocated funds to local workforce development boards, which directly or indirectly contracted with local agencies or firms to provide services for TANF clients. Georgia allocated funds to finance job search for TANF applicants to the local offices of the state Department of Labor. New York transferred funds and oversight for work activities to the state Department of Labor, which supervised the work activities of the county welfare agencies. Giving funds for employment services to workforce agencies whose core mission was to provide these services guaranteed that a pool of services was available to clients referred by the welfare agency.

Two features of the federal TANF legislation facilitated the increase in resources for employment-related purposes. Most importantly, the sharp drop in caseloads left states with surplus funds because TANF, as a block grant, was a fixed amount regardless of the state's expenditures for cash assistance. States reallocated this savings in cash assistance to their budgets for employment services, child care, and transportation. Reallocating the windfall to employment related services helped ameliorate the perennial problem of insufficient funds to impose a work requirement on everyone expected to work. States no longer needed to exempt large shares of their caseload from the work requirement due to a lack of capacity to serve them.

Second, TANF gave states more flexibility in purchasing services. Under prior federal law, welfare funds could not be used to purchase services that were "otherwise available on a nonreimbursable basis,"[6] that is, those services that governments made available to any low-income resident. These services were to be obtained through interagency "coordination," where the welfare agency negotiated agreements with other agencies to devote their resources to welfare clients. These provisions made the welfare agency dependent on the resources of other agencies and skewed the mix of services offered to welfare clients.[7] The TANF legislation did not contain these provisions, giving welfare systems more control in choosing the types of services, selecting the organizations to provide them, and imposing mechanisms to encourage performance on these organizations.

Although all states increased their spending for employment-related services, the states with high welfare benefit levels received a greater windfall and were able to spend more on these services than the low benefit states. The impact of the differences in expenditure levels between Michigan and Texas was especially evident because the states were similar in several respects, both requiring a Work First orientation for applicants and providing job search assistance for recipients through a decentralized workforce system. Staff in Michigan urged clients to work by offering transportation and child care assistance for both recipients and the working poor. Staff in Texas did not discuss transportation assistance as an inducement to work and exempted recipients with a child under age three from the work requirement, thereby avoiding the high cost of child care assistance for this group of children.

Mechanisms to Encourage Performance

Virtually all TANF funds allocated directly to local workforce organizations came with some form of accountability mechanism to encourage performance (Table 2-3). States allocated funds to purchase a narrow set of services and subjected local agencies to one or more performance goals in delivering them. The Georgia Department of Labor subjected their local offices to goals for job placements. Local contracts in Michi-

---

6   42 U.S.C. 685(b).
7   Hagen and Lurie, *Implementing JOBS: Initial State Choices,* and Hagen and Lurie, *Implementing JOBS: Progress and Promise.*

gan and Texas included performance goals such as the percent entering employment, the percent entering employment whose hourly wage rate is at least a specified amount, the percent employed at follow-up of 30, 60, or 90 days, and the average wage at follow-up. The New York Department of Labor allocated some funds on a performance basis, but most funds were allocated by the state welfare agency to county welfare agencies and did not contain performance goals. Similarly, the state welfare agency in Georgia did not impose performance goals on the funds allocated to local county agencies.

The activities of local workforce offices reflected these performance incentives. The workforce offices in Michigan placed all unemployed clients in job search, permitting education and training only for people who were already employed. The workforce offices in Texas gave primary attention to job search, although the Dallas offices permitted clients to attend its GED programs. The Georgia Department of Labor focused on job search and job placement. In contrast, the mix of services offered by the welfare agencies in Georgia and New York was broader, based more on an assessment of the client. In New York, the Suffolk County Department of Labor provided a wide range of employment and training services including job search, education, training, and work experience under a contract with the Suffolk County welfare agency that was not based on performance.

Project Zero in Michigan, which granted additional funds to sites for the purpose of employing the entire caseload, demonstrates the power of resources combined with a single performance goal. More than other states, workers in Michigan pressed clients to work with the promise of funds for child care, work clothes, and particularly transportation. At the time of the observations, Project Zero had already been effective in Hillsdale in employing clients and reducing caseloads substantially. In Wayne County, where Project Zero had been introduced more recently, workers in the workforce agencies frequently explained the availability of the extra services funded by Project Zero and the welfare agency created a Summer Enrichment Program for clients and their children providing virtually everything the family would need to participate, including child care, lunch, and door-to-door transportation.

The federal mandate for states to achieve a minimum rate of work participation among their caseload was putting more pressure on some welfare agencies than others at the time of the observations. The Michigan welfare agencies had no difficulty meeting the overall federal participation rate and had moved beyond it in taking on the goal of Project Zero, which was substantially more ambitious. In Texas, the state gave responsibility for meeting the participation rate to the workforce agencies (Table 2-3), where it was a primary measure driving their operations. The welfare agencies in Texas paid little attention to it. In New York, the welfare agency in Suffolk County, while formally responsible for meeting the participation rate, had in practice transferred this responsibility to the Department of Labor. As a result, the primary effect of the participation rate on the welfare agency was a set of procedures requiring workers to refer clients to the Department of Labor.

Not surprisingly, the welfare agencies feeling the pressure of the participation rate most were those that contracted with individual agencies for employment services and had responsibility for assessing clients and referring them to these services. All welfare agencies in Georgia were responsible for the work activities of clients after they completed job search with the Department of Labor, and in New York, the welfare agency in Albany County was responsible for the work activities of all clients (Table 2-3). Meeting the federal participation rate was a central goal of the welfare administrators in these agencies and they stressed this goal to supervisors and frontline workers.

The federal participation rate for two-parent families, which was about double the rate for single-parent families, was less of a driving force than the overall rate. Georgia did not try to meet the participation rate for this group, instead assisting them through a "separate state program" that was not subject to the federal work participation rate.[8] The Texas workforce agencies were not meeting the participation rate for two-parent families, a tiny share of the caseload, and the state later transferred them to the "separate state program." In Michigan, neither Wayne County nor Hillsdale County was meeting the higher participation rate for two-parent families, but the observations did not capture any special

---

8   A separate state program is financed by state funds, not by the federal TANF block grant.

initiatives for this group, perhaps because it was a small share of the caseload.

Under TANF, the federal participation rate motivated agencies to mandate work but, overall, it exerted less influence than the participation rate in the 1988 welfare reform legislation. TANF gave states credit for caseload reductions in calculating their participation rate, so the decrease in caseloads reduced the work participation rate that states actually needed to meet. But states could not initially predict the decrease in case-loads and the amount of the credit, leading them to pay some attention to the participation rate. As states learned when the rates were calculated, the credit reduced the minimum work participation rate standard dramati-cally; by 2000, it was only 5.2 percent in New York and was zero in the other states.[9] With credit for caseload reductions, all states in the study met the overall participation rate by a wide margin. States with difficulty meeting the participation rate for two-parent families simply transferred these families onto a "separate state program" not subject to the federal rules.

Investments in Information Systems

The observations of frontline workers revealed the importance of computerized information systems in determining eligibility and detect-ing fraud and, to a lesser degree, in monitoring clients' compliance with behavioral mandates. All states planned investments in these information systems in response to TANF, although the pace of change was more rapid in some states than others. Some of these investments were moti-vated by other management changes, such as the contracts with workforce offices and the mechanisms to encourage performance.

Texas was particularly ambitious in its efforts to promote inter-agency information sharing. At the time of TANF implementation, Texas was creating TWIST — The Workforce Information System of Texas — to link the databases of all the state's workforce programs, including the work program for TANF clients and the Child Care Management Sys-

---

9   U.S. Department of Health and Human Services, *Temporary Assistance for Needy Families Program Information Memorandum*, TANF-ACF-IM-2002-1, February 14, 2002.

tem. TWIST gave workers in the workforce agency the ability to read and enter selected items in the database of the welfare agency and gave workers in the welfare agencies the ability to read selected items in the workforce database. Workers in the welfare agency already had access to the databases of the state Attorney General's Office, the Health Department, and the Social Security Administration. As it was implementing TANF, the Texas welfare agency purchased information about clients from a private data broker, primarily to prevent fraud in the food stamp program. In another effort to reduce fraud, Texas had recently invested in a system to take photographs and finger-images of all applicants.

The Georgia welfare agency had just created a new computer system, one that required workers to enter information into the system as they interviewed clients, and was training workers to use it. Workers used the system primarily to determine eligibility for TANF, food stamps, and Medicaid. Unlike Texas, the system had no linkage to the database of the workforce agency. Bibb County perceived the state system to be insufficient for its needs and had developed two databases on its own, one to track the client's work-related activities and another to track the placement of children in child care.

Administrators in Michigan and New York talked less about current developments in their computer information systems, and these states appeared to be behind Texas and Georgia. Welfare workers in Michigan could read some information on the workforce agency's database but the systems were not linked. New York had invested in equipment to take photographs and finger-images of applicants but was still relying on an old system for other eligibility functions. Administrators in Michigan and New York acknowledged shortcomings in their states' information systems and referred to plans for improvements.

In summary, these system-wide management changes pushed local welfare systems to encourage clients to work and decrease their reliance on welfare. By using the workforce agencies to deliver employment services, giving them additional resources, and subjecting them to performance goals, the states created conditions making the employment of welfare clients a feasible goal for local welfare systems. This organizational framework, together with the federal work participation rates, placed pressure on local welfare administrators to accept their state's

goal of encouraging and supporting work by TANF clients. Computerized information systems tightened eligibility and improved coordination
among agencies. Reinforcing the work goal was the time limit on TANF
benefits, which gave welfare administrators a sense of responsibility to
prepare their clients for a life without welfare.

Management Changes
Within the Welfare Agencies

Under these pressures, welfare administrators faced the challenge of
changing the behavior of their frontline staff to focus attention on these
goals. The failure of previous welfare reforms to encourage and support
work had been attributed in part to the behavior of frontline staff, who were
criticized for using excessive discretion to exempt people from the work
requirement. This frustration with the welfare bureaucracy was sufficiently
strong that TANF allowed governments to contract with any type of public
or private organization to deliver TANF services, including cash assistance. When the TANF law was signed, Texas immediately sought to pri-
vatize its entire welfare operation, including cash assistance, and was
halted only because the administration of cash assistance was tied to that of
Medicaid and food stamps, which could not be privatized. Welfare administrators would need to find ways to focus the attention of their own staff on
moving clients into work and decreasing their reliance on welfare.

In the years leading up to TANF, scholars argued that major management changes were needed to change the behavior of workers in the
welfare agencies. Bane drew upon her experience as a welfare administrator in New York to argue that fundamental organizational change was
necessary to refocus the welfare system on emphasizing work instead of
providing cash assistance. Bane used the term "organizational culture" to
express the depth of the required change, calling for "a dramatic shift
from an organizational culture in which the dominant ethos is centered
around eligibility and compliance to one in which clients and welfare
workers are engaged in the common tasks of finding work, arranging
child care, and so on."[10] After examining the management of the WIN

---

10 Kane and Bane, "The Context for Welfare Reform," 2.

program in Massachusetts, Behn concluded that strong leadership could be effective in motivating staff to focus on clients' employment. Leaders must repeatedly emphasize the agency's goals and what each individual in the organization must do to accomplish these goals. While highlighting the importance of leadership, Behn recognized that leadership alone was insufficient to implement a policy — changes in administrative systems and procedures were important, too.[11] Which of these management approaches, if any, did local welfare administrators adopt to drive their staff to mandate and support employment-related activities?

Communicating the Work Goal to Welfare Agency Staff

Local administrators communicated the importance of employment physically — by banners and signs posted in the welfare agency that exhorted clients to work. These visible expressions of the work goal, along with the new names of the welfare agencies and job titles, announced to both clients and staff that the agency was not just distributing cash assistance.

In all local welfare offices, welfare administrators verbally communicated the goals of TANF to staff in meetings and in training sessions. Administrators in Georgia and Texas, like welfare administrators around the country, announced they were seeking to change the "culture" of their agencies to emphasize work. Every site gave workers some sort of training about new rules and procedures under TANF, like time limits for TANF recipients, referrals of applicants to the workforce agency, the Personal Responsibility Agreement, participation rates, and new rules about food stamps and Medicaid. The training ranged from in-house, informal, on-the-job-training in some sites to more formal, state-sponsored training in others. Because most of the training revolved around rules and regulations, its focus was predominantly on the details of determining eligibility for assistance.

The most visible effort to give frontline workers new skills unrelated to eligibility processing was in Michigan, where the state offered "Strength-Based, Solution-Focused Training," which was geared toward

---

11 Behn, *Leadership Counts*.

training staff to do needs assessments of clients and to be more "customer focused." But workers were skeptical about the value of the training, arguing that putting the skills into practice was difficult and took too much time. Moreover, as the encounters illustrate, they had little in the way of "solutions" to offer clients besides the limited services of the welfare and workforce agencies.

Although the encounters showed that staff understood the importance of work for welfare clients under TANF, they also showed that the primary task of the welfare agencies continued to be determining eligibility for assistance and doing so with few errors. Accuracy in determining eligibility and benefits remained an important goal to welfare administrators because the Quality Control system, while no longer operating for TANF, penalized states with excessive errors in administering food stamps. Because local offices administered the programs together, increasing or maintaining accuracy in administering TANF continued to be a high priority. The welfare agencies in Texas were particularly preoccupied with reducing error rates, with supervisors reviewing the computer screens filled in by the workers before authorizing assistance, but all the states were paying attention to errors. Local welfare administrators pursued the new work goals set by the states, but they did not discard the old eligibility goals.

Perhaps most importantly, administrators conveyed the importance of the work goal by inserting Work First into the routine procedures for determining eligibility. Changes in procedures demonstrated a change in the goals of the agencies. The increased capacity of the welfare system to offer employment-related services and the increased funds for child care assistance and transportation were further evidence that TANF required work. Even though determining eligibility was the primary task of the welfare agency, these substantive changes in procedures and resources were evidence of a new goal.

Routinized Procedures

At the front lines of the welfare agencies, administrators needed to control the behavior of frontline workers to ensure they referred applicants to Work First. The discretion of workers in determining eligibility for cash assistance had been tightly constrained for decades before TANF, but referral to work-related activities had been left to the judgment of workers. In implementing TANF, administrators needed to limit discretion in this area also. They did so by developing routine procedures for workers to follow in referring clients to the Work First agencies, procedures that structured and thereby constrained the behavior of both workers and clients.

The procedures were essentially the same in Georgia, Michigan, and Texas, the three states adopting Work First. When a client applied for assistance, the worker pended the application, or put it on hold, until the applicant attended Work First and the worker obtained proof of attendance. With proof of attendance, the worker finished authorizing assistance. This process was a way to influence the behavior of the client, who could not receive assistance unless she attended Work First, but it was also a way to influence the behavior of the worker. Because the applicant could not receive assistance unless the worker referred her to Work First, the application created pressure for the referral.

As shown by the observations, referral to Work First was highly routinized in all sites, entailing little collection of information about the applicant's ability to attend the required activities. Workers did not assess whether the applicant was able to attend Work First, but simply explained that referral to Work First was part of the standard process of applying for assistance. Some workers explained this early in the eligibility interview, while others explained this near the end. During the course of collecting information to determine eligibility, workers learned whether the few policies granting exemptions applied to the applicant. Because these policies rarely applied, they generally told applicants they must comply with the Work First mandate before authorizing assistance. Workers in New York could not grant exemptions until applicants went to specialized agencies for an assessment of their employability, removing this decision from the judgment of eligibility workers.

With accuracy still a goal for the welfare agencies, Work First was only one component of an eligibility process that continued to be routinized and stringent. The states' computerized information systems contributed to this routinization, demanding that workers collect the numerous items of information needed to complete the application for assistance and preventing them from taking shortcuts that would reduce the time spent determining eligibility. This was particularly true in Georgia and Texas, where computers sat on the desks of eligibility workers and prompted them to enter information. Even in New York, where welfare was administered by the counties, eligibility workers used the state's computer system and were controlled by its demands for information. A stringent process of fraud detection was observed to be a routine feature of the eligibility process for all applicants in New York and Texas. Routine home visits in Michigan, while not solely for the purpose of detecting fraud, gave workers the opportunity to scrutinize the client's home for expensive consumption goods and unreported household members and assets. While discussion of fraud was less routine in Georgia, it was frequent enough to indicate the welfare agencies operated some sort of fraud detection system.

In addition to computers, the behavior of workers was influenced by scripts and forms. In Michigan, the state welfare agency wrote a script for its workers to use during the orientation for applicants at the workforce offices. Workers did not always adhere to the script, but the variation in the orientations in Michigan was far less than the variation in other states. The Personal Responsibility Agreements in Georgia, Michigan, and Texas required workers to inform clients about the state's mandates. Other forms prompted workers to explain rules to clients, like the family cap in Georgia. Workers sometimes just asked the client to sign the form without explaining it to them, so the forms had limited success as a method of communicating information to the client. But the forms at least served as a method of reminding the worker to mention the mandate or rule. Moreover, workers then placed the signed forms in the client's folder, where a supervisor could review them to monitor the worker's behavior.

The repetitive explanations of complex rules and systems led workers to use acronyms and jargon in speaking with clients, a response to routinization that was universal across the sites. Workers used acronyms like WIA, TCC, and FEDS without spelling them out and terms like Work First, job readiness, assessment, and budgeting income without describing them. Few workers explained the earnings disregard and even fewer explained it accurately. They referred to numeric codes for the client's eligibility, employability, and other personal characteristics.

Medicaid had the most complex rules, with unexplained references to a spend down, transitional Medicaid, TP55, and other terms meaningless to the uninitiated.

In short, the demands of these procedures left welfare workers with little discretion in determining eligibility for assistance. They collected and verified information, entered it into the computer system, asked applicants for their signature on numerous forms, and explained the rules governing assistance. The computer system determined the family's eligibility and calculated the amount of the benefit, often followed by a supervisor's review of the entire case for accuracy. The work mandate was a relatively small component of this process, an add-on to the complex and time-consuming job of determining eligibility, which continued to be the primary task of the welfare offices in all the sites. Yet despite being a small component of the process, it was hard-wired into the process and difficult to ignore.

Referring clients to services after they became TANF recipients was a less routinized process, but workers had limited discretion in choosing work activities or supportive services. With state policy giving the choice of a child care provider to parents, very few workers were observed using discretion to refer a client to a specific child care provider. Except in Michigan and Albany County, workers had limited transportation choices to offer their clients. In Georgia, Michigan, and Texas, a limited array of job search, education, and training programs were arranged specifically for TANF clients and few clients were referred to services offered to the general population. This meant that the typical task of the worker was to decide which of the limited array of work activities was best for the client or which activity the client preferred, a process that typically took only a few minutes. In New York, where the range of available work activities was broader, workers engaged in a fuller discussion of their clients' backgrounds and interests before referring them to an activity.

Workers gave clients extra, more individualized attention when clients mentioned health problems or disabilities, either their own or their children's, that interfered with their ability to work. They also gave extra attention to problems raised by crime and, in all states but Texas, to domestic violence and substance abuse. Mentioning these difficulties prompted workers to ascertain the nature of the problem and ask for documentation or, less commonly, to refer clients to specialized staff who could assess their situation more completely. The assessment would determine whether they were unable to work and whether a referral to another program, most typically SSI, would be a possible alternative to welfare. Workers also gave clients individualized attention when they were out of compliance with the work mandates and threatened with a sanction.

Workers in the welfare offices often learned a great deal about the personal and family problems facing their clients, but they generally did not advise or counsel their clients about personal and family issues. The closest they came to counseling was to encourage their clients to work or to prepare for work by going to school or training. In Georgia, where the state required welfare workers to discuss family planning, workers told clients to learn about family planning services. They generally discussed family planning in the context of the Personal Responsibility Agreement, presenting the need to learn about family planning as a rule rather than as advice or counsel about a personal issue. Problem-solving with clients was primarily to resolve problems related to TANF and other public programs like Medicaid, SSI, and housing assistance or to refer clients to community services like food banks, discounts on utilities, and other private charities.

In discussing topics other than Work First, job search, and education and training, workers did little substantive advising or assessing. When conversations about topics such as child care and Medicaid were coded as advising or assessing, workers were generally explaining rules. Although activities with these codes were expected to be individualized, and were labeled as "individualized" in Table 3-4, a reading of the conversation indicates that many workers' activities that were coded as advising or assessing were, in fact, routinized explanations of rules.

Within states, the size of the site's caseload influenced the behavior of workers, both in welfare and workforce offices. In Michigan, workers in rural Hillsdale County and suburban Macomb County had more time to spend with clients than workers in Wayne County (Detroit), giving them more detailed explanations of the rules and more individual attention in discussing their problems and interests. In Texas, workers in the

Denton workforce office explained rules more clearly than those in Dallas and, because group meetings were smaller, could give individual clients more attention. In Georgia, the Bibb County welfare agency monitored its clients more rigorously than the welfare offices in Fulton County (Atlanta) and, with child care and work experience on site, appeared able to enforce the work mandate more widely.

Workers in Wayne County and New York — sites with large caseloads in high benefit states — treated clients with less patience and sympathy than workers in the other sites. Clients were also more recalcitrant in these sites, occasionally provoking angry responses in workers. These behaviors were particularly evident in Wayne, where observers used tape recorders. Workers in the low benefit states generally treated their clients with more respect than those in high benefit states. In Texas, where observers also used tape recorders, workers were respectful and clients more passive. Workers in Georgia were also respectful and sometimes expressed warmth toward their clients, who also tended toward passivity.

In the Albany County welfare office, the only site where workers were responsible for both determining eligibility and referring clients to a work activity, workers appeared to exercise more discretion than anywhere else. The office gave them authority to use discretion in assigning clients to a work activity and also in granting diversion payments to applicants. In addition, workers appeared to bend the rules in calculating benefits, using unsanctioned discretion. One worker told a client she would delay entering the client's earnings into the system, explaining that the client had not been working long. Another worker told a client she was budgeting her "loosely" because her pay was sporadic. Although it is difficult to attribute cause and effect, it is worth noting that the rate of decline in caseloads between 1995 and 2000 was lower in Albany than in any other site.

Leadership and Culture Change?

These routine procedures, computerized information systems, scripts, and forms strongly influenced workers to implement TANF policies. The role of leadership as described by Behn was weaker. To the extent local welfare agency administrators promoted the design and introduction of these tools for controlling the behavior of workers observed at the front lines, they acted as leaders. But with the system-wide policy and management changes supporting local administrators, introducing these changes did not require extraordinary leadership. Without judging the welfare administrators in the 11 sites, the likelihood that they all possessed unusually strong leadership skills is low. The one clear exception was the welfare administrator in Bibb, a community leader who used her negotiating skills to surround the welfare agency with a satellite office of the Department of Labor, a child care center, a teen center, and a building for basic education.

Bane's call for changing the "culture" of welfare offices from a focus on eligibility and compliance to a focus on work and self-sufficiency was echoed by welfare administrators around the country.[12] In Georgia and Texas, administrators adopted this language in describing a vision of their welfare agency where the employment of clients would be a primary goal. In practice, the encounters leave little doubt that TANF was successful in causing the welfare system as a whole to give more attention to work and to promote self-sufficiency. The question addressed here is whether a change in organizational culture was one of the management tools that produced this transformation.

The term "organizational culture" is a slippery concept that lacks a single definition. Scholars who have wrestled with the concept use terms like "the shared philosophies, ideologies, values, assumptions, beliefs, expectations, attitudes and norms that knit a community together."[13] Under this definition, the behavior of the members of an organization may change without a change in the organization's culture. While the study did not systematically examine organizational culture at this deep level, the survey of frontline workers did ask them what they perceived to be their agency's goals.

In the minds of frontline workers in the welfare offices, the eligibility goals were more important to their agency than requiring and encour-

---

12 For example, Thomas Corbett, "Changing the culture of welfare," *Focus*, Institute for Research on Poverty, University of Wisconsin-Madison, 16:2 (Winter 1994-1995).

13 R.H. Kilman, M.J. Saxton, and R. Serpa, "Issues in Understanding and Changing Culture," *California Management Review* 28:2 (1986); Irene Lurie and Norma M. Riccucci, "Changing the 'Culture' of Welfare Offices," *Administration & Society* 34:6 (2003).

aging work. The survey of these workers found they perceived the traditional goals of welfare agencies, namely determining eligibility for benefits accurately and in a timely manner, to be most important to the welfare agency.[14] This is not surprising, considering that 52 percent of the encounters in the welfare agency were for the primary purpose of determining eligibility for TANF, food stamps, or Medicaid. Accuracy in determining eligibility was still important for the Quality Control system in food stamps. Determining eligibility in a timely manner, or simply getting the job done, was still the major task of these workers. Because workers performed much of their work in the context of determining eligibility for assistance, the goals of the eligibility process ranked highest.

Their perception that eligibility determination was the agency's most important goal suggests stability in the organizational culture of welfare agencies, indicating that the attention given to Work First and other work-related activities was not the product of a change in the organization culture. Supported by the policy changes in TANF and the system-wide changes in management and resources, local managers could change the behavior of their workers by stating new goals and specifying new procedures. As Behn pointed out, administrative systems and procedures can also be effective management tools.

---

14 Norma M. Riccucci, Marcia K. Meyers, Irene Lurie, and Jun Seop Han, "The Implementation of Welfare Reform Policy: The Role of Public Managers in Front-Line Practices," *Public Administration Review* 64:4 (2004).

11

Conclusion

Prior to TANF, no federal welfare reform to encourage employment among recipients had been fully implemented by the states. This history of implementation failure led me to expect that states would implement TANF on paper, adjusting their welfare program enough to qualify for their share of federal funds, but would achieve little reform at the front lines where welfare policy is delivered. After observing conversations between staff and clients during the first half of 2000, I conclude that TANF's goals regarding employment did reach the front lines. When TANF ended the entitlement to welfare, states did not explicitly deny applicants entry to the welfare system but they imposed a work mandate as a condition of entry. This work-related mandate on applicants, imposed with few exceptions, became an embodiment of TANF's provision that welfare is no longer an entitlement.

From the perspective of the front lines of the welfare system, the staff practices that appear to have contributed most to the decline in caseloads were the work mandates and increasingly strict eligibility processes. Although it is impossible to measure the magnitude of their impact on caseloads, these practices could have accounted for much of their sharp decline. This final chapter summarizes the observations that support this conclusion, reflects on the study's methodology, and concludes with a brief discussion of the impact of TANF on poor families, who received no explicit attention in this implementation study.

Policy as Delivered and the Decline in Caseloads

The sharp decline in welfare caseloads after 1994 resulted from a confluence of two forces: federal, state, and local policies pushing families away from the welfare system and a booming economy pulling people into jobs. With both forces acting simultaneously, trying to measure the contributions of each is a difficult exercise. If I had not examined the front lines of the welfare system, I might have given most of the credit to the economy, doubting that local welfare systems could have implemented the policies sufficiently for them to account for a large share of the caseload reduction. But observing the front lines gave a vivid view of how local systems were using the provisions of TANF to push families away from welfare, convincing me that welfare systems were exerting a powerful force.

When TANF capped federal funding for welfare and declared that welfare was not an entitlement, outright denial of assistance to families who were financially eligible became a possibility. Some states had denied welfare to mothers who were financially eligible for assistance in the years before the U.S. Supreme Court declared welfare to be a statutory entitlement, raising the possibility that they might do so again. Waiting lists for child care and housing assistance set a contemporary precedent for denying assistance to families that are financially eligible. Even if states did not restrict entry to the welfare system by otherwise eligible families, time limits allowed them to hasten the exit of eligible families.

The observations revealed that workers did not invoke the lack of an entitlement to restrict access to cash assistance. They routinely mentioned the time limit, often using it to urge clients to prepare themselves for a life without welfare by finding a job or improving their job skills. But the rapid decline in caseloads occurring in Georgia, Michigan, and New York during the first half of 2000, when most of the observations were made, cannot be explained by the imposition of a time limit. The time limit in Georgia and New York did not trigger terminations until after 2000, and Michigan did not impose a time limit. In Texas, the time limit for adults was short enough for some to have exhausted their assistance, but the 60-month time limit for children had not yet triggered case closures.

The TANF rule that workers explained most often was the requirement to work. For TANF recipients, the federal law narrowed the exemptions from participation in a work-related activity and mandated participation as soon as the recipient was ready for work. For TANF applicants, the lack of an entitlement allowed welfare agencies to impose a work-related mandate during the application process and deny assistance to anyone who failed to comply. In all the states examined in this study, state level officials supported the TANF rule and devoted resources to increasing their state's capacity to mandate work. Increased capacity in workforce agencies and more funds for child care and transportation meant that, unlike previous reforms, a lack of services did not undermine the work requirement by driving staff to be lenient in granting exemptions.

The capacity to impose a work-related mandate on applicants for assistance was apparent at the front lines of all the sites. Work First, consisting of an orientation at a workforce agency in Michigan and Texas and a period of job search in Georgia, was a routine part of the application process. Welfare agency staff did not assess whether the applicant was able to attend Work First, but simply explained that attendance was part of the standard process of applying for assistance. Constrained by strict procedures, staff rarely exercised discretion to exempt applicants from Work First or, in New York, another immediate work activity. Significantly, no workers said they were exempting an applicant due to a lack of capacity at the workforce agency.

Most welfare agencies imposed the work mandate more consistently on applicants than on recipients. Once families were on assistance, workers gave more scrutiny to their problems with employment and exempted some recipients from work. Recipients who were able to work received more individualized treatment and were referred to the limited array of work activities that had been arranged for TANF clients. The welfare offices in Fulton County (Atlanta) and Wayne County (Detroit) had not yet engaged all recipients in a work activity, as indicated by observations of assessments of long-term recipients who were not employed. But under the pressure of the time limit in Georgia and the Project Zero performance goal in Michigan, the agencies were learning whether these recipients faced problems preventing employment or could be pushed into the labor force.

Prerequisites to mandating work were the capacity to finance child care for TANF clients and a sufficient supply of child care slots. The infusion of funds for child care that accompanied TANF was evident when staff assured applicants and recipients they would receive child care assistance if they worked. Lack of money for child care was no longer a reason, or an excuse, for not working. However, the conversations also revealed that Michigan was the only state offering child care assistance to all the working poor, including families not on TANF. Conversations in Georgia and Texas mentioned waiting lists for child care assistance for low-income families not receiving TANF, and several administrators believed that some TANF applicants were applying in order to receive assistance with child care. The supply of child care slots for healthy children appeared to be sufficient, particularly during standard business hours, but slots were less plentiful for children with physical or mental problems and for parents who worked during other times or who lived in suburban and rural areas.

In summary, workers in all the sites routinely mandated participation in an employment-related activity and offered to provide welfare clients with child care assistance while they participated. After decades of haphazardly enforced work requirements, the consistency of the mandate to participate in a work-related activity was a major accomplishment of TANF. Workers were unfailing in enforcing Work First as a condition of eligibility for assistance. Participation in Work First delivered a clear message to applicants: Welfare was not an entitlement and, sooner or later, recipients would need to find employment.

Welfare staff delivered this message during a strict eligibility process that used sophisticated computer systems to verify eligibility, monitor behavior, and detect fraud. Eligibility determination continued to be the focus of their attention, in part because the quality control system in the food stamp program demanded accuracy. Considering the public attitudes that led the nation to end the welfare entitlement and impose a time limit on assistance, it is not surprising that the welfare system would continue to restrict access by the older method of applying the eligibility rules strictly. The fixed amount of the TANF block grant gave states another reason to apply eligibility rules rigorously, since they received no additional federal funds if they allowed caseloads to increase and they reaped a windfall if caseloads decreased.

While eligibility workers across the sites used Work First to deliver the same message, the goals of Work First and the package of policies and processes created by the states to mandate employment varied. Work First could serve two policy goals: increasing employment and diverting applicants from welfare. Both goals were achieved simultaneously when applicants found a job that paid enough to make them ineligible for welfare, thereby diverting them from the program. But only the second goal was achieved if a Work First program diverted applicants from welfare but they failed to find a job. Another possibility, one alluded to by administrators who spoke of "miracle jobs" found by applicants just as they were required to participate in Work First, is that applicants were already working when they applied for welfare but were not reporting their income. Yet a fourth possibility is that applicants did not comprehend the imperative to attend Work First and were denied assistance without understanding why. Because the diversion of applicants could worsen the economic well being of families, the difference in the states' emphasis on these two goals was a critical dimension of their TANF programs.

Michigan and Texas were at opposite ends of the spectrum in their emphasis on these goals even though their Work First approach was similar, consisting of an orientation at the workforce agency for all TANF applicants. Michigan sought to increase the employment of all low-income families, whether or not on welfare. Job search assistance was the primary service provided by the workforce offices. Child care and transportation assistance were available to TANF applicants and recipients and also to low-income families who were working but not receiving welfare. Once on welfare, the earnings disregard provided a financial incentive to work and, while not explained routinely, was built into the computer system that calculated benefits. The welfare offices used sanctions to enforce work, but workers met with clients to give them the opportunity to come into compliance with the work mandate.

Texas, in contrast, adopted Work First as a way of diverting applicants from assistance in order to reduce the caseload. The welfare agency offered no child care or transportation assistance to help applicants attend the workforce orientation, making the orientation a hurdle in the application process. At the orientation, workers told applicants they could qualify for child care assistance if they took a job immediately and withdrew their application. Like Michigan, job search assistance was the primary service provided by the workforce offices but, unlike Michigan, workers in Texas never discussed the earnings disregard, telling clients they would be ineligible for assistance if they worked. Once on welfare, transportation and child care were available to TANF recipients in a work activity but the state did not assist low-income families with transportation and devoted sufficient resources to child care to assist only a fraction of all low-income families. Sanctions were imposed on recipients without a conciliation process and, perhaps for this reason, the rate of sanctions was high.

Georgia, like Texas, adopted Work First as a way of diverting applicants from assistance, operating a job search program for applicants that created a high hurdle during the application process. But unlike Work First in Texas, job search assistance in Georgia was designed not only to divert applicants from welfare but also to help them find work. Applicants met with staff at the Department of Labor to learn about available jobs, and the welfare agencies offered child care and transportation assistance for applicants searching for work. Despite the full-family sanction in state policy, welfare agencies made efforts to avoid imposing sanctions by their conciliation process.

Texas was an outlier among the four states in its efforts to limit welfare use. Policies to divert applicants were explicit, information systems to detect applicant fraud were the most sophisticated, and the sanctioning process offered clients the least protection against misunderstandings and errors. The time limit on adults was the shortest of the four states and the welfare system's responses to clients' problems like substance abuse and domestic violence were minimal. These efforts to limit welfare use mirrored the state's low benefit levels, which themselves made welfare unattractive. Texas paid a three-person family a maximum monthly benefit of $201, compared to $280 in Georgia, $459 in Wayne County, and $703 in Suffolk County. TANF in Texas was so different from TANF in

Michigan and New York that they can hardly be considered the same program.

The diversity and complexity of state programs complicate efforts to estimate the relative importance of the various aspects of TANF that contributed to the sharp decline in welfare caseloads. From the perspective of the front lines, however, the single most important factor appears to be the restricted access to welfare by mandating a work activity, whether the goal of the mandate was employment or diversion.

Reflections on the Methodology

Few studies of policy implementation observe the point of service delivery. This is no accident. Observing conversations between people and analyzing their content is labor intensive, and methods for analyzing qualitative data are less developed than those for analyzing quantitative data.[1] For researchers who are considering using this approach, I will point out several aspects of the method that could be improved by future studies. This section first discusses the selection and size of the sample, the technology for recording the conversation, and the coding of the conversation. It then discusses the strengths of this approach for learning about policy as delivered.

In selecting the encounters for observation, the objective was to obtain a representative picture of the activities of all types of frontline workers in their face-to-face contact with clients. All types of frontline workers, not just those determining eligibility, potentially have the power to influence the experience of clients coming to the welfare system. According to several of the administrators interviewed in preparation for the observations, even clerks in the reception areas could provide information that encouraged or discouraged families from applying for welfare and other assistance.

---

1   Two useful volumes for qualitative analysis are John Lofland and Lyn H. Lofland, *Analyzing Social Settings, A Guide to Qualitative Observation and Analysis*, 3rd ed. (Belmont, CA: Wadsworth Publishing Company, 1995), and Matthew B. Miles and A. Michael Huberman, *Qualitative Data Analysis,* 2nd ed. (Thousand Oaks, CA: Sage, 1994).

The first step in selecting the encounters was to obtain a roster of workers in each site listed by job description, and to survey a sample of workers in each job position to learn how much time they spent in face-to-face contact with clients per week. With this information, it was possible to estimate the total amount of time workers in each job position spent with clients and the total for each job description as a percent of the total in the site. This distribution was then used to calculate a quota of hours of observations of workers in each job description. Encounters became part of the study when the workers being observed met with clients.

Clients were neither selected prior to the observations, nor were they observed again except by chance. Because clients commonly made multiple visits to the welfare and workforce offices, workers had multiple opportunities to collect information, explain rules, and engage in the other activities analyzed here. If a topic was not discussed during a particular encounter, it might have been discussed during a prior or subsequent visit. Without information about other visits, the observed frequency of discussion of a topic could be lower than the actual frequency over all the client's visits. This means that the observed frequencies presented in the tables must be interpreted as minimum estimates of the actual frequencies.

Alternatively, the study could have selected a sample of clients and followed them over time. As the sample flowed through the paths of the system, clients would encounter workers in all job positions. Although attrition from the sample would occur as clients left the welfare system, workers in all job positions would be observed if the sample were sufficiently large. With this approach, it would be possible to observe the client's entire treatment by the welfare system and to learn whether a particular topic was discussed with the client at any time. The observed frequencies of discussion of topics would equal the actual frequencies. The disadvantage of this approach is its higher cost. Observers would need to be stationed in the offices at all times to observe subsequent visits, which are often unpredictable, and would need to remain in the offices over an extended period to observe all phases of the treatment.

The size of the sample, 969 encounters, was large in some ways but small in others. It was a large sample for the labor-intensive tasks of qualitative analysis, requiring over 2,000 hours of work by coders and many hours by me. The sample was also large for the encounters taking place for the primary purpose of applying for TANF, food stamps, or Medicaid, ranging from 36 to 50 percent of the encounters in states. The sampling procedure undersampled the time of workers in job descriptions with many contact hours with clients and oversampled the time of workers in jobs with few contact hours, but considering the similarities in the conversations of eligibility workers, an even smaller sample of encounters with them would have provided sufficient information. At the other extreme, too few exit interviews with clients leaving welfare were observed to understand what information was given to them or to draw any conclusions except that few clients had formal exit interviews, indicating this is not a reliable opportunity for conveying important information to them. A larger sample of encounters for the purpose of conciliation and sanctioning would also have been warranted considering the complexity of the issues discussed. Making sense of the workers' discussion of Medicaid would also have required a larger sample.

Using tape recorders during the observations of the encounters produced a more detailed record of the conversation than handwritten notes, as indicated by the frequencies of the topic and activity codes. Permission to use tape recorders had been requested from welfare administrators in all the states, but those in Georgia and New York were reluctant to grant permission, perhaps expecting that verbatim transcripts would raise criticisms of their agency. Their reluctance was understandable, but the data collected by tape recorders did not paint a more negative picture of the agencies than the data collected by handwritten notes. To the contrary, the taped conversation showed more comprehensive explanations of the rules, more justification for the behavior of the workers, and more information about the workers' efforts to deal with their client's circumstances. If administrators anticipated that verbatim transcripts would place their agency in a less favorable light than handwritten notes, their concerns were unwarranted.

Coding the conversation during the encounters was a trial for everyone, both the coders and me. Although the graduate student coders were trained and monitored carefully, they did not have the in-depth understanding of the welfare system needed to recognize all the features of TANF that should have been coded. When this became apparent, a former welfare caseworker was hired to read all the encounters and improve the accuracy of the topic codes. In addition, the use of five coders, while intended to speed the coding process, substantially reduced the reliability of the activity codes. Even if a single person had applied the activity codes, choosing among 34 codes to characterize an activity might have been too difficult a task. Further research could refine the codes used here to make more reliable distinctions among the activities of workers.

Despite imperfections, this study has the strength of quantifying the practices of workers, thereby permitting comparisons of the amount of attention given to one topic versus another. The frequencies in Tables 3-3a and 3-3b are powerful evidence that the welfare agencies gave selective attention to the provisions of TANF, focusing the attention of workers on promoting job preparation and work. Promoting marriage, reducing out-of-wedlock pregnancies, and encouraging the formation and maintenance of two-parent families received little or no attention. The frequent discussion of participation requirements and the scant attention to the earnings disregard, one-time diversion assistance, and the earned income credit shows that workers discussed mandates far more than financial incentives.

Observing the front lines of welfare agencies during this extraordinary period in the history of the welfare system was personally satisfying. Studying the implementation of the JOBS program had made me a skeptic about the likelihood that TANF would be implemented, but seeing first hand what was happening on the ground was persuasive. Observing workers was also satisfying because it demystified the processes inside welfare offices, showing how routine procedures, scripts, forms, and computer systems structured the activities of workers. Finally, I found the conversation between the workers and clients to be endlessly interesting, which, considering the amount of time I spent reading them, was a blessing.

TANF and Poor Families

The successful implementation of a work mandate and the decline in caseloads says little about the impact of TANF on poor families. The contentious partisan politics that produced TANF did not give systematic attention to the immediate impact of the legislation on poor families, exposing them to an increased risk of poverty of unknown magnitude. Considering the potential power of the fundamental changes in the law to harm the well being of children, it was reckless legislation. My doubts that TANF would be implemented were matched by my fears that poor families would suffer if it were.

Fortunately, the risk that TANF would throw many families into poverty has not materialized. As welfare caseloads fell following TANF, the rate of poverty among female headed families with children under 18 years also fell, declining from 41.9 percent in 1996 to 33.0 percent in 2000.[2] While the 33.0 percent poverty rate was still high in absolute terms, it was the lowest rate on record. The rate of poverty increased during the recession that began in 2001 but it did not approach its pre-TANF level. Studies of families that left welfare show that about 60 percent of adults were employed at some point during the first 13 weeks off welfare and over 70 percent began to work during their first year off welfare.[3] But their employment was frequently unstable and wages were generally low, so that many of these families remained poor. Families where adults were not employed after leaving welfare relied on an often unstable mix of support from family and friends, absent parents, and private charities.[4] For families still on welfare, the time limit had the salutary effect of directing the attention of some states to the underlying problems that prevented them from working.

In focusing resources on reducing welfare caseloads, states reallocated their savings in cash assistance to their budgets for child care, transportation, and other services to support work. Maintaining caseloads at low levels will require a continuing allocation of resources to these services. As seen in the four states examined here, the lack of funds for child care and transportation were the most common barriers to work among welfare applicants and recipients, and the ability of the welfare system to

2   U.S. Census Bureau, *Historical Poverty Tables*, http://www.census.gov/hhes/poverty/histpov/hstpov4.html.

3   Gregory Acs and Pamela Loprest, *Leaving Welfare, Employment and Well-Being of Families that Left Welfare in the Post-Entitlement Era* (Kalamazoo, MI: W. E. Upjohn Institute for Employment Research, 2004).

4   Sheila R. Zedlewski and Sandi Nelson with Kathryn Edin et al., *Families Coping Without Earnings or Government Cash Assistance* (Washington, DC: The Urban Institute, 2003).

offer families assistance to pay for these supportive services was a pre-requisite to mandating work. Because the cost of these supportive services often exceeds the cost of simply paying a mother to stay home with her children, reducing caseloads does not necessarily reduce costs. Moreover, without continuing expenditures on Medicaid and food stamps, families relying on the earnings of low-wage workers are likely to have less total income than those relying on welfare.

Moving families off welfare into employment changes the form of the subsidy to low-wage families from cash assistance to assistance with child care and transportation, but it does not eliminate the need for a subsidy. As long as families must rely on low-wage jobs, particularly those lacking health insurance, they will need to rely on both these work supports and on Medicaid and food stamps. The Earned Income Tax Credit raises the income of these families, but it still leaves family income hovering around the poverty line. Without policies and programs for raising their wages, they are destined for a livelihood at the margin of self-sufficiency. While the new world of welfare has just begun to play out, experience so far points to the need for more thought about ways to increase the wages of low-skilled workers.

APPENDIX TABLE 1. DEFINITIONS OF TOPIC CODES

CODE	*TOPIC: WHAT THEY ARE TALKING ABOUT*
Programs:	
food stamps	*food stamps (including expedited food stamps)*
Medicaid	*medicaid (local terms may be different, e.g. "medical"), transitional Medicaid after leaving welfare for work, Medicaid for children only/children's health insurance program (CHIP)*
child care	*child care use, child care providers, child care reliability, child care costs/payments/reimbursements, transitional child care after leaving welfare for work, child care for low-income families not on welfare*
emergency assistance	*emergency cash assistance provided through the welfare office*
one-time diversion assistance	*one-time diversion assistance; may be cash or a one-time payment for a specific item like car repairs*
transportation	*clients' transportation including car ownership/reliability, value of car, rides from other people, public transportation, gasoline, car repairs, driver's license, car insurance, traffic tickets, etc.*
earned income credit	*earned income tax credit reduces income taxes for people with earnings*
other government services	*unemployment insurance (UI), Supplemental Security Income (SSI), Social Security, Home Energy Assistance Program (HEAP), housing programs (e.g. public housing, Section 8, emergency housing assistance), veterans benefits, foster care, child protective services, etc.*
community services	*food banks, homeless shelters, hospitals and health clinics, family planning clinics, budgeting classes, discounts to low-income customers by gas, electric, and telephone companies, etc.*
Policies:	
absent parent	*identity, location, circumstances, etc. of non-resident parents OTHER than discussions of specific child support enforcement topics*
child support enforcement	*child support orders, paternity establishment, collections, including reporting this to the welfare office, pass-through of collections to the family, appointments with child support enforcement officers, problems*

participation	*client's participation in mandatory education/employment activity (the work requirement), substance abuse program, or other mandated activity. Failure to participate without good cause results in a sanction. Participation rules apply to parents but not to other caretakers like grandparents.*
sanctions	*reduction in benefits for failure to comply with program rules without good cause*
earnings disregards	*a share of earnings are not counted in determining the welfare grant*
entitlement	*welfare is no longer an entitlement or right; or client is expected to become self-sufficient (i.e., off welfare) or independent*
benefits without TANF	*reference to the availability of food stamps, Medicaid and/or child care for people who leave TANF or who never come onto TANF. Also code the program being discussed (e.g., food stamps, Medicaid, or child care).*
time limits	*limit on the months of welfare payments*
Personal Responsibility Agreement	*Personal Responsibility Agreement or contract*
school attendance of children	*explaining rules and/or monitoring of children's school enrollment and attendance*
immunization of children	*explaining rules and monitoring of children's immunization status, shot records*
family cap	*a family's welfare benefit is not increased with the birth of an additional child*
marriage	*discussion or activity that appears to promote marriage and the formation of two-parent families*
fraud	*accusation or investigation of possible client fraud, referral of the case to the agency's fraud unit, references to finger-imaging*

Client's Education/Employment:

education (past, current or future)	*education, including high school, adult education, GED programs, college (past, current or future)*
employment (past, current or future)	*regular paid work (past, current or future)*
training (past, current or future)	*vocational and other training programs (past, current or future)*
work experience (past, current or future)	*unpaid work activities, including workfare, work experience, and community service (past, current or future)*

job readiness/job search (past, current or future)	*orientation, job readiness activities, job search, and job placement (past, current or future)*
education/employment unclear (past, current or future)	*one of the above education/employment activities but unclear which one (past, current or future)*

Other Topics:

housing and utilities	*client's housing problems, including problems with rent, mortgage payments, utilities, housing quality, landlord, etc. Do not include who lives with client and dollar amounts unless these raise problems.*
health insurance	*health insurance OTHER THAN Medicaid, such as Medicare, veterans' programs, and private health insurance*
health, disability, and mental health — client	*client's health status, health problems, disabilities*
health, disability, and mental health — others	*health status, health problems, disabilities of spouse, partner or children*
substance abuse	*drug or alcohol use, problems, treatments of clients or other family members*
pregnancy	*pregnancy of client or family member, prenatal care*
family planning	*additional children, birth control use, family planning services*
parenting	*client's problems with child's behavior, parent/child interactions, parents as role models*
family problems	*client's problems with spouse/current or former partner, domestic violence, relationship problems with other family members*
crime	*problems raised by crime, such as family members in prison, stolen property, etc.*

APPENDIX TABLE 2.   DEFINITIONS OF ACTIVITY CODES

CODE	*ACTIVITY: WHAT THE WORKER IS DOING*
Advising:	
collecting info intentions	*asking the client about her intentions, plans, or expectations*
collecting info needs	*asking the client about needs other than cash assistance, such as Medicaid, food stamps, child care, transportation, other services*
explaining options	*describing alternative activities, programs, providers, and courses of action available to the client and asking client about preferences*
invoking personal beliefs	*invoking personal beliefs, values, and experience to advise and counsel client*
translating rules/benefits	*advising based on interpretations of agency rules, available benefits, and rule-based consequences; explaining a rule in light of the client's particular circumstances, activities, or needs*
using professional expertise	*using professional expertise, training, and experience to advise and counsel client and/or to attempt to resolve immediate problems*
Assessing:	
assessing employment	*assessing the client's vocational abilities, interests, and preferences by asking questions, administering a test, asking client to fill out a form or questionnaire, discussing educational or vocational interests*
assessing services	*assessing the client's needs for services such as child care, transportation, substance abuse programs, mental health services, and housing*
Collecting documents	*collecting documents verifying information about a topic listed above*
Collecting information about circumstances	*asking questions about the client's situation or actions regarding a topic listed above, other than monitoring attendance/participation at mandatory activities*
Completing or signing forms	*asking client to fill in and/or sign form, with or without explanation of what is in form or reading form to client*
Excepting or exempting	*telling the client an exception or exemption is being made in this case; postponing enforcement of a rule*
Explaining rules	*explaining rules, requirements, benefits, services, application procedures, other procedures, and how the process works*

MIS verification *using computer systems and finger-imaging to collect, cross-check, or verify information about the client, either on-the-spot or with computer-generated reports; include using computer systems to monitor attendance/participation; include references to problems with computer systems*

Providing Employment Services:

providing job placement *referring client to a specific employer with a possible job opening*

providing job readiness/job search *preparing the client to search for work and assist in job search*

Verifying:

contacting for verification *contacting or phoning a landlord, employer, school, or other person or institution to verify information about a topic listed above, or telling client this will be done*

monitoring via client *asking the client whether and/or when she attended or participated in a mandatory activity*

monitoring via outside source *informing the client that the worker has information about attendance/participation from an outside source, such as attendance rosters, phone call from service provider, employer, computer system*

sending for verification *sending the client to somewhere or someone to get verification of information about anything, even if the quotation has no topic code*

verifying via client *asking for and/or getting from the client information verifying attendance/participation, such as a letter or form*

CODES NOT USED IN THE ANALYSIS

CODE	ACTIVITY: WHAT THE WORKER IS DOING
explaining consequences	*explaining consequences for failure to comply with rules and procedures; warning that benefits can be denied or reduced for failure to comply*
authorizing benefit	*authorizing cash assistance, other benefits, services*
denying benefit	*denying cash assistance, other benefits, services*
active dissuasion	*actively dissuading or discouraging someone from cash assistance*
informing of rights	*informing the client about rights to benefits, rights to an appeal or a fair hearing, and other rights*

acting on sanctions	*referring or explicitly not referring client to the concili-ation/sanctioning process; authorizing or explicitly not authorizing a sanction; explaining how client can lift sanction or lifting a sanction*
sending to mandatory ac-tivity	*sending or referring client to another person or organi-zation to apply for or receive assistance, engage in ac-tivity, receive an assessment, or pursue another activity; client is told she must go to secure or keep benefits*
sending to voluntary ac-tivity	*sending or referring client to another person or organi-zation to apply for or receive assistance or service, en-gage in activity, receive an assessment, or pursue another activity; client has the option of going or not going*
positive reinforcement	*commenting, describing, enumerating clients' positive behavior, traits, potential*
expressing sympathy	*for example, "I'm sorry to hear that..."*
admonishing	*negative comments about client; criticizing client's past or current behavior; criticizing client's attitude*
sending for investigation	*sending the client or the client's case to be investigated or pursued by a fraud unit, child protective services, child support enforcement*
mentioning	*simply mentioning a topic without doing any of the activities above*

CODE	*ACTIVITY: WHAT THE CLIENT IS DOING*
disclosing problems	*disclosing specific problems facing the client, other than a lack of income*
requesting other assis-tance or service	*requesting assistance other than TANF, food stamps, Medicaid, child care, or other government assistance*
declining	*declining, rejecting, or withdrawing from a program, service, work activity or employment; declining or re-fusing to provide information or documents; declining to pursue child support; refusing to comply with a rule*
inquiring about rules or benefits	
inquiring about rights	
underground economy	*disclosing work or income that is not reported for in-come tax purposes*

ENCOUNTER WORKSHEET

Office_____   Encounter number_____

Unit_____   Observer_____

Job title_____   Date_____

Worker number_____   Begin time:_____   End time:_____

Meeting space_____

Group meeting or stream (explain)_____
    (Complete section III only.)

Individual meeting_____
    (Complete all sections.)

I. OBSERVATIONS

a. Clients present and relationship; advocates/translators:

b. Adult client(s): race_____ sex_____ language_____ other_____

c. Observe whether the worker and client appear to know each other:
    yes_____   no_____

Encounter number _____

II. DEBRIEF OF WORKER

a. Who initiated the meeting? Worker_____ Client_____

b. Is this your client? yes_____ no_____ If yes, when was the last time you communicated with her?_____

c. What was the primary purpose of meeting? For example, application for assistance (which programs?), redetermination (which programs?), request for supportive service(s) (which?), monitoring/disciplinary, employment services, resolve problem (explain), etc.

d. What was the disposition (check as many as apply)?

	Next step in application/ recertification process (pended)	Authorized	Denied	Already receives
TANF	_____	_____	_____	_____
food stamps	_____	_____	_____	_____
medicaid	_____	_____	_____	_____
child care	_____	_____	_____	_____
other (explain)	_____	_____	_____	_____

mandatory referral to: office/agency_____ for _____   (benefit, service, activity,

optional referral to: office/agency_____ for _____   etc.)

other action (explain)
no action (explain)

e. What factors explain the disposition of the case? Why did you take the action you did?

f. Did you exercise your professional judgment? If so, how? What other options were available to you?

Encounter number _____

III. DEBRIEF OF OBSERVER

a. Why did the client(s) come in? Briefly describe the circumstances leading them to come in.

b. What happened during the encounter?

c. Briefly describe if employment issues were addressed and, if so, how.

d. Comments, if needed (difficulties observing the interaction, unusual aspects of worker or client circumstances or behavior, insights)

Index